Claude Simon
and Fiction Now

Other Books by John Fletcher:

The Novels of Samuel Beckett (Chatto and Windus)

Samuel Beckett's Art (Chatto and Windus)

New Directions in Literature (Calder and Boyars)

Samuel Beckett: His Works and His Critics with Raymond Federman (University of California Press)

Beckett: A Study of His Plays with John Spurling (Eyre Methuen)

CRITICAL APPRAISALS SERIES

General Editor: John Fletcher

CLAUDE SIMON

and

Fiction Now

JOHN FLETCHER

CALDER AND BOYARS

LONDON

First published in Great Britain 1975 by Calder & Boyars Ltd.
18 Brewer Street, London W1R 4AS

© John Fletcher 1975

ISBN 0 7145 1014 9

Printed in Great Britain by
Ebenezer Baylis & Son Limited
The Trinity Press, Worcester, and London

for Harriet

CONTENTS

	page
Acknowledgements	9
Foreword	11
Biographical Note	15
Introduction: The Post-Modern Situation—Tradition and Renovation	19
A Novelist's World: Claude Simon's Major Themes	57

Cross Sections

1 *The Palace* and *The Third Book about Achim*	97
2 *The Flanders Road* and *August 1914*	117
3 *The Grass* and *The Middle Age of Mrs Eliot*	135
4 *Histoire* and *A House for Mr Biswas*	156
5 *The Battle of Pharsalus* and *The Leopard*	175

Conclusion: Humanism, Tragedy and the Contemporary Avant-Garde	197
Bibliographical Note	229
Index	231

ACKNOWLEDGEMENTS

I should like to thank my colleagues for their kind assistance: Malcolm Bradbury and Ihab Hassan for providing me with advance copies of important publications of theirs which I wished to discuss; Melvin J. Friedman for supplying hard-to-come-by copies of American editions of Claude Simon's novels; and Colin Butler for his comments on the first section of the third chapter. I also benefited from colleagues' criticism when I read early drafts of parts of this book before graduate or research seminars: in this connection I particularly wish to acknowledge the penetrating critique made of the section on style in the second chapter by linguistics faculty at the University of East Anglia, and the comments of colleagues in French studies (especially John Cruickshank, Peter France and Anthony Cheal Pugh) when I presented the fourth section of the third chapter in its provisional state to a graduate seminar held at the University of Sussex in December 1972. Furthermore my own graduate and undergraduate students (particularly successive generations of participants in my 'Neo-Modernism' course) have contributed much, including the odd phrase here and there in the text; I am grateful to them for giving me something while I was teaching them.

I have occasionally paraphrased my own words used previously in other contexts; in particular I wish to make acknowledgement to the following journals in which early drafts of parts of this book first appeared: *Critical Quarterly*, the Claude Simon special issue of *Entretiens*, *International Fiction Review*, *Journal of European Studies*, *Journal of Modern Literature*, *Kolokon* and *UEA Bulletin*.

A word about critical apparatus: the footnotes are provided for the benefit of more specialist readers and can safely be ignored by others; sources of quotations are usually given in brackets immediately after citation of the text in question, and where a page reference is preceded by the letter 'F', this indicates that my source is the original French text and not a translation; book titles are given in English where a published English translation exists, otherwise titles are left in the original; and where such a translation is available—as specified in the copyright acknowledgements below—I use it either unmodified, or in slightly altered form to bring it closer to the original text. All other translations are my own.

I am grateful to the following publishers and copyright holders for permission to make quotations from the following works: *August 1914* by Alexander Solzhenitsyn, translated by Michael Glenny (The Bodley Head Ltd); the novels of Claude Simon translated by Richard Howard (Jonathan Cape Ltd); *The Third Book about Achim* and *Two Views* by Uwe Johnson, translated by Ursule Molinaro and by Richard and Clara Winston respectively (Jonathan Cape Ltd); *A Farewell to Arms* by Ernest Hemingway (the Executors of the Ernest Hemingway Estate and Jonathan Cape Ltd); *The Sound and the Fury* by William Faulkner (Curtis Brown Ltd, London, on behalf of the Estate of William Faulkner); *Time Regained* by Marcel Proust, translated by Andreas Mayor (Chatto and Windus Ltd); *The Leopard* by Giuseppe di Lampedusa, translated by Archibald Colquhoun, and *Doctor Zhivago* by Boris Pasternak, translated by Max Hayward and Manya Harari (Wm. Collins Sons & Co. Ltd); *The Nigger of the Narcissus* by Joseph Conrad (the Trustees of the Joseph Conrad Estate and J. M. Dent & Sons Ltd); *A House for Mr Biswas* by V. S. Naipaul (André Deutsch Ltd); *Sentimental Education* by Gustave Flaubert, translated by Robert Baldick (Penguin Books Ltd); and *The Middle Age of Mrs Eliot* by Angus Wilson (Secker and Warburg Ltd).

                                                            John Fletcher

FOREWORD

Since about the turn of the century, and more so than at any other time previously in his history, Western man has been preoccupied with the question of the 'modernity' of his culture. The 'modern' has for some while now been a term of praise or blame, depending on your point of view; and as an object of active investigation it has preoccupied, and continues to preoccupy, anyone trying to keep abreast of the frequently disturbing and disorientating achievements of our time.

This is particularly true of the writers, artists and thinkers who are the subject of this series, which is concerned primarily with the phenomenon variously known as 'neo-modernism' or 'post-modernism', i.e. work produced roughly since the Second World War which explores media in a more or less radical way. Earlier writers are not of course excluded, but they will only be considered if they can still be shown to exert a cultural influence on our contemporary world. In other words, the series will concentrate on present-day innovators of one kind or another working in the tradition of the great moderns, now dead, such as Joyce, Proust and Thomas Mann. It will not concern itself with the ups and downs of the volatile avant-garde, but only with such contemporary writers, artists, works, genres and movements as can be said to satisfy at least one of the following criteria:

1   that they have affected in a perceptible way current styles or attitudes;

2   that they already present an appreciable opus or corpus of creativity;

3   that they are demonstrably 'masterly' in the sense of

having made a real impact on the contemporary arts and stayed in the forefront of cultural endeavour.

The series aims to offer a fresh and original way of approaching the works of our contemporaries, and render accessible what is challenging and often difficult. Although the stress will fall mainly on creative writing, there will also be a place for artists working in other media and in fields generally considered peripheral to literature proper. All forms of contemporary artistic endeavour hang so much together that none can be scrutinized in isolation, and the series as a whole will urge the organic nature of art in a period of rapid and often disconcerting change.

In this book on contemporary novelists from different countries Claude Simon receives special attention, because I believe him to be the greatest fiction-writer of his generation (I consider Beckett and Nabokov even greater, of course, but they belong to a rather earlier period); this is how I justify the more detailed examination of his works which this study proposes. All previous books which have been devoted in part to his fiction (and at the present moment there is no existing monograph which deals exclusively with him) have discussed this in the context of the 'new novel' or *nouveau roman* movement in France. But the *nouveau roman*, especially for the 'common reader', is only a small part of contemporary writing—some might say the least attractive part. This book therefore situates the greatest of the 'new novelists' in the wider context of post-modernism generally. For post-modernism embraces different kinds of experiment and different explorations of reality: some of its aspects are clearly radical and aggressively innovatory; others are new 'only in the sense', as Jean Alter has put it, 'of pressing forward with the normal evolution of modes of expression.'[1] It is my view, now the dust has settled somewhat, that the *nouveau roman* belongs to the latter category, while the contemporary American novel (which, for me, is the only other vital fictional enterprise in the world today) belongs to the former;

and this is because, for all their daring, Alain Robbe-Grillet and his colleagues are pro-art, whereas the great Americans headed by Norman Mailer are decidedly not. This is one of the reasons why, despite my admiration and respect for its achievements, I barely mention the contemporary American movement in this book; it is so fundamentally different from the European novel (and of course for all his Caribbean origins V. S. Naipaul is a European in this sense) that the two simply cannot be compared. The other reason for my reticence is that a fine study of the contemporary American novel has already been written: it is Tony Tanner's *City of Words*. I have (all proportions kept) attempted to write a book parallel to his, and have tried not to overlap with it. In the context of my own work, this study represents a narrowing of focus from my earlier and more general book *New Directions in Literature*, where Claude Simon could only receive the attention possible in a short chapter.

This essay discusses his entire fictional output, which is of course by no means even in quality. The early novels are conscientious efforts, but ultimately insignificant, and it is not difficult to entertain reservations about the very latest books. For, perhaps old-fashionedly in an age of explication, this study is frankly evaluative: I think the reader expects a critic to sort out the sheep from the goats, and does not like the issue evaded. Naively some may think, but quite correctly, the publisher's blurb for Simon's novel *Triptyque* asked: 'isn't the best criterion for judging a literary work quite simply the pleasure which reading it gives rise to?' As long as we are clear what is meant by 'pleasure', I see little wrong in the sentiment expressed. Too often critics, and those of the school currently dominant in Paris in particular, appear to be suggesting that the more neuter a work can be made to sound, the better it must be.[2]

My approach to the study of Simon's novels is thematic rather than chronological. The introductory chapter tries to define the general context of post-modernism, while the second surveys Simon's fiction from a number of synoptic angles. The third attempts to situate Simon *vis-à-vis* other outstanding contemporary novelists like V. S. Naipaul and Solzhenitsyn, by comparing each of his major novels with another—by a fellow writer—to which it bears some kind of thematic relationship; while the concluding chapter explores the ways in which contemporary avant-gardes approach the issues of human meaning and destiny with which all great fiction has traditionally had to concern itself.

I should just add it happens, rather fortuitously, that Claude Simon is an esteemed personal friend whom it is always a pleasure for me to be with. However, the friend has contributed nothing to this study except for the occasional anecdote. We rarely talk much of his work, and never of its interpretation: my subject is the writer as manifested in the published novels. That the distinction is a meaningful, indeed crucial one, is something I hope can be taken for granted.

Norwich, January 1974.   John Fletcher

FOREWORD—NOTES

1 *Nouveau roman: hier, aujourd'hui* (Paris: 10/18, 1972), vol. I, p. 35.
2 If my tone becomes as polemical as those I discuss, perhaps I can plead—as I am sure they would—that 'qui aime bien châtie bien'.

BIOGRAPHICAL NOTE

Things as they are
Are changed upon the blue guitar
    —Wallace Stevens

Claude Eugène Henri Simon was born at Tananarive in Madagascar, then a French possession, on 10 October 1913. Both his parents were French: his father's family came from Arbois in Franche-Comté, his mother from Roussillon, both wine-producing areas. His father, a cavalry officer, was killed early in the First World War, and Simon was brought up by his mother's family (and in particular by his uncle) in Perpignan. His secondary education took place at the rather exclusive Collège Stanislas in Paris, after which he spent a few months at Oxford and Cambridge (where he had his first love affair, with an English girl), but he does not appear to have ever formally taken a degree at a university. As a youth he was, if anything, a keen rugby player. The career he had in mind was to become a painter; it is not clear how long he spent trying to establish himself as an artist, but by the outbreak of the Second World War he had probably given up his ambition, realising he lacked *la main*, plastic ability—his great regret, he has said, is not having succeeded in becoming a painter. But his painterly inclination subsists; he is perceptive about contemporary art, as his interest in Rauschenberg and Bacon shows, and he still constructs 'assemblages' of shells and drift-wood he finds on the seashore, and covers large folding screens with his collages. Such graphic talent as he possessed clearly surfaces in the fiction, which offers many sharp verbal vignettes, like snapshots of scenes or events.

He became a cavalryman like his father, but served in the ranks in the 31st Dragoons both during his military sevice at Lunéville in 1934-5, and during the period of mobilization 1939-40. Between these two bouts of soldiering he travelled widely, to Russia, Germany, Italy and Greece, and he was, like the hero of *Le Sacre du printemps*, involved for a time in gun-running for the Republicans in Spain. He narrowly escaped death at the Battle of the Meuse in May 1940 and was captured and sent to a camp in Saxony. He managed to persuade his captors that he was not a white French soldier but a coloured trooper; his colonial birth, his darkly tanned complexion, and a yarn he spun about Madagascan tribes being blue-eyed enabled him to claim transfer to a POW camp in France, from which he escaped with relative ease in November 1940. One of his sharpest memories of captivity is of the time he was denounced to the German authorities as a Jew by one of his comrades; fortunately he came up before an officer who despised such treachery and was let off without the intimate physical examination normally carried out on males in such circumstances. When he had escaped he joined the resistance movement in Perpignan.

After the liberation he returned to Paris, where he now lives in a small flat in the Latin Quarter during most of the year, and in the summer goes to Salses in Roussillon where he owns a house inherited from his mother's family (and before that from the First Empire general who was their common ancestor). He is a wine-grower by profession and lives mainly off the income from the sale of the dessert wines produced by his medium-sized estate. He is twice married and in recent years has travelled round the world on lecturing engagements. Honours include the Prix Médicis for *Histoire* and the degree of Doctor of Letters *honoris causa* from the University of East Anglia.

Politically he has always been a man of the left, but *gauchisme*'s disorder and contempt for free speech hold no attractions for him, and he has even clashed with Sartre over the point. He would seem, if a label is required, to be a kind of liberal anarchist and does not appear to have ever belonged to any formal political party. In common with a number of leading French intellectuals he signed the famous 'Declaration of the 121' on the right of insubordination in Algeria. And in his youth he threw in his lot with the Spanish Republicans, but like Orwell, Koestler and others, he seems quickly to have become disillusioned by the cynical opportunism of the party political machines (*The Palace*, among other things, is an elegy on the death of a great hope, of the '*illusion lyrique*' of which Malraux wrote so eloquently at the time). There may, indeed, be certain contradictions in his own feelings, which lead to fertile tensions in the novels. He seems in some matters to hold attitudes towards established values which one might describe as aristocratic, perhaps *élitist*; as the scion of a 'good' family it would be surprising if he did not. And on the other hand one may discern an anarchistic dissatisfaction with the *status quo* and a very real concern for the underdog and the exploited. It is significant in this respect that he adopts as the epigraph to *The Wind* a profound observation of Paul Valéry's: 'Two dangers continually threaten the world: order and disorder'. His own position, I suspect, oscillates between those two poles, and the debate between the older and the younger man in *Le Sacre* bears this out. Perhaps he would have been happiest as the ancestor to whom he refers so often that one feels he identifies with him: the aristocratic soldier who voted for the king's execution and became a general under Napoleon Bonaparte. Simon must often have wondered if he were not a reincarnation of that eccentric forbear who established the family's fortune, and then left his descendants to litigate over a diminishing inheritance in a manner worthy of characters from a Balzac novel (the Franche-Comté properties were finally disposed of at the end of the Second World War).

He began writing fiction early in the war and produced novels like *Le Tricheur* and *Gulliver* which were strongly influenced by models (American in particular) in vogue at the time. But he started to delve into his own experience with *Le Sacre du printemps*, which deals in part, as *The Palace* does wholly, with the Spanish Civil War. *The Wind* is still an imitative construction, but is set in Simon's native Roussillon. He began to liberate himself from his influences when he wrote *The Grass*, an even more personal novel; at the centre is a character modelled upon his own aunt, who abandoned her Arbois house as she fled from the Germans in 1940, and after changing trains many times arrived several days later in Roussillon with not a hair out of place, with her handkerchief still immaculate, and with only a trace of dust in the creases of her shoes (see p. 144 below). *The Flanders Road* reflects his war experiences; *Histoire* offers us a (probably rather idealized) portrait of the uncle who brought Simon up; *The Battle of Pharsalus* is to some extent concerned with a trip to Greece made by the author and his wife; *Les Corps conducteurs* is concerned both with a writers' congress in Latin America which Simon attended (and by the rhetoric of which, one suspects, he was mortally bored), and also with his reactions to the prodigies of the U.S.A., while at least one episode of *Triptyque* draws on childhood memories of the Jura. But none of this matters ultimately; as Beckett once put it, 'the author is of no interest.' It is the words that count, the novelist's basic material: language; those implements of human speech which as Beckett again expressed it in a beautiful phrase, 'vous font voir du pays avec eux d'étranges voyages.'

INTRODUCTION

The Post-Modern Situation—Tradition and Renovation

Oh! Blessed rage for order, pale Ramon,
The maker's rage to order words of the sea
—Wallace Stevens

I

'Do we have a "rage for order"?' asks Frank Kermode rhetorically in his essay 'Modernisms', published in Bernard Bergonzi's important symposium *Innovations* (Macmillan, 1968), consciously echoing the serene lines quoted above which close Wallace Stevens's poem 'The Idea of Order at Key West'; and, like Stevens, Kermode considers that we do. For although he distinguishes two phases of modernism—which he designates respectively as palaeo-modernism, whose 'peak period . . . must be placed somewhere around 1910-25', and neo-modernism, which postdates the Second World War—he believes in their fundamental if diverse continuity. 'There has been,' he writes, 'only one Modernist Revolution, and it happened a long time ago . . . There has been little radical change in modernist thinking since then.' He reinforces this point a little further on:

> Neo-modernists have examined . . . various implications in traditional modernism. As a consequence we have, not unusually, some good things, many trivial things, many

19

jokes, much nonsense. Among other things they enable us to see more clearly that certain aspects of earlier modernism really were so revolutionary that we ought not to expect—even with everything speeded up—to have the pains and pleasures of another comparable movement quite so soon.

In consequence Frank Kermode rejects the two other possible views of modernism—Cyril Connolly's, as expressed in his survey *The Modern Movement* (1965), that 'it is virtually all over', and Leslie Fiedler's proposition in a famous essay (also in *Innovations*) that the new art is so radical, both aesthetically and socially, that its proponents should be called 'the New Mutants'. Kermode's sense of continuities is qualified in its turn by another chronicler of the fortunes of modernism, Ihab Hassan, who writes in a 'paracritical bibliography' published in *New Literary History* (Autumn, 1971) that 'we will not grasp the cultural experience of our moment if we insist that the new arts are "marginal developments of older modernism;" or that distinctions between "art" and "joke" are crucial to any future aesthetic'. To Kermode's categories palaeo- and neo- (which presuppose variations upon an on-going theme rather than any radical discontinuity), Hassan prefers the more definitely final terms 'modernism' and '*post*-modernism' as his formulae. Like Fiedler, he takes much more seriously than does Kermode the 'apocalyptic' quality of recent art which the works of Cage, Burroughs and Rauschenberg possess; and unlike Kermode, he is not inclined to consider that such manifestations merely reveal 'that the Last Days are good for a giggle'. In other words, where Kermode views neo-modernism as a 'marginal development' on palaeo-modernism, Hassan sees his post-modernism (for it is quite clear they are both talking about the same movement) as being much more radically and disturbingly distinct. The scenario, as Hassan would sketch it, goes something like this:

We have all in recent years become preoccupied with the

special quality of the art of our own century, and have come
to look upon what has happened since the early 1900s as
constituting a divide or rift which separates us irrevocably
from such crises of the past as the Renaissance, or the Romantic
agony. The recent cataclysm can be situated, with some degree
of assurance, in the years before and immediately after the
First World War, and its tremors were provoked by artists
like Proust, Joyce and Mann in the novel, Strindberg, O'Neill
and Pirandello on the stage, Yeats, Rilke and Eliot in poetry,
Debussy, Stravinsky and Bartok in music, and Cézanne,
Picasso and Klee in painting. Then, as if the shock administered
to our sensibilities by this upheaval were too great to bear,
there seemed to occur a lull, even a reaction. During the
1930s and 1940s people began to belittle, even to reject
violently, the absolute dedication to art of these practitioners.
Writers like George Orwell and Louis-Ferdinand Céline,
Gottfried Benn and Alberto Moravia, set a new tone of
asperity, of austerity, of ironic casualness, which—as was
intended—contrasted with what was seen as the Apollonian
dignity and majestic decorum of the previous generation. In
France, for example, Gide's elegant, measured periods quite
suddenly looked old-fashioned beside the harsher cadences of
Malraux and Sartre writing under the influence of the recently
translated laconic and ungenteel prose of a Dos Passos or a
Hemingway; and Valéry, of all people, sounded effete beside
the colloquial brashness of Aragon. This is of course not the
whole story by any means: others carried on as if nothing had
altered, but they attracted less attention at the time and tend
not to provoke much discussion now.

Then gradually, and apparently unpredictably, a new
tendency began to assert itself vociferously in the late 1930s
(*Nausea* and *Murphy* were both published in 1938), and we
still live in its shadow. In the often violent reaction to the
social and political concerns of the previous generation, of the
movement which received its testament, as it now turned out
to be, in Sartre's *What Is Literature?* of 1947, this new force was

ostentatious in its preoccupation with forms and structure, taking up again, after an interval, the aesthetic obsession of earlier modernist writers, but with a difference: the new 'post-modernism' was much more drawn to anarchism, iconoclasm and anti-formalism than its precursor, as well as much more self-consciously an heir to dada and surrealism, and much more interested in both nihilism and play, in subverting structures than in exploiting their full potential. The 'crucial text' of post-modernism in Hassan's view is not *Ulysses*, for all its 'contemptuousness of its own formal and stylistic elaborateness', because it derives from and makes studied reference to a whole tradition of epic and mock-epic, but *Finnegans Wake*, in which destruction is a mode of creation, and iconoclasm and remake go hand in hand. We still have not adjusted to all the consequences of that radical gesture of Joyce's mature years. So it is not surprising that his disciple Samuel Beckett should be the acknowledged high priest of this black apostolate, and that its idiosyncratic votaries are called William Burroughs, John Barth and Michel Butor in the novel (Hassan is alert to the coincidence of the frequent occurrence in post-modernism of the initial B), Edward Albee, Harold Pinter, Peter Weiss and Fernando Arrabal in the theatre, Allen Ginsberg in poetry, John Cage in music, and the followers of Marcel Duchamp in the visual arts. Hassan is quite clear about who is the remote progenitor of these lusty and rebellious infants: it is our old friend the Marquis de Sade. The line Ihab Hassan traces from Sade to Beckett in his book *The Dismemberment of Orpheus: Toward a Postmodern Literature* (New York: Oxford University Press, 1971), deftly hopping 'the age of Novalis and Rimbaud in order to reach the present swiftly', is, he admits, 'hypothetical'. The theme he pursues through his major figures Sade, Hemingway, Kafka, Genet and Beckett is silence, the 'sovereignty of the void': a silence that may be either nihilist or plenary, or both ('contrapuntally') at once. His controlling image, the dismemberment of Orpheus at the hands of the Maenads for having 'offended life in some hidden

and original manner', appears a shade tenuous as a link between
the literary figures who are selected as being somehow
exemplary of Hassan's argument, but who tend to have a
rather fashionable air about them—and little wonder, since
with the possible exception of Hemingway they inhabit the
familiar pantheon erected by French critics like Blanchot and
Bataille. But none of this really matters: Ihab Hassan has a
vision, which he presses with considerable conviction. The
true meaning of the avant-garde, for him, is that Orpheus now
consents to being dismembered, and he sees this attitude on
the part of the artist as the culmination of a long evolutionary
process.

Whether it is itself a stable attitude is another question.
There are signs of a new outlook developing within post-
modernism itself, and in particular a return to political
involvement. A quarter of a century after the publication of
What Is Literature? the French avant-garde, or at least that
section of it grouped around the review *Tel Quel* and its editor
Philippe Sollers, is once again heavily influenced by marxist
thinking on the role of literature in a capitalist consumer
society. How *Tel Quel* will manage to reconcile the extreme
formalism of its literary theory with its militantly antibourgeois stance in political and social philosophy is as yet
difficult to predict. But John Cage's scores, cut-up fold-in
novels, ready-mades and photo-realism are by no means the
last word of the avant-garde; if anything, such *dernier cri* is
beginning to sound a trifle dated.

Indeed, the danger with the Hassan/Fiedler version of the
new modernism is that it tends to overemphasize the flashier
and more strident avant-gardes, the sort egregiously characterized by the products of the Warhol factory. On the other
hand, because we are in the middle of the phenomenon it is
not easy to reconcile such odd bedfellows as the beat poet
Allen Ginsberg and the Roman Catholic novelist Muriel Spark,
and yet both writers exemplify important, if rather different,
aspects of the movement. Nevertheless, we do seem to be able

to discern a pattern, at least through the contrast with what
has gone immediately before; and it is natural we should look
for some term which will adequately describe it. The 'new
literature' is obviously unsatisfactory, for the same reason that
mirages are always one jump ahead of the parched traveller.
Claude Mauriac's neologism 'aliterature', for which Hassan
has considerable liking, is as inaccurate in its way as Martin
Esslin's phrase 'the theatre of the absurd': not all post-modern
writing can be described as 'aliterature', any more than all
contemporary experimental drama is preoccupied with the
absurd.

Frank Kermode, as we have seen, has coined the rather
unpretty term 'neo-modernism', which has the virtue of
being precise. But the difficulty with Kermode's version of
the contemporary situation is that it does not account very
adequately for the big slump in modernist values in the twenty-
year period between about 1930 and 1950. On the whole I
share Kermode's view that palaeo- and neo-modernism are
essentially continuous and that the development of the new
forms can be seen 'as following from palaeo-modernist
premises without any violent revolutionary stage'; that neo-
modernists are 'stealthy classicists' and that both phases share
the conviction 'research into form is the true means of
discovery, even when'—as with Beckett—'form is denied
existence'. I share, too, his belief that neo-modernism has
thrown up 'some good things' (as far as I am concerned they
have been produced by, amongst others, the writers who are
the subject of this book), just as I feel the same distaste as he
does for the excesses and muddle often associated with neo-
modernism's more eccentric manifestations. My own version
of the new modernism, while it derives from his, will attempt
to account for the impression of hiatus we experience as we
look back to the Second World War decades; and it goes
something like this:

Neo-modernism emerged in France about 1950 and spread
fairly rapidly to most countries of predominantly European

civilization, though not without strong local opposition in several places, which led to their undergoing its influence later than others did. Moreover, it has, for obvious reasons, had no perceptible impact in the Soviet Union, though there has been some echo in those other member-countries of the Communist bloc which have achieved a certain degree of freedom for artists, such as Poland and Czechoslovakia; Martin Esslin rightly includes playwrights from these nations in *The Theatre of the Absurd*. And—with the exception of Latin America—the Third World has proved largely indifferent to neo-modernism; indeed, the reaction has occasionally been hostile, as was shown at the 1964 Formentor conference when delegates from developing countries expressed their disgust at the award of the International Publishers' Prize to *The Golden Fruits* by Nathalie Sarraute, an author whose concerns seemed utterly remote from those exercising readers in their home countries: 'are we to be national writers,' one of them pointly asked, 'or Parisians?' In fact just as modernism sprang from and remained largely centred upon Europe and places mainly colonized by Europeans, so its reincarnated form has tended to spread little beyond the same confines. But wherever it has spread, it has been a cosmopolitan rather than a regional phenomenon. Its characteristic figures are writers like Nabokov, Beckett, Ionesco and Arrabal, who may have their roots in a national tradition, but no longer contribute to it. Their works are like apple-grafts: the trunk is of one variety, the graft (a different language and milieu) another, and the fruit a hybrid. Even a writer like Borges, who writes in his mother tongue and resides in the same country in which he was born, is a cosmopolitan figure, a man of universal culture whose work transcends the confines of his own nation and is addressed to those whose reading is as eclectic as Borges's own.

As an aesthetic movement, neo-modernism is primarily rooted in three media: the novel, drama and the film. It shows less interest in lyric poetry, at least of the more traditional, i.e. the non-concrete variety, or in dance, or in music (at least of a non-electronic kind). In this it differs from another movement that originated in France, symbolism, which was rooted in poetry, music and dance; and unlike that other French-inspired movement, surrealism, it maintains only a fairly episodic interest in the visual arts. So it will principally be with the so-called new novel, the new wave in the cinema, and the not necessarily absurdist 'theatre of the absurd' that I shall be concerned in presenting my own version of neo-modernism. All three of these artistic manifestations arose in France in the early fifties.

Why this was so is a complicated problem of the sociology of art which it is impossible to answer satisfactorily in the present state of our knowledge. But it may be possible to give some idea of the political and social climate in which it arose, and which goes some way towards suggesting an explanation. To do so we need to go back to the period before the Second World War. The rise, diffusion and triumph of fascism in a number of European countries, and the consolidation of Stalinism in the Soviet Union, cast a pall of political dread not only over the countries directly affected but over most others in the civilized world. These developments in the political sphere were of course often triggered off by crises in the economic domain, such as runaway inflation in Germany and the rever-berations of the 1929 Wall Street crash. New, aggressive, totalitarian régimes raised once again the threat of war which the generation that survived 1914-18 had hoped to have seen exorcized for ever. And in this general climate of unsettlement and tension it was natural that palaeo-modernism should fall into abeyance, plunge beneath the surface like a river in limestone country, and re-emerge only when conditions altered. It took some time for the shock administered by the horrors of the First World War to affect what was most dynamic in creative endeavour, but this it did, and by the mid-1920s palaeo-modernism was losing its impetus. It never disappeared entirely, of course; the magazine *transition* was published during the 1930s, Beckett began his literary career in that decade, and Joyce published *Finnegans Wake* at the end of it, but nothing of this created anything like the impact provoked by the appearance of *Journey to the End of the Night* in 1932 and *Man's Estate* in 1933 by Céline and Malraux respectively, those two voices so profoundly characteristic of the thirties, or in a more popular vein by the publication of *All Quiet on the Western Front* a year or so previously. Once war had broken out, France suffered further severe shocks: the collapse of her army and occupation by the enemy realized in concrete terms the imprecise fears of the uneasy peace. After 1940 intellectuals had the opportunity to engage in clandestine activities of resistance to the invader, and at last the issues became as simple as the life hard and dangerous. The majority opted for resistance, active or passive according to their situation and opportunities. Nearly every name of importance in modern French literature is associated with the resistance under one guise or another. Some, like Malraux, took to the maquis and narrowly escaped torture and death. Others, like Samuel Beckett, acted in a humbler but still dangerous capacity as collectors and transmitters of information. Others again, like Sartre, Eluard, Mauriac, Jouve, Aragon and so on, militated in literature, overt or clandestine, and Camus helped produce the underground newspaper *Combat*. It was naturally in the area of journalism and propaganda that the intellectual was most effective, as German efforts to trace secret presses showed. The size of printings and extent of distribution of clandestine publications reached impressive levels, and Camus's famous article of May 1944—'For five hours they shot French people'—exposed in the best traditions of journalism the mass execution at Ascq. Of course, a handful of writers adopted the opposite ideological stand and collaborated actively with the occupying forces; their journalism in the tolerated, pro-German press aroused the strongest feelings of resentment. Robert Brasillach, one of the best of them, was executed at the Liberation; another, Drieu la Rochelle, committed suicide. The rest were small fry, like Lucien Rebatet, and survived.

But even if finer points of humanity were sacrificed both during and after the war, the main issue was clear-cut and admitted of few doubts: one was either for or against the Vichy régime. But the euphoria resulting from the success of the liberation of France did not long survive the complexities of the postwar world and particularly the development of the cold war. By 1950 the spirit of the Resistance, of comradely brotherhood in the face of a common enemy, was dead. The Communist Party had retreated into its Stalinist bastion; the Fourth Republic had settled down to its wrangles; Madagascar, Morocco, Indochina and Algeria were so many episodes of which the liberal intellectual could feel only ashamed, or torn apart and impotent, as Camus was over Algeria. Guilty memories of Dresden and Hiroshima haunted minds formerly accustomed to suppose that one side had held the monopoly of evil. By 1950 the atmosphere was therefore ripe for a reaction against commitment in literature, or *littérature engagée*, the concept of which had grown out of the experience of writing under the occupation and been provided with an elaborate theoretical basis in Sartre's essay *What Is Literature?* of 1947. But whereas during the Resistance literary commitment posed few difficulties for the writer, after the war the issues became so complex that they admitted of no clear-cut stand that was not fraught with inconsistencies: the history of Sartre's bewildering love-hate relationship with the French Communist Party is a case in point. Quite suddenly, around 1950, it began to be felt that *littérature engagée* was too simple and naive, with its rash claim to be able to alter life, rather than simply to reflect it as it is.

This, then, was the atmosphere of disenchantment in which, in May 1950, the first of the 'absurdist' plays, Ionesco's *Bald Prima Donna*, was performed in Paris, and in which, ten months later, Samuel Beckett's novel *Molloy* appeared. The impact of the two events was immediate, and their significance far-reaching; it is now quite clear that in so far as any single occurrence can mark the beginning of a new era, the arrival of Beckett and Ionesco to the forefront of the literary arena was just such a turning-point. And yet neither Beckett, nor Ionesco, nor Arthur Adamov, who achieved notoriety at the same time only to fade away later, were young Turks. In 1950 Beckett was forty-four years old, Adamov forty-two and Ionesco thirty-eight; all had been around literary Paris for several years, writing and working in relative obscurity. They were, therefore, mature men, who certainly owed little or nothing to such contemporary fads as Saint-Germain-des-Prés existentialism, to which they tended at first to be assimilated by commentators who were slow to perceive how radical was their originality. In any case, their literary allegiances lay further back, and were formed before the Second World War. Beckett had in his youth been influenced by the aesthetics of the circle of writers grouped around the magazine *transition* (published between 1927 and 1938), in particular of course by the Joyce of *Work in Progress*. Surrealism, too, had been a minor influence on him, and it had had a major impact in Ionesco and Adamov's formative development. In other words, the movement was launched by men who had been young in the inter-war years, and who also—and this was quite new in the history of French literature—were all of alien origin. Adamov was of Armenian extraction, Ionesco Rumanian, and Beckett Irish. Ionesco was always the most naturalized of the three—he is now, of course, a member of the French Academy—but throughout his life Adamov continued to speak French with a heavy accent, and Beckett has never renounced his Eire citizenship. This foreign background goes some way towards explaining why, although they wrote in perfectly fluent French, their tone sounded so radically different from that of the reigning native intellectuals.

They were, however, soon followed by Frenchmen of the next generation, who had been children when surrealism was in its heyday, and teenagers when the war broke out. Robbe-Grillet (born in 1922) submitted his second novel *The Erasers* to Beckett's publisher and it appeared in 1953; Michel Butor, four years his junior, followed suit in 1954 with *Passage de Milan*. Older writers were sufficiently impressed to modify or develop their style and thus become drawn into the same current: Nathalie Sarraute, born in 1902, who had published her first book as early as 1938, when it had passed virtually unremarked; Claude Simon, born the same year as Camus (1913), who had already published four books with other firms before he joined the Editions de Minuit in 1957; and Robert Pinget, born 1920, who had launched himself unnoticed in 1951 with *Entre Fantoine et Agapa*, the source of much of his later writing and especially of his masterpiece *L'Inquisitoire* (1962). Such disparate individuals have never constituted a 'school' or close band of friends as the surrealists did, and they are not all even published by the same firm, though Minuit issue the bulk of their work.

It follows that there was no one source for this literary revolution—or, more accurately, resurgence of an earlier revolution—though it is possible to trace a lineage which most writers I have just mentioned would not repudiate, and which for all practical purposes goes back to Flaubert. He was probably the first writer to take the novel completely seriously as an art form with rigorous principles of its own. In doing so, he envisaged a 'book about nothing', a book without 'external attachments' which would, as he put it, 'stand by itself through the internal forces of its style as the earth stands without being supported, a book with hardly any subject, or at least with an almost invisible subject'. Flaubert himself, of course, never wrote any such book, but his ideal of the novel as a perfect formal structure, owing little to the world outside it, was taken up after 1950 as a battle-cry in the attack on 'committed literature', which was seen as owing too much to external considerations. One might think that this was nothing more than the old business resurrected of 'art for art's sake', and no doubt there was an element of that in it. But with a difference: these writers did not retreat to ivory towers, but continued—

as intellectuals—to take an active interest in national and international affairs. Most of them were, for instance, signatories to the famous 'Declaration of the 121' on the necessity of military insubordination in Algeria, and they were prosecuted in consequence. But they no longer felt able to weave allusions to, and attitudes against, current or past injustices into their creative works, except in quite incidental ways. Claude Simon, for instance, set *The Palace* in Barcelona during the civil war, but his novel is an elegy, quite unlike Malraux's *Days of Hope* which is set in the thick of the struggle in 1937. And if Marguerite Duras focuses her screenplay *Hiroshima mon amour* on the occupied French town of Nevers, and the devastated Japanese city, her main concern is with the grief over a first love which a successful actress and fairly happily-married woman has buried in her psyche, until the day when a chance encounter in present-day Hiroshima permits her to exorcize it in a hysterical but memorably liberating cry, 'but it was my first love!' It is of note, too, that both *The Palace* and *Hiroshima mon amour* flout deep-rooted French political taboos: Simon in demythifying the heroics of the struggle against Franco, Duras in giving her heroine a German soldier as a lover while her countrymen were resisting the invader; and yet both writers have identified themselves with left-wing causes, Marguerite Duras even militantly so.

Flaubert (to return to him) is usually portrayed as a detached, even cold author, but his detachment was more apparent then real: there is no such thing, of course, as complete detachment on the part of the writer in his fictions, any more than there is such a thing as total realism. It is all a matter of degree. The narrator in *Madame Bovary* certainly seems detached if you compare him with the narrator in a book by Balzac or by Dickens, where the narrative voice is much more insistently in evidence. Both *Hard Times* and *Madame Bovary* open with a scene set in a schoolroom, for instance; but the manner is very different. Flaubert's narrator identifies himself at once as one of Charles Bovary's school-fellows;

but after the initial paragraphs he only reappears two or three times more throughout the whole novel. He might be supposed to serve as the silent objective reporter of the events related, adding nothing of his own; but he is, in fact, a mere front for Flaubert himself, who intervenes surreptitiously at intervals to make comments of a general nature about people, society, or existence, like this one provoked by Léon, the clerk, Emma's second lover:

> For every bourgeois, in the heat of his youth, be it only for one day, one minute, has believed himself capable of huge passions and high adventures. The most mediocre libertine has dreamt of the harem; every clerk bears in his heart the remains of a poet.
>
> (*Madame Bovary*, Part III, ch. 6)

Flaubert is able in this way to comment on the general implications of the particular happenings his narrator is describing: because he holds the reporter's impassive mask over his face he beguiles us into assuming that he too is detached. Which he certainly is not, of course: he gave the game away when he confessed privately, 'Madame Bovary, c'est moi.' Dickens, on the other hand, has no need for such subterfuges. Although his narrator does not introduce himself, he is very much in evidence from the outset, manipulating our vision and appraisal of the opening scene by his choice of angle and imagery:

> The scene was a plain, bare, monotonous vault of a schoolroom, and the speaker's square forefinger emphasized his observations by underscoring every sentence with a line on the schoolmaster's sleeve. The emphasis was helped by the speaker's square wall of a forehead, which had his eyebrows for its base, while his eyes found commodious cellarage in two dark caves, overshadowed by the wall. The emphasis was helped by the speaker's mouth, which was wide, thin, and hard set. The emphasis was

helped by the speaker's voice, which was inflexible, dry, and dictatorial. The emphasis was helped by the speaker's hair, which bristled on the skirts of his bald head, a plantation of firs to keep the wind from its shining surface, all covered with knobs, like the crust of a plum pie, as if the head had scarcely warehouse-room for the hard facts stored inside. The speaker's obstinate carriage, square coat, square legs, square shoulders—nay, his very neck-cloth, trained to take him by the throat with an un-accommodating grasp, like a stubborn fact, as it was—all helped the emphasis.

(Hard Times, Book I, ch. 1)

In passages like this Dickens's language is overt in its direction of his reader's feelings and attitudes, and most of the time it works superbly well (think of the atmospherics of *Bleak House*, for instance, generated by the opening litany on fog, both literal and metaphorical); but sometimes it is too blatant, and the reader refuses to co-operate. Flaubert offers us very little of such flamboyant drama, but his subdued and subtle devices are sometimes more effective, as in the famous sequence of short and long sentences which bridge sixteen years of his-torical time in the existence of his re-creation of the 'super-fluous hero', Frédéric Moreau:

> He travelled.
> He came to know the melancholy of the steamboat, the cold awakening in the tent, the tedium of landscapes and ruins, the bitterness of interrupted friendships.
> He returned.
> He went into society, and he had other loves. . .
>
> (Sentimental Education, Part III, ch. 6)

By similarly discreet rhetorical devices, Flaubert leads us, in his earlier novel, to sympathize with his foolish, romantic, thoroughly misguided but fundamentally rather decent heroine Emma Bovary. And another of his most remarkable creations—

2

a real *défi de maître*, this, since the material is so negative—can be found in the late short story 'A Simple Soul', the principal character of which is the illiterate, idolatrous servant woman Félicité. He holds us fascinated with the changing personality and narrowing vision of this person as fifty years and about as many pages pass over her in order, as he put it, 'to make sensitive people weep, being one of them myself.'

Flaubert's modernity, like Baudelaire's, clearly announces new attitudes which half a century later were to come to dominate the literary world. It has been said of modernists that they are romantics, albeit stealthy ones, and with a difference: that they have a sense of, and feeling for, the ironic. It has also been said that modernism seems to have something to do with 'the intersection of apocalyptic or modern time and the timeless symbol, with the ironic relationship between contingent history and the formal wholeness of art'. The origins of such attitudes can clearly be discerned in Flaubert. After him, the great writers of modernism—Henry James, Conrad, Joyce, Proust, Kafka, Faulkner and Virginia Woolf—are of course also rightly looked upon as important precursors in the field of experimental fiction: precursors, indeed, whose achievement is not likely soon to be surpassed, and whose formal innovations are still being absorbed. The palaeo-modernist novel, with its high degree of technical sophistication, particularly its tendency towards interiorization or turning structurally in upon itself, and also what Malcolm Bradbury has called its 'air of exhausting itself formally in each new work', sets the standard against which neo-modernist fiction has to be judged.

The transition between the novels of high modernism, and the works of the *nouveau roman* which began to appear after 1950, was provided by books whose authors probably had quite different intentions in mind. The apparent neutrality of the opening lines of Ernest Hemingway's *A Farewell to Arms* (1929) offered French writers who were young in the inter-war years an example of what they saw as 'constat literature', although the flat, even subdued tone of the prose conceals the impassioned and rather naive quality of the novel's denunciation of war and exaltation of the thirties version of the drop-out syndrome. The sentimentality of the story, the hip remarks about life being a 'dirty trick', the tedious harping on a 'good time' (until the hero is redeemed by true love from boozing and wenching) do not detract from the beauty of the opening paragraphs. The famous Hemingway rhythms in these sentences are based on one of the most ancient of prosodic measures, the hexametre. This occurs in the phrases italicized in the following extract:

> In the late summer of that year we lived in a house in a village that looked across the river and the *plain to the mountains*. In the bed of the river there were pebbles and boulders, dry and white in the sun, and the water was clear and swiftly moving and *blue in the channels*. Troops went by the house and down the road and the dust they raised powdered the leaves of the trees. The trunks of the trees too were dusty and the leaves fell early that year and we saw the troops marching along the road and the dust rising and leaves, stirred by the breeze, falling and the soldiers marching and afterwards the road bare and white except for the leaves.
>
> The plain was rich with crops; there were many *orchards of fruit trees* and beyond the plain the mountains were brown and bare. There was fighting in the mountains and at night we could see the flashes from the artillery. In the dark it was like summer lightning, but the nights were cool and there was not the feeling of a storm coming.
>
> (*A Farewell to Arms*, Book I, ch. 1)

Hemingway, like Erskine Caldwell and John Dos Passos, has exerted an immense influence on French writing, largely through the translations of Maurice Coindreau, who has done for this phase of American fiction what Baudelaire did for Edgar Allen Poe, that is to incorporate it into the native tradition. American writers presented an example of freshness, of direct, blunt, even brutal transcriptions of modern urban and industrial reality, in a world where man was shown as dehumanized and nature sterilized by the machine, by the conveyor belt in the factory and the combine harvester on the land; the city's *lumpenproletariat*, the dispossessed share-cropper of the plains, found their spokesmen in novels that provoked widespread enthusiasm when they were translated into French. Let us now try to listen to the paragraphs quoted above with a French ear; in translation of course the rhythms largely disappear with the Biblical 'ands', leaving only a flat, neutral tone which was widely imitated:

> Cette année-là, à la fin de l'été, nous habitions une maison, dans un village qui, par-delà la rivière et la plaine, donnait sur les montagnes. Dans le lit de la rivière il y avait des cailloux et des galets, secs et blancs au soleil, et l'eau était claire, et fuyait, rapide et bleue dans les courants. Des troupes passaient devant la maison et s'éloignaient sur la route, et la poussière qu'elles soulevaient poudrait les feuilles des arbres. Il y avait également de la poussière sur le tronc des arbres, et cette année-là, les feuilles tombèrent de bonne heure, et nous voyions les troupes passer sur la route; poussière soulevée; chute des feuilles détachées par la brise; soldats en marche, et de nouveau la route solitaire et blanche sous les feuilles.
>
> La plaine était couverte de récoltes. Il y avait de nombreux vergers, et, à l'horizon, les montagnes étaient brunes et dénudées. On se battait dans les montagnes, et le soir, nous pouvions apercevoir les éclairs de l'artillerie. Dans l'obscurité, on eût dit des éclairs de chaleur; toutefois les nuits étaient fraîches et l'on n'avait point l'impression qu'un orage menaçait.

The direct result of this kind of writing was the first part of Camus's novel *The Outsider*, which Robbe-Grillet admires, although he has reservations about what happens to it later in the novel because, he claims, the book isn't 'written in as *purified* a language as the first few pages might lead one to suppose' (*Snapshots and Towards a New Novel*, p. 85; nor, as we have noted, is *A Farewell to Arms*). And this comes about naturally enough, Robbe-Grillet points out, since Camus's 'intention is to reveal to us, as Pascal put it, "the natural misfortune of our condition".' What Robbe-Grillet seeks is the rigorous exclusion of such 'anthropomorphism'; he wants the neutrality of tone to be consistent and thorough-going, as it undoubtedly is in one of his own early texts:

> The coffee-pot is on the table.
> It is a round, four-legged table, covered by a piece of red and grey checked oilcloth. The background to the checks is neutral, a yellowish white which might once have been ivory—or white. In the middle is a tile, being used as a table-mat; its design is entirely obscured, or at least made unrecognisable, by the coffee-pot standing on it.
> The coffee-pot is made of brown china. Its shape is that of a sphere, with a superimposed cylindrical filter equipped with a mushroom-shaped lid. The spout is an S with attenuated curves, with a slight bulge at the base. The handle might be said to be shaped like an ear, or rather the outer rim of an ear; but it would be an ungainly ear, too rounded and with no lobe, which would thus be shaped like a 'pot handle'. The spout, the handle, and the knob of the lid are cream-coloured. All the rest is a very even light brown, and shiny.
> There is nothing else on the table; only the oilcloth, the tile and the coffee-pot.
>
> (*Snapshots and Towards a New Novel*, p. 3)

Robbe-Grillet backed up the example of writing of this kind

in a carefully argued theoretical attack against the indulgent humanism of the previous generation, and particularly Sartre's view of literature. In advocating a fresh approach to the purpose of writing he diverges radically from the tenets Sartre expounds in *What Is Literature?*. For Robbe-Grillet, the writer's first duty is to his art, which he alone is equipped to advance; his effectiveness in the political arena is no greater than any other citizen's, and may well be smaller. In line with this scepticism about the efficacy of ideological commitment there is advocacy of a new approach to characterization and psychology in fiction. Nathalie Sarraute, in her essay *The Age of Suspicion*, claims that the novelist no longer 'believes' in his characters (we have come a long way since Flaubert made himself ill by sharing so intensely in Emma Bovary's sufferings under arsenic). Even if the writer does still believe in his characters the reader no longer will. The history of the novel reveals increasingly elaborate and sophisticated devices being invented by authors to convince their increasingly sceptical readers of the 'reality' of their fictions. In this writers have managed to keep only a step or two ahead, and then not always: we have all experienced annoyance with stories in which we find the characters 'unconvincing'. The new novelists maintain that they no longer can be made convincing, so the writer might as well own up to his impotence and not seek to deceive anyone about the reality of his creations. Detailed psychological analyses of the feelings and motives of a character sound more and more 'phoney' to the reader. So, instead of doing a 'straight' study of a jealous man in the classical manner, Robbe-Grillet wrote a novel which itself constitutes a fit of jealousy, becoming gradually more and more irrational and fanciful as the obsession feeds upon itself. In this way Robbe-Grillet's novels are themselves, as much as his essays, an aesthetic.

The same is true of Nathalie Sarraute. Her interest lies in the area of wordless, instinctive behaviour which, like a subterranean power, or like 'tropisms' in biology, governs our relations with other people. Since she cannot analyse the unsayable verbally, she indicates through dialogue, interior monologue and situation the antagonisms, resentments and sudden sympathies which activate her characters. Moreover, time in the *nouveau roman* is never a straightforward matter of hour added to hour and day to day, since the human imagination is continually extending crucial very brief moments (such as the seconds during which a road accident takes place), and drastically compressing much longer stretches of duration, like tedious periods of work. Nor is the order in which events actually occur often respected by the human memory; so the new novel is similarly disrespectful of it, rarely signalling its transitions by tense or otherwise from present to past time and back again. And sometimes the human consciousness harbours flagrant inconsistencies, even logical impossibilities of the sort that occur in Robbe-Grillet's novel *The House of Assignation*, where the mysterious circumstances in which Manneret has died make it imperative for Johnson to quit Hong Kong, so before he leaves he asks Manneret to lend him the money he needs, and so on. The new novelists therefore believe that it is quite legitimate for the novel, like the mind, to stretch, abridge, shuffle and repeat, with or without variations, any particular occurrence or event. They are also convinced by developments in phenomenology in recent French philosophy that the external world can only be taken at face-value, and that there are no hidden depths, which might harbour malevolent feelings towards man, to such things as the notorious root of the chestnut tree which, in Sartre's novel *Nausea*, seems to claw at the hero Roquentin like a vulture's talon. On the contrary, writes Robbe-Grillet, 'man looks at the world, but the world doesn't look back at him,' though it may willy-nilly act as a focus for his emotions, and like the centipede in *Jealousy*, or like the piece of string in *The Voyeur*, release their pent-up force just as contact with an earth will discharge static electricity; but it always remains passive and irremediably external, totally unaffected by the touch which matters to man who is 'no more, from his own point of view, than the only witness'. But if he can learn to live with the smooth, meaningless, mindless and amoral surface of things he will, says Robbe-Grillet, 'reject communion' with them, and in doing so 'reject tragedy' which inevitably follows when he is made aware of their utter indifference. Robbe-Grillet thus flatly refuses to embrace the 'tragic' vision of an 'absurd' world which he finds in the work of Camus and Sartre; the world is not absurd, he argues, it is simply there. He likewise rejects the accusation that his own writings are 'inhuman'; by constantly maintaining that everything in the novel must be seen from a human, circumscribed and relativistic point of view, and that nothing pseudo-human should be posited about the external world, Robbe-Grillet claims that he is more genuinely a humanist than his predecessors, whose anthropomorphism tended to belittle man in relation to the surrounding hostile universe.

The reader of novels inspired by this new attitude is not treated to the hectorings of authorial rhetoric, but expected to co-operate with the writer in the joint elaboration of a world which is open to infinite development by the reader's imagination. His activity is therefore creative, prolonging that of the author, which is only to be expected in an era which 'is less sure of itself and more modest, perhaps because it has abandoned the idea of the omnipotence of the individual'. From this it follows that form must logically be prior to content: neither writer nor reader will know in advance what the novel is going to 'contain', what it is going to be about: they will both discover that in the process of creating it. The novelist can have no previously determined 'message' for which he merely requires a vehicle to put it across, or if he has, he can only expect to produce the most dreary *roman à thèse* written didactically, to a formula. The true artist, on the contrary, starts writing in order to find out what it is precisely he wishes to convey. Content can only be a function of form, and the determining factor in all literary creation must be the formal decisions (how long?, what tense?, from which point of view?, etc.) taken in the very process of the undertaking. To write according to a prior ideological commitment, as Sartre recommends, is therefore a contradiction in terms as far as Robbe-Grillet is concerned.

Of course, as I have already indicated, the new approach threw up works before theory, which has tended always to be *post hoc* and indeed to leave largely out of account aspects of the works, such as humour or myth in Robbe-Grillet's case, which are if anything more significant than those on which the heaviest stress is laid in the essays. And in any case independent figures like Beckett and Genet had already been writing for some time oblivious of the theory, but within its general spirit and certainly affecting its elaboration by their example (*Towards a New Novel* contains a short study of Beckett, for instance). For there can be no doubt that Beckett's novels are new in a more radical way even than Robbe-Grillet's, because they call into question the validity of the expressive act itself. But even though he and Genet stand outside all schools and coteries, rarely discuss their work in public and never theorize in a general fashion about it or its place in the contemporary movement, they are clearly two of the major figures in the neo-modernist revival. Now that several years have elapsed since *Molloy* appeared it is evident that this current, greeted at first with the derision that hails all avant-gardes, represents a profound renewal in literary aesthetics, one which maintains rhetoric even in its anti-rhetoric, and holds to the highest ideals of art even when it appears at first sight to be anti-art. For of course neo-modernism is not anti-art, it is opposed only to a certain kind of art, which it considers outdated and thus irrelevant to the contemporary world. This includes conventional socialist realist art just as much as conventional bourgeois art. It is concerned to drive the money-changers out of the temple, not to tear down the icons: 'far from making a clean sweep of the past,' says Robbe-Grillet, 'it is on the names of our predecessors that we find it easiest to agree, and our only ambition is to continue where they left off' (*Towards a New Novel*, p. 137). And this they certainly have achieved. In a talk critical of Robbe-Grillet's theories Bernard Bergonzi argued that 'the novel cannot, in fact, escape from the limitations of lineality and chronology' (*The Listener*, 23 March 1967), but I believe that both in theory and in practice Robbe-Grillet and others have shown that it can, indeed, escape from these limitations, while still remaining recognizably a fictive structure enriching and extending our experience of the world we inhabit.

This, then, would be how I would describe and define neo-modernism. I have laid most stress on the novel, since a novelist is the subject of this book, but in the theatre and the cinema it is obvious that a similar exploration into formal possibilities is taking place. Narrational chronology, consistency of characterization, conventional dialogue, all are subverted in the search for fresher, more vivid, more natural and more genuine forms of the medium. Superficially unconventional, Harold Pinter's plays have a classical rigour about them; and even though nothing much may appear to 'happen' in them in the traditional sense of theatrical development, they generate considerable tension by timing and the judicious use of silence. They are certainly as dramatically expressive, if not as rich, as the great works of palaeo-modernism, *A Dream Play* or *Three Sisters*. And in the cinema the directors of the 'new wave' acknowledge a clear debt to the classics of the film, to Lang, Ford and Hitchcock, while developing a free, loose style which differs radically from the more rigid structures that were necessitated by less flexible and sophisticated equipment. And in this medium, too, neo-modernism has already produced its own masterpieces, films like *Zabriskie Point* directed by Antonioni and *Persona* directed by Bergman, which in terms of subtlety and range can compare with anything palaeo-modernism created in the silent film. In none of these areas, fortunately, do we appear to be near to seeing an end to what Kermode sees as modernism's distinguishing characteristic, its

'formal desperation': the restless play with structures
continues to excite us. And in the forefront of this endeavour
stands one of neo-modernism's greatest novelists, Claude
Simon.

II

Wallace Stevens's 'rage for order' has him by the throat, too,
as we shall see in the chapters that follow. But before embarking on that, let us explore the affinities his work reveals
with the great palaeo-modernists to whom he has acknowledged a debt. Like his coeval Camus he has been profoundly
affected by Dostoyevsky, by the unique density and intensity
of his novels which are features (all proportions kept) of
Simon's writings also. But a more specific influence can be
discerned in his early books. The second he published, *La
Corde raide*, takes its epigraph from Dostoyevsky; novels like
Le Tricheur and *Gulliver* could be said to be rather sombre in
their Dostoyevskian preoccupation with mystery and sensational crime, and their concentration on dark and even evil
forces at work in human affairs, corrupting, polluting and
destroying people's feeble attempts to achieve happiness and
tranquillity; and *The Wind's* hero is a kind of Dostoyevsky
innocent, a Simonian 'Idiot'. But after *The Wind* this influence
fades as the mature writer outgrows the young man's literary
enthusiasms; for what he tried to imitate in Dostoyevsky was
an atmosphere, the rather feverish tone, without at the same
time sharing the religious and social assumptions underlying
the original. In so far as they possess a Dostoyevskian flavour,
Simon's early works do not rise much above laboured pastiche.

From Joseph Conrad, on the other hand, Simon learned
something much more lastingly important: how to construct
a fiction. The books of his apprentice years all show him
exploring and developing techniques copied from the Polish
master, who is for him 'the father of the kind of novel which

has freed itself from extra-literary preoccupations like message, realism and psychology' (*Le Monde Hebdomadaire*, 6-12 April 1967), and he refers interviewers to the preface of *The Nigger of the Narcissus* which he believes to be a text of crucial importance in his own development. There Conrad writes:

> Fiction—if it at all aspires to be art—appeals to temperament. And in truth it must be, like painting, like music, like all art, the appeal of one temperament to all the other innumerable temperaments whose subtle and resistless power endows passing events with their true meaning, and creates the moral, the emotional atmosphere of the place and time. Such an appeal to be effective must be an impression conveyed through the senses; and, in fact, it cannot be made in any other way, because temperament, whether individual or collective, is not amenable to persuasion. All art, therefore, appeals primarily to the senses, and the artistic aim when expressing itself in written words must also make its appeal through the senses, if its high desire is to reach the secret spring of responsive emotions. It must strenuously aspire to the plasticity of sculpture, to the colour of painting, and to the magic suggestiveness of music— which is the art of arts. And it is only through complete, unswerving devotion to the perfect blending of form and substance; it is only through an unremitting never-discouraged care for the shape and ring of sentences that an approach can be made to plasticity, to colour, and that the light of magic suggestiveness may be brought to play for an evanescent instant over the commonplace surface of words: of the old, old words, worn thin, defaced by ages of careless usage.

Simon shares completely the emphasis Conrad lays upon visualization, on making palpable, on creating a sensuously experienced world, rather than on conveying a message. In his own case, he is not concerned in *The Flanders Road* to analyse the political and moral dilemmas of the period, the sort of thing which occupies nearly all of Sartre's attention in *Roads to Freedom;* nor, in *The Palace,* does he go in for the sort of ideological conversations which take up so much space in Malraux's novel *Days of Hope.* On the contrary: in the first book he reconstructs, even reconstitutes, a moment on a road in the war zone with such vividness that not only did one of the participants recognize it at once after twenty years, but the rest of us who were not there carry the feel of it in our imagination long after reading about it. And in *The Palace* the requisitioned luxury hotel of the title is faithfully resurrected before our eyes by such details as the 'huge couch . . . uphol-stered in faded red or rather pinkish moiré silk, still in rather good condition along the back, but worn on the seat, frayed in ladders of parallel fibres fine as hairs' (pp. 19-20) which is soon stained with grease when one of the characters leans his rifle against it.

More concretely, we find Simon in *The Wind* adopting the sort of devices of narrative reconstruction (it is not for nothing that the novel is subtitled 'Attempted Restoration of a Baroque Altarpiece') elaborated by Conrad in *Under Western Eyes* and other works. In *Lord Jim,* as in *Heart of Darkness,* Marlow is the narrator, but he is not omniscient. Indeed, in *Lord Jim* he is not introduced until the fourth chapter, and some of his information is gleaned only 'a long time after' from 'an elderly French lieutenant' whom he met 'by the merest chance', 'one afternoon in Sydney', and whose story is related in chapter twelve. Similarly, in *Under Western Eyes* Conrad's narrator, the ageing teacher of languages, is by no means in full possession of all the information needed to tell Razumov's story. He acquires this only gradually, from a variety of sources, one of which is Razumov's personal diary, but part of the truth is revealed only at the very end of the novel when, the narrator tells us, 'I heard for the first time of Razumov's public confession in Laspara's house', a crucial episode about which only a 'very summary' version had been available. This is very like the technique Simon's schoolmaster narrator adopts in *The Wind*: he picks up information, from which the story is built up, in a variety of ways. He learns a lot, of course, from the protagonist Montès, but other people, like the lawyer, tell him things too. The very Conradian device of situating a marginal observer, like Marlow or the language-teacher, within the narrative, and making him its principal constructor, is seen operating at its purest in *The Wind*, which is for that reason still a rather derivative novel. But by *The Grass* Claude Simon reveals that he has transcended and absorbed this very necessary and fruitful influence. He will still employ time-shifts like Conrad, unfolding his narrative in piecemeal fashion as memory or association dredges up fragments of information buried in the narrator's consciousness; he will continue to follow Conrad's example and employ dialogue, or free indirect speech, as a vehicle for conveying facts about the situation; and, like Conrad introducing Nostromo almost surreptitiously, he will still slip in vital details amongst a lot of secondary material. But he will no longer employ, as a kind of safety net, an omniscient narrator of the kind that has to tell us about Decoud's end in *Nostromo* since in the nature of things no one else could have observed it. *The Grass* is transitional in this regard: although the whole story is told very closely from Louise's point of view, her consciousness does not constitute the sole theatre in which the story is enacted. Although the next novel, *The Flanders Road*, alternates between first- and third-person narration (between 'I' and 'Georges'), nothing occurs outside Georges's mental sphere. And in *The Palace*, the whole novel is enacted in the student's mind, and is compounded of his memories of the past and his impressions of the present. Thus by the early 1960s Simon had fully absorbed the lessons of Conrad, and had begun to surpass them.

The other influences which Simon sustained are more obvious and more generally shared with other 'new novelists'. Proust's flexible construction of time in *La Recherche*, where he moves over long stretches with few temporal indications to give an impression of generality is widely followed today, not least by Claude Simon in a novel like *Histoire* which covers half a century of human history. Just as in his account of Swann's love affair with Odette Proust ranges over months and even years of time, or in his later volumes glides freely between the Dreyfus case and the occupation of eastern France by the Germans in 1914-18, so *Histoire* moves us from the narrator's father penning laconic postcards for his fiancée, the narrator's future mother, to the hero himself trying to sell the chest in which the cards have been stored all those years. There is a distinction, of course: Proust is genuinely vague about time, even indifferent to matters of chronological exactitude, partly because the writing of his novel was spread over many years, whereas Simon deliberately adopts imprecison from the outset. The result, aesthetically speaking, may be similar, but the intention is different.

Simon is quite overt about his debt to Proust. He quotes him frequently (in *The Battle of Pharsalus* even systematically, as part of the plot, using a technique dubbed 'intertextuality'), and his style presents some analogies with Proust's; they both use long, complex periods for instance, and where Proust subordinates, Simon tends to parenthesize, so that the cumulative effect of such syntax will often sound very similar. Let us compare two passages which illustrate this rather well. They both describe old women. In Proust's case the famous though now eclipsed actress Berma is presiding over a dreary tea-party while the rest of fashionable society is toasting the current queen of the Paris stage. Proust's description rises to a superb climax of pathos and grandeur:

> Berma's daughter was too well aware of the ignominy which in her mother's eyes attached to Rachel, she knew that she would die of despair at the thought of her daughter begging for an invitation from the former prostitute. So she told the young man and her husband that what he

suggested was impossible. But she took her revenge as she sat at the tea-table by a series of little grimaces expressive of the desire for pleasure and the annoyance of being deprived of it by her kill-joy mother. The latter pretended not to see her daughter's cross looks and from time to time, in a dying voice, addressed an amiable remark to the solitary guest. But soon the rush of air which was sweeping everything towards the Guermantes mansion, and had swept me thither myself, was too much for him; he got up and said good-bye, leaving Phèdre or death—one scarcely knew which of the two it was—to finish, with her daughter and her son-in-law, devouring the funeral cakes.

(*Time Regained*, tr. Andreas Mayor)

In Simon's example the narrator's mother, like a spectre at a feast, haunts evenings of chamber music, cadaverous and painted in her armchair. Characteristically, this passage peters out since the face reminds the narrator of something analogous, and as always the association causes an abrupt change of topic; but before this occurs we can feel a crescendo effect not unlike Proust's:

each bending over, complimenting her pretending to ignore the face with the brightly-rouged cheekbones that seemed day after day not to shrink but to be turning into some kind of sharp-edged object (as if everything that happened to be on either side of the ridge of the nose were gradually being filed down, pushed back, until it seemed that there was no longer anything left but a profile as thin, as lacking in depth and substance as a sheet of paper), beginning already to assume, with its jutting cheekbones brightened with rouge by a supreme coquetry or rather a supreme and arrogant defiance, that consistency of an inert substance or rather rendered inert by suffering: something like leather or even the papier-mâché of carnival masks, Punch with his absurd and terrifying expression caused by some irremediable outrage, some irremediable wound, and she—or what was left of her—entrenched behind it.

(*Histoire*, pp. 46-7)

Again like his contemporaries, Simon has derived great benefit from a study of narrative methods, especially interior monologue, as practised by Virginia Woolf and James Joyce; of Joyce, in particular, much could be said: Simon always mentions his name admiringly, and *Ulysses* seems to be affectionately parodied in *Histoire*, pp. 32-3. The raising of the pun (above its status in *Tristram Shandy* as a mere embellishment) to high art in *Finnegans Wake*, where it becomes an integral and all-embracing element of total structure in fiction, was probably just as inspiring an example to Simon as *monologue intérieur* which, in common with many others of his generation, he imitated from *Ulysses*. Joyce's later verbal profusion lies behind several contemporary works, not least Simon's recent novels, where the proliferative potential of linguistic components is exploited to the full. Borges's method also follows from Joyce's, as does Nabokov's. And Joyce's magpie-like plagiarism, plundering sources of widely differing kinds in many languages, perhaps can be accounted for in terms of the exile's doubts about what constitutes his real fatherland, his authentic spiritual and cultural roots. Nabokov is the greatest of the post-modernists who have followed Joyce in this path (as the puns on Lolita and Dolores make clear); Nabokov's heroes, Pnin and Humbert, are exiles who seek their bearings in an alien tongue and a strange, even hostile culture.

The importance of *Finnegans Wake* in post-modernism includes but also transcends layout, typography, marginalia and footnotes, though innovations in this field are being pursued by Michel Butor and others. It also transcends the kind of circularity where the serpent bites its tail, though this aspect of the *Wake* is taken up in Beckett's *Molloy* and Simon's

The Battle of Pharsalus, to mention them only. The essential Joycean legacy for post-modernism is what Ihab Hassan calls, rightly I am sure, a 'metalanguage [created] from the chaos of the world's phonemes, fusing the Viconian modes of hieroglyph, metaphor and abstraction', and Stephen Heath, in stressing the role of pastiche and self-pastiche in the *Wake* (by which I think he means much the same thing as Hassan does in speaking of Joyce's 'ruthless self-parody'), likewise draws attention to a crucial aspect of Joyce's modernity. We may observe it recurring in the phenomenon of intertextuality, a more and more common device in the French novel. As Stephen Heath puts it, 'the situation of the nouveau roman is post-Joyce: Joyce, that is, is a major element in its situation, [which] is that work of textual reactivation in which the work of Joyce represents so important a stage.'

This self-consciousness of fiction in fiction is what is archetypally modernist. Shem is writing a book which is the *Wake* itself; this is the case with Proust's narrator, too, of course, but Joyce goes further in offering the 'parody of a parody'. Such are Nabokov's *Pale Fire*, Robbe-Grillet's *Project for a Revolution in New York*, and Simon's *The Battle of Pharsalus* in which the central figure O. is alternately author of and protagonist within the fiction, in a text that presents itself as being, so to speak, 'self-generated'. This is what I understand by Hassan's term 'parodic reflexiveness' in which 'the genre, with its multiple, fractured and ambiguous perspectives' comes of age. Of course, there may be drawbacks in Joyce's method and in its imitators'; Hassan's rhetorical question, 'Without hope of redemption, will not such ['lapsarian'] irony turn secretly into despair or even malice?' commands an answer which it is yet too early to give. But Hassan himself indicates the possible alternative tradition within modernism, Picasso's 'pagan wit'. I think we have some of that in Simon's baroque, pantheist side, his sheer celebration of life's processes in spite of their tragic destination. But he gives his sensuous impulse rigour by sharing with other post-modernists in continuing the Joycean heritage of proposing rational control of the pullulating and effervescent energies of the world.[1]

Simon owes, too, a general debt to French pathfinders in the modern like Louis-Ferdinand Céline and Michel Leiris. But, more markedly than any of his colleagues, he has been profoundly influenced by William Faulkner; so much so, in fact, that some critics have tended to dismiss his work as little more than pastiche of the great Southern writer. In reality, Simon probably owes no more to Faulkner than he does to Conrad, but because the latter's style is not so obviously personal it is harder to accuse Simon of copying it. He admires Faulkner primarily for developing the 'sensorial' rather than the 'intellectual' possibilities of literary creation, but he has his reservations, in particular over Faulkner's habit of delivering himself of moral observations of 'staggering banality, of lamentable conformity'; 'it would be interesting', he says, 'to separate out in Faulkner's work the admirable passages in which he wrote so superbly (about people, things, animals, smells . . .) from those in which he philosophizes and moralizes' (*Le Monde Hebdomadaire*, 6-12 April 1967).

These objections, together with the gradual and necessary quality of the evolution of Simon's style over the years (which will be examined in the next chapter), makes it very improbable that anything like pastiche is a satisfactory description of the connection between the two writers. There may, however, be a case for supposing unconscious imitation, even in such a selfconscious novelist. It is true that Simon shares certain technical devices with William Faulkner and may have derived them from him. Random soundings in one of Faulkner's most characteristic works[2] show his fondness for colons and parentheses, both of which are standard features of Simon's practice. For example:

. . . accepting the fact that he must value above all not

her but the virginity of which she was custodian and on which she placed no value whatever: the frail physical stricture which to her was no more than a hangnail would have been. Knew the brother loved death best of all and was not jealous, would (and perhaps in the calculation and deliberation of her marriage did) have handed him the hypothetical hemlock (p. 10).

Simon's 'comme si' certainly seems to be modelled on a favourite Faulknerian phrase, as for example in:

> . . . the light dwindled slowly, yet at the same time without altering its quality, as if I and not light were changing, decreasing . . . (p. 187)

This last quotation reveals, as would many another ('. . . and her laying up there in the house, waiting to die . . .', p. 435) Faulkner's predilection for the present participle and, more generally, for a rhythmical prose that presents undeniable analogies with Simon's.

The issue becomes even more complex if we refer to the Faulkner texts which Simon would most likely have read, the French translations (by Maurice Edgar Coindreau and others) which appeared before the last war. In this respect *Sanctuaire*, translated by R. N. Raimbault and Henri Delgove, is particularly revealing: one might almost say that it unconsciously 'Simonizes' Faulkner's American, converting it on occasion into phrases the rhythms of which the Frenchman himself might easily have created—as for example in the following fragment:

> Elle ne répondit rien. Elle pensait au train pavoisé d'oriflammes et qui était déjà à Starkville; aux tribunes bariolées; à l'orchestre avec le gouffre étincelant du basson; au pentagone verdoyant pointillé de joueurs accroupis poussant des cris brefs et glapissants comme

des oiseaux de marais dérangés par un alligator, qui,
incertains d'où vient le danger, immobiles, prêts à
s'envoler, s'encouragent l'un l'autre avec de brusques
appels, absurdes, plaintifs, circonspects, éperdus.[3]

At this point in the novel the original reads 'encouraging one
another with short meaningless cries, plaintive, wary, and
forlorn'. This already reveals an undeniable Simonian flavour,
but the French translation does so even more in its dropping of
the last copulative and in the resulting concatenation of epithets
separated only by commas. And the end of the twenty-ninth
chapter reads in translation, even more than in the original,
just like several of the Claude Simon climaxes we shall be
examining:

> Horace ne les entendait pas. Il n'entendait pas les
> hurlements de l'homme qui s'était brûlé. Il n'entendait
> pas le feu, bien qu'il se tordît toujours vers le ciel avec
> la même violence, comme s'il eût trouvé en lui-même
> son propre aliment, silencieux comme une voix furieuse
> au milieu d'un cauchemar, comme un rugissement muet
> sorti des profondeurs paisibles du néant.

In fact, the whole atmosphere of *Sanctuaire*, especially its
brooding concern with squalor and evil, reminds one of
Simon's first two novels, *Le Tricheur* and *Gulliver*. Simon was
clearly impressed by American writing, and by Faulkner's in
particular, like many other French novelists of his generation;
it will be remembered that Sartre devoted early essays to
Sartoris and *The Sound and the Fury*, and Camus's admiration led
to an adaptation of *Requiem for a Nun*.

The obvious occasional similarities between Simon's style
and French versions of Faulkner should not, however, blind us
to the differences. For all its elaboration, Faulkner's writing—
compared with Simon's—is relatively unselfconscious. It has
a deceptive spontaneity lacking in Simon. It does not attempt

to be 'intellectual', but only to imitate the thought processes
and speech rhythms of Southern people. Simon's language on
the other hand is a highly imaged artefact, deliberately and
painstakingly developed for a purpose which owes little to any
other writer (except, marginally, to Proust in the matter of
time and memory). In any case he has shown in his most
recent works—*Les Corps conducteurs* and *Triptyque*—that his
style is not static and immutable, and that he is able to discard
the long, sinuous periods of his middle novels when his
thematic interests change; for there is little that can be called
Faulknerian about these books. And in some respects Robbe-
Grillet is closer to Faulkner's practice, as is shown particularly by the 'hole in the narrative' aspect of both *Sanctuary*
and *The Voyeur*; the rape of Temple in the first case, and the
assault and murder of Jacqueline in the second, are 'burned'
out of the story, and have to be reconstructed by the reader's
interpreting, detective-like, various signs and indications that
individually are enigmatic but which cumulatively amount to
proof.

Nevertheless, it is clear from an investigation of Claude
Simon's sources and debts that, like other neo-modernist
writers, he has selfconsciously carved out a place for himself
in the fictional tradition he shares with his contemporaries.
Like them, he builds on what has gone before; like them, too,
he modifies and develops his inheritance. In extending what
he has learned from the practice and example of the great
modernists he has created a fictional œuvre which is uniquely
personal. It presents similarities, of course, with the work of
other *nouveaux romanciers*, but cannot be confused with their
explorations. What Simon has created, he has created alone.
Like all great artists, he has fashioned his own instrument by
trial and error in the never-ending task—and never-satisfied
ambition—of expressing his own vision of reality in the
universal medium of language.

INTRODUCTION—NOTES

1 The preceding two paragraphs are based on remarks made by me as member of a panel, chaired by Bernard Benstock and devoted to the theme of the relationship between *Finnegans Wake* and the postmodern imagination, which took place in Dublin (as part of the Joyce Symposium proceedings) on 15 June 1973. The panel discussion followed the reading of a paper on this subject by Ihab Hassan, from which I draw my quotations. I quote too from Benstock's study *Joyce-Again's Wake* (Seattle and London: University of Washington Press, 1965), pp. 118-19, and from *The Nouveau Roman* by Stephen Heath (London: Elek, 1972), p. 29. I also make passing reference to Heath's essay 'Ambiviolences: Notes pour la lecture de Joyce', *Tel Quel*, no. 50 (Summer 1972) and no. 51 (Autumn 1972).

2 *The Sound and the Fury*, *As I Lay Dying* (New York: Random House, Modern Library Paperbacks, 1946).

3 Paris: Gallimard (Le Livre de Poche), 1964, p. 57.

A NOVELIST'S WORLD:
Claude Simon's Major Themes

Ecrire, cet étrange plaisir solitaire
—Claude Simon

Claude Simon is, first and last, a novelist. What he has written or published outside the canon of his fiction is of little significance. But, for the record, this is what it appears to be made up of. There are the interviews, replies to literary *enquêtes* and questionnaires, public lectures and so on, which constitute an unsystematic and partial exposition of the theory, or aesthetic, of the kind of novel-writing Simon practises; but he is not a propagandist or polemicist like Robbe-Grillet or even Nathalie Sarraute, and so far he has shown no interest in collecting these scattered pieces. I doubt even whether he attaches very much importance to them; they were all produced in response to a stimulus exerted from outside (a journalist's questions, an invitation to lecture) and were not, like Robbe-Grillet's statements, provoked by any inner compulsion to make explicit what have been called 'les sentiers de la création'. In fact, in his contribution to a series bearing that title, published by Skira, Simon writes: 'As far as I am concerned, the only "paths of creation" are those opened up step by step, that is word by word, by the very progression of the writing' (*Orion aveugle*, preface). In other words, for Claude Simon the act of writing alone can uncover, and then only partially, the principles which govern its functioning, so that all 'theory' is inevitably *post hoc*, descriptive of a state of affairs that lies already behind in the past. Hence no doubt the fact that Simon sees no utility in giving these utterances a more permanent form.

Apart from composing theoretical statements, Simon has had one play performed. It was called *La Séparation*; it was based on *The Grass;* it consisted, drama critic Jacques Lemarchand writes, of 'four interwoven monologues' and was not very effective theatrically;[1] it was staged at the Théâtre de Lutèce, a small experimental playhouse in Paris, in the spring of 1963, was taken off after a few performances, and has not been published; nor is it likely to be. Like Henry James, Simon writes superb dialogue in his novels, but he has no sense of theatre, no feeling for ways of filling a stage with movement and life. Although he would like to write a filmscript, no one has yet invited him to do so, and he has done nothing in this medium at all.

The only other published works, apart from the novels, and a kind of prose poem called *Femmes* which was illustrated by Joan Miró, are the early essay in autobiography *La Corde raide*, from which I shall have occasion to quote fairly frequently in this study; various pre-publication fragments from the novels (these appeared in various journals—*Tel Quel*, *Lettres Nouvelles*, and so on—and rarely show variants of any significance); and a rather indifferent short story called 'Babel' which Simon now repudiates. And that is all.

The novels, then (and even so not the entire canon, of course), are what really count, and they alone are the subject of the present study. Since there are now almost a dozen of them, it would help, I think, if I suggested certain broad groups or categories into which they appear naturally to fall. The first remark that has to be made is that all Simon's fiction is based, to a greater or lesser extent, on his personal experience: he has declared, not quite truthfully, that he is unable to invent anything by himself. As a reading of *La Corde raide* and acquaintance with the basic facts of his biography make clear, he certainly exploits personal memories in his novels, but refracts and distorts these, often in quite radical ways. He takes full advantage, in fact, just as Proust did, of the artist's prerogative to modify and adapt reality to fit his aesthetic purposes. Just as Proust's Combray is an idealized, even mythified version of Illiers, and his Balbec resembles the real Cabourg only in incidentals, so Claude Simon charges places, people and real occurrences with a significance quite transcending that which they originally represented. His setting for *The Palace* is and is not Barcelona; *The Wind* may be located in Perpignan, but it need not be; *The Grass* is based, like *Histoire*, only partially on family documents and souvenirs; and *The Flanders Road* draws only fragmentarily on Claude Simon's own war experiences (there is nothing about his successful escape, for instance: Georges spends the whole period in captivity). But, when that is said, the fact of an at least partial degree of personal experience does enable us to place the novels into three broad groups, as follows: firstly novels dealing with the period immediately preceding and that immediately following the Second World War (*Le Tricheur*, *Gulliver*, *The Wind*); these are perhaps the least 'personal' works in Claude Simon's fictional output, and so it is not surprising if they read occasionally as if they were written to a formula, to a pattern imitated from Simon's acknowledged masters in the art of the novel; secondly novels dealing with the Spanish civil war (*Le Sacre du printemps*, *The Palace*); these draw so obviously on Simon's own experience that little comment is needed, except (as Leon S. Roudiez has perceptively pointed out) *Le Sacre* is really just a first draft for *The Palace*, which makes a much better book 'by fusing the two consciousnesses into one [so that] the same person confronts his own civil war experience in Spain with the total experience of what he has become many years later';[2] thirdly novels dealing with the period during and after the Second World War, with particular reference to the fortunes of the narrator's family; all the other works enter this category more or less directly. At least one episode of *Triptyque*, as I have said, is set in the Jura of Simon's boyhood; *The Flanders Road* draws on his battle experience; *The Grass* recalls the sale of the family property in the Jura; *Histoire* is based on postcards in the possession of the author and forming part of the family inheritance; *The Battle of Pharsalus* not only contains memories of the same family which appears in *The Flanders Road* and *Histoire*, but also describes a journey to Greece, which must be based in part at least on travels in the Balkans which Simon has undertaken with his Greek wife. The only exception here might be thought *Les Corps conducteurs* (part of which appeared first in *Orion aveugle*), but even this is fairly transparently based on the author's visits to the United States and Latin America, the latter in connection with a writers' congress, the proceedings of which are quoted in the novel verbatim and at ironic length.

Of course, the novels are not watertight, but are all connected up by an internal system of references, especially of names: Odette occurs in *Le Tricheur* as well as in *The Battle of Pharsalus*, where the Proustian associations of the name are more prominent; a man called Charles crops up in several of the books, starting with *Le Tricheur*, and cousin Corinne looms large in the novels from *The Flanders Road* onwards. The reader is reminded both of Balzac, with his *retour des personnages* through the *Comédie humaine*, and of Faulkner with his complex Yoknapatawpha relationships, but there are differences. Unlike Balzac, Simon has not sought to make his early novels fit retrospectively into a later schema; and unlike Faulkner, he does not give us enough clues to construct a family tree in any detail. All that is established about the Simonian family is that Georges, a central character in *The Flanders Road* and *The Grass*, is related via his father to peasants of Franche-Comté origin, and through his mother with Roussillon petty nobility (the 'Reixachs'); a De Reixach (Georges's commanding officer in *The Flanders Road*) has married Corinne, the sister of Paulou and daughter of Uncle Charles, who brought up the narrator of *Histoire* and *The Battle of Pharsalus* after his father's (and Charles's brother-in-law's) death early in the First World War. How much, and how little, of this pattern is modelled on Claude Simon's own family background can be judged by a glance at the Biographical Note at the head of this book. Clearly some of it is straight from life, but less than one might at first suppose. But whatever may be the case as far as Simon's immediate relations are concerned, there is no doubt that an ancestor crops up frequently. His portrait, which Simon has inherited and a photographic reproduction of which has been published,[3] is referred to in *The Flanders Road*, particularly the crack in the paint which led the young Claude to imagine that the picture showed the blood streaming from a temple wound after the ancestor allegedly shot himself. This forbear was a member of the Convention and, as we have seen, voted for the execution of Louis XVI, became a general under Napoleon, and founded the family fortunes. But the fortunes started to decline from the Second Empire onwards, as we are told in *Le Tricheur* (p. 68), the very first novel; and the greatest of all Simon's books, *Histoire*, shows us the sunset of those fortunes, since the narrator is reduced to selling off his remaining heirlooms. The heroic figure of the regicide general is likely to show up again; Simon published some notes about that (in the review *Minuit*, no. 3, March 1973), which he sees as a first step towards a new novel in which this character will loom rather large.

It is evident, I think, that Simon's use of personal information is selective and usually distorted, perhaps in quite simple ways. The ancestor's name is given as Laverne in *Le Tricheur*: in Salses, the author's family is known as Lacombe (and that is the name which appears on bottles of table wine from the family vineyards); and the Jura peasant is given, in the fiction, the surname of Thomas, which is about as common as Simon. But as Vivian Mercier puts it, 'Simon weaves fiction around his authentic documents';[4] what interests him in, say, his war experiences is not so much his own remarkable survival but the strongly emotive image of rout and débâcle which not only underlies *The Flanders Road*, but coincides with a deeply-felt conviction that all is flux and shifting chaos, which war serves merely to render more obvious. As John Sturrock perceives, a novelist like Claude Simon who deals in memory is bound to reflect the genuine ambiguity everyone experiences as to whether 'some of the contents of his memory are fact or fiction',[5] so that it finally matters little, even if it could be ascertained, what is true and what is invented. Because some of the facts are true the novels are guaranteed a basic degree of authenticity; but the fact that a great deal is imaginary makes them artefacts, works of art that structure life rather than merely reflect it.

As to how the progression in these works figures itself in the author's own mind, Simon has been quite explicit. Interviewed by Ludovic Janvier, he spoke of his 'slow, groping evolution'; he saw his first phase as ending with *The Wind;* a second period was inaugurated by *The Grass*, and ended with *Histoire;* and a third began with *The Battle of Pharsalus*, in which for the first time he allowed himself to be governed not by what he himself wished to say but by what the writing itself said, by its own 'internal dynamic'.[6] We might see the first phase as being apprenticeship, in which he tried a number of different plots and situations in his attempt to find an authentically individual voice of his own. For this reason, these novels are not discussed in any great detail in this study. The second period can be seen as maturity, when Simon had not only established his characteristic manner, but had also started to mine the rich vein of family history that I have just discussed. In my view, these novels—especially *The Grass, The Flanders Road* and *Histoire*—constitute his highest achievement as of now, the early 1970s. His more recent works—particularly *Les Corps conducteurs*—I am less happy about. They seem to me to betray uncertainty, and to be excessively influenced by theories (picked up from others, Jean Ricardou in particular) of the alleged autogeneration of texts. Nevertheless Claude Simon is still in the prime of life, and out of his current restless experimentation an altogether new manner may evolve. He has done it before; by dint of patience and constant trying he found, with *The Grass*, how to transcend the category of the talented but minor novelist in which his early books put him. Perhaps, in much the same way, texts of the *Corps conducteurs* variety will enable him to pull off that most difficult of artistic feats, a complete self-renewal and the creation in a quite different idiom of another series of masterpieces. If this does happen, Simon will quite clearly become one of the great novelists of this century, and take his place naturally among the masters he reveres: Joyce, Faulkner, Beckett and Proust.

But for the present such considerations must be speculative. Before we turn to a more detailed discussion of the major novels of Simon's maturity, I should like us to consider first, in synoptic fashion, three important aspects of the fiction: how it handles the theme of time, which is so central to it; how the narrator operates in the novels; and what the characteristic features of Simon's style and narrative technique are.

Time and Duration

In his study of Jean Genet, Richard N. Coe describes the dilemma in which man finds himself in relation to time: he is 'caught between two irreconcilable forces', Coe tells us, 'that of the instantaneous present, his *être*, his consciousness; and that of sequence, which takes acts or words more or less at random out of the present and situates them in an unattainable past, whence they continue to dominate the present, yet themselves lie for ever out of reach'.[7] Sartre made a similar point in his famous essay on Faulkner, collected in *Situations I*, when he said that the past is never lost but remains to haunt the present, like an obsession. Simon would agree that the past is like a spectre, one that cannot be exorcized. 'There is a profound tension in his novels,' John Sturrock writes, 'between the urge to reconstruct the past as densely and plausibly as possible, and the perpetual recognition that any sort of certainty dies with the event.'[8] This is because, when things are perceived by man, that act of perception itself deforms what is perceived; and when perceptions are remembered later, the act of memory deforms those perceptions too; and, finally, when the memories are written down, the very act of writing deforms further what has twice been deformed already. No wonder Claude Simon once stated, with little exaggeration:

> All I know is that the world is on the move, that it's changing all the time, that life is a kind of perpetual motion, constant revolution, continual destruction and reconstruction, that what was true yesterday is no longer true today, that nothing perhaps is true . . .[9]

This remark was made outside the context of the fiction, but in his novels Claude Simon reiterates the same point. His treatment of time and of the way human memory and perception attempt to control and organize it reveals a profound scepticism about the nature of reality. The novels are usually articulated around an event which is only half-remembered, and at least partially imaginary;[10] this is then painfully reconstructed in a narrative process which invariably omits to do more than confirm a rather hopeless quest. This occurs in *The Flanders Road*, where Georges's sexual failure with Corinne is paradigmatic of his wider failure to reconstruct the past as it was, and in *The Palace*, where the middle-aged hero is compelled to accept the impossibility of recreating the Barcelona he knew so intimately as a young revolutionary in 1936.

Time attracts a surprisingly extensive range of epithet in Simon's writings: it is at various points described as 'solid' or 'rigid', 'gelatinous' and 'liable to putrefy', 'stagnant' and 'viscous' like sludge or a thick clay 'in which the instant resembles a spade slicing the dark earth and revealing the myriad wriggling worms' (*The Wind*, p. F163), and—of course—'inexorable', 'mechanical', its progress as irreversible as the hands of antique clocks jumping forward with the staccato rhythm imposed on every second by the action of the pendulum and giving the impression that time consists of a conglomeration of solid lumps, a 'succession of solidified fragments' or 'of fixed, frozen, motionless images' (*The Palace*, pp. 59, 73). This dual aspect of duration—its liquid, mobile quality, its resemblance to haemorrhage, ceaseless flow, and its divisible, fragmentary nature—is continually insisted upon. A wheel turns so quickly that it attains a kind of 'vertiginous immobility' (*Gulliver*, p. 90), but equally the way notes are played on a piano reveals the 'myriad particles which make up duration' (*Gulliver*, p. 132). This means that time can be telescoped, can stand still or expand, like the cottony, spongious substance it appears to be. When it is contracted the effect is usually comic, 'as in films where a facetious projectionist suddenly alters the speed of the frames [so that] our actions, however trivial or however momentous, are seen as disorganized, absurd, hilarious agitation' (*Le Sacre du printemps*, p. 226). When time stands still, as in the assassination sequence described in *The Palace*, the result is intensely dramatic and yet oddly risible; witness this instance too, from *The Flanders Road*:

> I saw Wack who had just passed me leaning over the neck of his horse his face turned back toward me his mouth open too probably trying to shout something which he didn't have air enough to make heard and suddenly lifted off his saddle as if a hook an invisible hand had grabbed him by his coat collar and slowly raised him I mean almost motionless in relation to (I mean animated by almost the same speed as) his horse that kept on galloping and me still running although a little slower now so that Wack his horse and I comprised a group of objects among which the distances were modified only gradually he being now

exactly over the horse from which he had just been lifted
wrenched slowly rising in the air his legs still arched as
though he were still riding some invisible Pegasus who
had bucked and made him fall slowing then and somehow
making a kind of double *salto mortale* on the spot so that I
saw him next head down mouth still open on the same
shout (or advice he had tried to give me) silent then lying
in the air on his back like a man stretched out in a
hammock and letting his legs hang down to the right and
left then again head up body vertical his legs beginning to
come together hanging parallel then on his stomach arms
stretched forward hands open grabbing snatching something like one of those circus acrobats during the seconds
when he is attached to nothing and liberated of all weight
between the two trapezes then finally the head down
again legs apart arms outstretched as though to bar the
way but motionless now flat against the roadside slope
and no longer moving staring at me his face stamped with
a surprised and idiot expression I thought Poor Wack he
always looked like a fool but now more than ever. . .

(pp. 119-20)

Wack's discomfiture as described here is comical, yet the
dramatic seriousness of the incident is equally palpable, and
the stress on the immobile nature of the moment reminds us of
the opening passage in Malraux's novel *Man's Estate*, where the
terrorist Tchen is poised in the act of murder. When time is
expanded, it provokes intense unhappiness, as with Bernard,
for whom a very short period—only a few seconds—is so
dragged out as to appear to be 'measured not in arbitrary,
ridiculous units of duration, but in sufferings' (*Le Sacre du
printemps*, p. 228).

Equally, time may be abolished, wiped out, either by the
recollection of vivid or painful sensations (*The Wind*, p. F175),
or by historical or family documents, 'the very skin of dreams,
of ambitions, of vanities, of futile and imperishable passions'

(*The Flanders Road*, p. 44), which bring the past back to life in all its vivid immediacy. There are moments of Proustian recall in *Le Tricheur*, when a character is transported back in time, especially to childhood, by a posture or sensation out of the normal run of things, but in the mature novels this derivative method is dropped in favour of other devices. In *The Battle of Pharsalus*, for instance, the Latin lesson is the pivot round which the narrator not only articulates memories of his boyhood, but also reaches back into the remote past, via 'the name PHARSALUS figuring in a Latin textbook and disfigured on a signpost beside a road in Thessaly' (p. 127). (This, incidentally, is, one of the few novels to contain references to events roughly contemporaneous with the writing: in this case, a left-bank student demonstration of the 1968 variety—see pp. 146-7). Such links are not surprising, since we are told in *The Palace* that time, like alcohol, has the capacity to preserve 'things and people indefinitely' (p. 40); from this state they are occasionally to be resurrected by the 'swarming and rigorous disorder of memory' (*Histoire*, p. 230), by 'exacting and tyrannical recollection' (*Le Tricheur*, p. 37). And this is just as well, since 'forgetfulness is worse than death'; something not remembered has ceased to exist, and memory must act like a camera and 'snap' reality, as the only way to prevent it from disappearing for good (*Le Tricheur*, pp. 100, 121, 154). The narrator himself, therefore, often 'photographs' things in a state of change, like the bucket of water tossed on the ground in *Le Tricheur* (p. 59), or the group of people in *Histoire* in the positions variously occupied by them (p. 226). He also 'records' aural impressions of great vividness, such as the singing of birds heard as the noise of battle dies away (*The Flanders Road*, p. 167), and he registers with a certain delay, as in *Femmes*, the sounds which accompany the movements of his characters: 'the ball rising heavily greyish and long afterwards you heard the thud of naked feet slapping the leather . . .' (p. 11). This is all carried one step further in *Les Corps conducteurs*, where 'shots' as it were are repeated in different parts of the book, thus creating an effect of simultaneity in which past and present cease to be readily distinguishable. 'Memory', comments Yves Berger on Simon's method, 'takes no account of time-perspectives.'[11]

This explains why the flashback (and even the flashforward) are structural elements of major importance in Simon's fiction. There is a continual urge to get back in time, to 'be yesterday' (*Le Sacre du printemps*, p. 208); and *Le Sacre* in particular relies heavily on flashbacks to 1936, from which stance it looks forward in time to the war period (there is a passage on prison camps on p. 260 which anticipates similar descriptions in *The Flanders Road*) as well as to 'maintenant', the period of the main action, i.e. 1952. But these movements in the temporal status of the text are carefully signalled in *Le Sacre*. This is no longer true in *The Flanders Road* or *The Palace* or *Histoire*—all being novels which rely heavily on flashback—where the evidence for a time-shift must be sought internally, via the context, rather than from any external signposts like dates at the head of the page. Such indications were also largely lacking in *Le Tricheur*, which is one of the reasons why this first novel is so prophetic of future developments in Simon's fiction; at the most a blank gap in the text alerts the reader to the presence of a narrative set in an earlier time (*Le Tricheur*, p. 68), but often even this aid is lacking. The lineage thus clearly extends from this novel of 1945 to *Triptyque* (1973), where an added dimension is supplied by the manner the stories start to be told in reverse, like a film run backwards through the projector, because the narrator imagines the reader doing the same, thumbing back in search of a passage misread or not paid proper attention to (p. 131).

I imagine it will be evident from what I have quoted that Simon's attitude to time is not detached: it is a passionate meditation on the inert, sluggish nature of duration, and the relative impotence of memory, and still less art, to make much impression on it. He has two remarkably vivid images which make this situation concrete so effectively that I should like to conclude this section with them. In the first, he contemplates an old broken-down clock which was slowly rusting, 'corroded in its turn by the time it had attempted to nibble away' (*Gulliver* p. 321). In the second image, he contrasts the continually-renewed virginities of the natural world, the unending cycles of burgeon and harvest, with the inevitable progression of decrepitude in man. But, curiously, he sees the natural world as being damned, while man enjoys a boon which nature envies him: 'the privilege of dying' (*The Wind*, p. 254). In other words, man triumphs in spite of his transitory nature, even because of it; unlike the clock, he is not mocked by an ambition to control time which has itself been defeated by time; and unlike the vegetable world, he is spared the fatigue of eternal renewal. Time, aware of its unassailable durability, can afford to leave perishable man secure at least in his dignity: a dignity arising from the clear-sighted acceptance of the fact that, sooner or later, he will die, and that the memory which is his unique weapon in the struggle against time will be erased as perfectly as if it had never existed.

Self and Narrator

The issue of the status of the narrative voice in fiction—of the '*voix-qui-parle*'—is central to the modernist novel, and Simon's work is no exception. Like other writers, he probes the ambiguous relationship between author and narrator which is so typical a feature of modernism, but he extends the investigation to include perception of flux and change, a perception which is characteristically his own.

On a purely technical level, Simon moves from the kind of fiction which employs a plausible narrator, such as *The Wind* where a *lycée* teacher, rather like Conrad's teacher of languages in *Under Western Eyes*, supplies an objective but not omniscient point of view, to a new form of novel in which the reader is addressed by the text itself. Leon S. Roudiez discerns the origins of this evolution as early as *The Flanders Road*;[12] certainly it comes to the fore in *The Battle of Pharsalus* and dominates *Les Corps conducteurs* and *Triptyque*. And we have indeed come a long way from the rather unsubtle use of younger and older variants of the same person's point of view in *Le Sacre du printemps* when we pass, via the gradually re-vealed narrator of *The Wind*, to the complex 'observer observed', the narrator called O. who is also an actor (and sometimes actress) in the drama of *The Battle of Pharsalus*. Let us investigate this evolution in a little more detail.

The narrator in *Le Tricheur* is for the most part of the omniscient third-person variety, with the occasional drop into stream-of-consciousness. But some sections (such as Louis's attempt at purchasing a revolver) are narrated in the first person, no doubt to achieve greater vividness and immediacy. And as in the novels Simon was imitating, there is an element of ambiguity over pronouns like 'I' and 'he', which makes it uncertain to whom they refer. Careful and alert reading is necessary if the author's rare and oblique indications on the subject are not to be overlooked. This is to some extent a literary gimmick, of course; but it also reveals early on in Simon's career a profound scepticism about the nature of the self and its vaunted stability.

In *Gulliver*, a novel of more traditional manufacture under-taken, he now says, to prove to his critics that he could compose one,[13] the narrator is omniscient and third-person, but tends even so to concentrate on one main character's fortunes at a time. This is of course essential to the structure of *Le Sacre du printemps*, which assigns different parts to different points of view, the older man's and the youth's, and these are narrated in the first or in the third person. Where the first-person voice is used, it is presented either as stream-of-consciousness, or in the shape of a sort of confession to a silent and invisible narrator who, as in Conrad, is assumed to transmit the words direct to the reader under quotation marks. It is tempting to speculate on the reasons which impelled Simon to adopt this elaborate and clumsy device. One certainly was his need to objectify certain conflicts he felt within himself when, around the climacteric of forty, he wrote the novel. Bernard's critique of his step-father, who was a young firebrand himself in his time, is clearly a kind of autocritique on the part of the author; but it is also a self-justification, an apologia, which the middle-aged Claude Simon addresses to the young man he was and has since ceased to be. Many people know that if they were able to meet their eighteen-year-old former self, they would face some sharp and even cruel questioning. In *Le Sacre du printemps*, which ends with a long conversation between Bernard and his mother's husband in which nearly all the talking is done by the older man, we get special pleading on behalf of those who have had to compromise with life. This will probably convince most readers over thirty-five, and anger those under twenty. It is a fascinating debate on a common moral dilemma; but it has very little to do with the art of fiction. Precisely what is wrong with *Le Sacre* (otherwise a warm and even wryly comic novel) can be seen clearly by contrasting it with *The Palace*, a much better book though still not one of Simon's best. It is curious that he felt the need to write two rather similar novels in order, so it would seem, to work out of his system feelings of guilt at his own *embourgeoisement*, at the loss of the revolutionary faith which inspired his youth. The pain, the nostalgia and the regret that such a loss inspires give *The Palace* its uniquely poignant tone. But this is only re-write and embellishment of *Le Sacre du printemps*. What is more germane to our present interests is the perception of multiplicity in the self. Man, the author seems to be arguing, is composed of many elements, even of all the experiences that make up his life-story, so that the middle-aged visitor to postwar Barcelona is

> able to hear that part of himself which had the form of a
> lanky American . . . having a dialogue with that other
> part of himself which had the form of a bald man wearing
> something that looked like a uniform, and he too exhausted,

both of them occupying that part of himself which had the
form of a little square of the old part of the city with, closing one of its sides, the obscure façade of the church . . .
and on another of its sides the still open bar of the
requisitioned hotel where they (the American, the
Italian and the student—or rather those three parts, those
three fragments of himself which were an American, a
Rifle and a young fledgling) were lying, and opposite them
a jewelry store with its iron grille lowered

(*The Palace*, pp. 171-2)

The narrator in *The Wind* is, as we have noted, a detached
observer who attempts to reconstruct the events involving
Montès in the same way as a picture-restorer uses different
solvents and cleansing agents to resurrect the pristine freshness
and colour of a canvas (the novel's subtitle is a reference to
this restorative action). For the first time in the fiction the
narrator is identified; and for the last time also. The device
must have struck Simon as being too derivative to be used
again. Accordingly *The Grass* has an omniscient but hidden
narrator, which is more or less Louise's own consciousness
(see p. 146 below). The same applies to *The Flanders Road*, *The
Palace* and to some extent to *Histoire*, though in this last novel
we see the full development of what, up to this point, is
embryonic, namely the increasing interchangeability of
characters and the fluidity of 'he' and 'I'. In earlier novels
people like Louise saw themselves 'doubled', that is they had
the uncanny and unnerving sensation of watching themselves
perform actions and of hearing themselves make utterances.
But in *Histoire* we begin to have the narrator entering the skin
of one of the characters, speaking in his or her voice in the
first person, and then slipping out again and referring to the
character once again in the third person. And as we have seen,
the narrator of *The Battle of Pharsalus* slips smoothly into and
out of both male and female characters: all are indifferen-
tiatedly labelled O.; as Moran in Samuel Beckett's *Molloy*,

O. writes at the end of the book the same words we have read at the beginning, making the novel circular. It also brings it right into Claude Simon's own study, since O. writes in a situation very similar to that depicted in a drawing by Simon which is the first illustration published in *Orion aveugle* (p. 5). The identification—and at the same time the distantiation—of narrator and author is now complete; almost to the extent that he is Claude Simon, O. is removed from him, into a further and more impenetrable realm of fictiveness.

In *Les Corps conducteurs* the narrator appears to have disappeared altogether, making the text its own narrator. There is no privileged point of view either in this novel or in *Triptyque* which follows it. This last book turns upon itself, as it were, in the very act of its being read: it exposes its devices self-consciously, even assertively. The narrator has become co-extensive with the author; but in the process the author himself is fictionalized out of existence, and the text is, in a literal sense, its own generator. And in becoming so it does not hesitate to exploit its author's previous works: from *Histoire*, particularly, it dredges both characters (such as Lambert) and situations.

It is now apparent, I think, how Simon brings the situation of the narrator into line with the general perception of mobility and change which lies at the heart of his vision. Over the years he has moved from traditional-style narrators, which are necessarily rigid by definition, to a position in which extremely volatile and fluid narrational situations are the norm. Whether such a development makes for fiction of real quality is a moot point, but what is certain is that Simon has revealed an impressively consistent impulse over the years, as well as a will to self-renewal which does him great credit.

Style and Technique

In common with all modern writers, Claude Simon is very

3*

selfconscious about his art and what he is trying to attain in writing novels, though like most writers he stresses that the final elaborated product goes far beyond anything he had originally in mind.[14] I propose here to look more closely at the question of style and narrative technique in order to illustrate how Simon's aesthetic operates on the level of the text we are presented with. I begin with an examination of his prose before turning to the wider issue of the construction of the fictions, of which style is only one aspect, though of course a crucial one.

Since Simon's prose evolves gradually from one manner to another, the most accurate way of taking a view upon it is to examine the novels in chronological order. In *Le Tricheur* we find, not unexpectedly, that the present and the perfect tenses predominate, as they do in *The Outsider* by Albert Camus which was written at about the same time. They give the prose a feeling of immediacy and a certain starkness; the perspectives supplied in more conventional writing by the use of the past historic tense are deliberately abolished here. Furthermore, one notes an unusually high density of present participles even in this first novel, and this feature will of course tend to proliferate. Early on, perhaps, the present participles are related rather closely to finite verbs; but in the mature fiction they increasingly supplant finite forms and stand in lieu of them. Simon's marked preference for verbal surrogates in '—ing' is easily explained, and critics have not been slow to do so. John Sturrock accounts for it by pointing out that 'things cannot be said to begin or end in Simon, they appear and disappear. . . . This form of the verb, used as a narrative device, denies the action it describes any recognizable beginning or end,' situates it within 'a succession of movements in which one movement merely replaces the other, divorced from any external temporal reference and its implications of a narrow, non-dynamic causality', and ensures that 'the importance of the agent in any action' is diminished 'because it can easily turn the agent into a victim, struggling with forces outside his control'. This leads Sturrock to conclude, I am sure rightly, that the present participle comes to dominate Simon's fiction precisely because 'his theme is defeat', and that the moments of failure of his characters can best be recorded in the continuous form of the verb.[15] Brian T. Fitch explains the frequency of present participles in Simon's writing by pointing to the fact that 'they describe an action which constitutes a stage, however unimportant, in the unbroken movement of the narration', thus preserving the even and depersonalized progression of a story which stands outside of normal chronological time.[16] And Claude Simon himself has stressed the fertile ambiguities which can be engendered by a consistent recourse to this part of speech: 'all I am affirming in using it', he has said, 'is a version, an image, not something which happened on a given day, within a so-called "reality", but which takes place precisely at the moment of writing.'[17]

Another characteristic feature of Simon's prose style is his tendency to accumulate synonyms, particularly adjectives, in an attempt both to render his descriptions more precise (in much the same way as a dictionary invariably offers more than one definition of any given word) and, at the same time, to suggest that total accuracy is impossible. As if to underline the point, he often draws attention to these multiple epithets by placing them, unusually for French syntax, before the substantive they qualify. An early example is the very last phrase which concludes Le Tricheur: 'cet illusoire et apaisant afflux.' Though perhaps not particularly remarkable in itself, this formulation looks forward to the much more elaborate and baroque phrases of the mature prose. And as an example of the accumulation of synonyms, an allied feature of later writing, one could take this group: 'frénétique d'orgueil, d'amour, d'appétit, de conquêtes' (Le Tricheur, p. 126).

Two other features of Simon's style can be discerned in this first novel. One is the habit, which Flaubert inaugurated, of beginning sentences with 'and', Et, or even with 'and then',

Et puis. This simple device stresses the continuity between one sentence or phrase and the next, and helps to give Simon's prose its 'unbroken' aspect. The other characteristically Simonian formula which occurs with unusual frequency in his first attempt at writing fiction is 'as if', *comme si*, which introduces images or parallels. There are a couple in the very last sentence of the book. The purpose of this device is obvious: it enables the narrator to suggest illustrative analogies, and thus constitutes another example of Simon's tendency to proliferate adjectival descriptions.

La Corde raide, though not a novel, reveals in its prose an intensification of the use of these techniques, perhaps because by its very nature it is a more rhetorical work. In the closing passage of the book the relative absence of copulatives gives a strong air of rhythmic repetition to the prose, and an animistic metaphor ('palpiter et s'ouvrir') leads to the elaboration, in the final sentence, of a complex image in which the narrator feels that he is being penetrated by the thrusting life of the natural world, that the sap of the trees is flowing through his own veins, 'filling me with memory, with the recollection of the days to come, submerging me in the peaceful gratitude of sleep'.

Gulliver represents to some extent a regression: the imperfect tense is more common than the present participle, but when the latter does occur Leon S. Roudiez considers that 'it affirms the permanence of past within present' and thus 'makes it clear that the [main] character is blind as far as future consequences are concerned'; the tense is 'so closely associated with a major theme as to make its subsequent development appear absolutely organic.'[18] Roudiez here perceives that even in a minor work like *Gulliver*, and one which the author now repudiates, style and theme are intimately related. To have established this so early in his literary career, even in a pot-boiler, is a major achievement to Simon's credit. We shall see throughout the *œuvre* developments in form and structure going hand in hand with the widening of the thematic compass.

Although in respect of present participles *Gulliver* reveals a relative numerical decline, adjectives piled up before the noun are just as much in evidence, sometimes clumsily so, as in 'quelque glorieux, horrible et infructueux forfait' (p. 162). This is the case also with *Le Sacre du printemps* (cf. 'l'incolore, humide et cacaphonique conglomérat', p. 105), but unlike *Gulliver* there is heavy exploitation here of the present participle. The following is probably the most dramatic instance; it describes the death of Ceccaldi at the hands of political opponents. Because the event is imagined by the hero, and because the moment of death, as Malraux has shown, is in a manner outside of time, suspended for ever in a sort of liquid state of non-being, there are about a dozen present participles in the passage:

> And he was able to plunge into this gelatinous, transparent time, going back through this dimensionless and perspec-tiveless matter, imagining him, after the boat had turned the end of the jetty, returning towards the town, noticing then perhaps the shadows of the two fascists just as they had already seen them the day before on this same jetty, understanding then perhaps, dining alone, impassive but alert . . . hearing perhaps, on his feet behind his half-opened door, the two men pronounce his name, going to his suitcase, taking out his revolver, standing with his face towards the door, opening fearlessly, watching . . .
>
> (*Le Sacre du printemps*, p. 202)

In translation there is some ambiguity as to whom the participles refer to; in fact, from 'returning' onwards, they agree with the object of the hero's meditations, Ceccaldi. But graceless and even obscure as a literal translation like this must be it does, I think, show how the '—ing' form of the verb functions in Simon's narrative: to suspend the moment, to emphasize the passivity of the agent, and to present the individual as impotent to alter his fate. We find the same thing in *The Wind*, where the participles give a feeling of imprecise but continuous duration which accords with the kind of myopic distortion through which Montès perceives the world, his 'fundamental inaptitude for being aware of life' (p. 153). In the same novel there are many instances of the dynamic *et* to indicate 'some kind of change, progression or climax',[19] as well as of the dramatic colon; we see both devices at work in a sentence which begins like this: 'And further still: the human race reduced . . .' (p. 154). Not unnaturally, sentences in *The Wind* tend to be longer than in previous novels, with parenthetic insertions performing much the same function as subordination in the Proustian period, namely to appear to be encompassing a rich but barely controllable material which is continually eluding the novelist's attempts to contain it within the bounds of articulate language.

In *The Grass* these features recur, together with an increased frequency of temporal indicators like 'puis', 'maintenant' and 'encore' which underline the growing importance of considerations of succession and simultaneity; Simon is beginning here to dispense with copulatives and to practise ellipsis. He is thus occasionally able to give his prose an almost telegraphic quality in which the essentials are flashed at the reader from a continuum, an even texture which matches better than previous styles the author's awareness of barely perceptible but profoundly significant ebb and flow in the flood of life.

The Flanders Road pushes all this one stage further—by reducing the frequency of commas, by piling as many as four adjectives before a noun—and adds a hint of uncertainty by the use of phrases like 'pour ainsi dire' and 'semblait-il', expressive of hesitancy. This, once again, is in strict conformity with the theme of the novel, which turns on the ultimate unknowability of even the most seemingly concrete events, like the death of an officer in action.

In *The Palace* we find perhaps the most far-reaching exploitation of the Simonian parenthesis, since even brackets within brackets are not uncommon. To a certain degree Simon clearly thinks parenthetically (his non-fictional prose shows this); but however many brackets he opens he is punctilious about closing them, and reproaches the surrealists for failing to do so in their disappointing essays in automatic writing.[20] His brackets are 'an indication that each moment of Simon's text is a focus of multiple associations . . . the proliferating clauses that crowd in between the subject of a sentence and its verb . . . are the actual substance, the gelatine, in which people and events are trapped, the insufficient but menacing paradigm for time itself', remarks John Sturrock with considerable acuteness.[21]

Histoire, as we would expect, orchestrates all these devices with astonishing ease and skill. In the following extract (which returns obsessively to the central episode of *The Flanders Road*, Reixach's death) we find them all: the participles suspending time, the parentheses braking the action, the rhetorical colon, the dynamic 'and', the accumulation of words of similar meaning, and the elaborate analogy introduced by 'comme si':

But this: that road lined with smoking debris, and he with all that remained of his squadron, that is a single second lieutenant, a cavalryman and his orderly, that jockey with a nutcracker's face he had taken from his mad old aunt, making him trade the famous cerise cap for these colours, pink shirt, black cap, which you would have said had been chosen to order for Corinne from some advertisement for lingerie in the fashion magazines, and the wounded lying in the ditches shouting to him not to go on, that he would get himself killed, and he ignoring them, merely saying to the other officer (speaking in that high nasal voice he probably inherited from his Arab ancestors, that is from the Arab ancestor who must have impregnated one of the great-great-grandmothers of the Barons de Reixach before Charles Martel had had time to arrive, so that he too was, like his horses, an Arab cross) with only a hint of irritation, of boredom: '. . . for a few bastards hiding behind the hedge with a pop-gun . . . ,' and not even finishing, continuing—arrogant, at most slightly vexed, offended— at the regular, calm gait of his mare in the middle of that vernal suddenly dangerous landscape (like the banal and dangerous setting of the avenue with its monotonous ochre façades, empty sidewalks, empty roadway, closed shops): the dangerous meadows spangled with daisies, the dangerous edges of the woods, the dangerous hedges, the dangerous orchards: as if all nature, in complicity with the murders, were holding its breath in expectation of the kill, had suddenly turned into something both indifferent and perfidious, green, sparkling in the sun- shine, strangely silent, strangely motionless, deserted, concealing what invisible gazes, what invisible death . . .

(*Histoire*, pp. 158-9)

Even so, there are a couple of new elements. One is the virtual suppression of all full stops except at certain moments in the novel where their use is indispensable in picking out a key word,[22] with the result that the whole book is characterized by a marked syntactical contraction and density. The other is the extensive and expressive use of dialogue presented without quotation marks and full stops, but with capital initial letters indicating a fresh sentence. Here is a good example; Richard Howard's translation captures the flavour rather well, and even manages to find a satisfactory equivalent for the bit of schoolboy smut at the end about 'sauter la sauterelle':

she opened the door she was carrying that big music briefcase her cheeks were pink because of the cold It was the year she had begun wearing stockings She stopped and stared at us

This is my friend Lambert I said Bernard Lambert

he bowed ceremoniously Pleased to make your ac- quaintance Mademoiselle

hello she said She started across the room

I see you're studying music he said
what?
she stopped
what you're carrying he said What do you play?
she stared at him Piano she said She shot me a glance
and took a step at the same time He stood in front of her
holding out one hand toward the briefcase May I look?
again she stopped What?
what you're playing
once again she looked at me then she began to walk
away opened the door and disappeared
Damn he said Talk about a piece of cake Who's that?
my cous . . .
do you lay her?
what?
I said: do you lay her? Hey that's a good one, layer cake
Do you lay her cake?
come on I said we'll go up to my room Let's go
                                        (*Histoire*, p. 186)

To cope with an even more complex interweaving of themes
The Battle of Pharsalus falls back on typographical devices, like
the use of italics for extended extracts from other works.
Simon is right to think this novel represents a new departure
for him. It is much more a magpie of a book, not only quoting
extensively but also imitating and pastiching. For instance,
there is a section of Proust which reads as if it has been put
through Raymond Queneau's mangle, and we are also treated
to a fragment of Baedekerese (French text, pp. 178-9, 241).
But the real change in Claude Simon's style became apparent
in *Les Corps conducteurs*, where the sentences are shorter again,
light and without parentheses; on the other hand there are no
paragraphs, so the prose still retains a massive appearance.
Finally, *Triptyque* offers itself frankly as a stylistic ragbag. Parts
are written in a familiar Simonian manner (with participles,
parentheses and analogies), but other sections read like

pastiche of Robbe-Grillet, with the same deadpan pseudo-scientific precision in descriptions, the same painstaking, gradual reconstruction of scenes whose initial innocence quickly evaporates before the all-pervading menace of the situation which is ultimately revealed. The tone of the book is distinctly cool, even bland, and there is an apparent objectivity. Gone are the long sinuous sentences with their constant disgressions and qualifications, their extended similes and multiple synonyms, seeking nervously to hedge the truth ever more firmly about. Gone, too, is the often distracting rhetoric about life and destiny. *Triptyque*—a most impressive essay in the art of narrative, by the way—is written in a spare and unemotional manner which makes no concessions to sentiment. The baroque, flamboyant Simon has gone; a restrained, classical writer has taken his place. We can expect him to go on writing in this new idiom he has perfected, since if this survey of his stylistic development establishes anything, it is that he does not act on impulse; that his recent manner has evolved gradually and logically from one stage to the next. His aim throughout has been 'to convey not so much the meaning of events as their weight, their fullness, their odour';[23] hence in his mature style the richness and variety of the lexis, and his concern with organic qualities and with assonance; hence, too, the way his words form chains and seem to be reproducing themselves spontaneously. This noble, poetic idiom makes possible much that is impressive in his fiction, above all its humanity and compassion and humour, for this is style fully appropriate to the matter and influences it profoundly. The style has matured as the vision has deepened, for the two have clearly interacted upon each other from the outset. As Simon himself has argued, the texture of the writing is not just an involved way of saying something basically quite simple, but the most straightforward manner he can find of conveying something highly complex. His early novels are naive affairs, and the style is similarly embryonic. But his later fictions are profound and subtle meditations on time, memory and the aesthetic act itself, for which an organic narrative manner, rich in synonyms, amplifications, qualifications and illustrative analogies, is indispensable. In evolving that style Claude Simon has shown himself to be one of the most inventive prose artists of our time.

It is not possible, of course, to separate stylistic considerations from the wider issue of narrative structure and technique. I have chosen to do so, however, since after this chronological survey I propose to deal with Simon's fictional methods in a more synoptic fashion, even if it means blurring certain historical distinctions between novels written over a period of thirty years. I think such an approach nonetheless has advantages, if only in enabling us to grasp by means of a single overview the ambitious complexity of Simon's fictional aesthetic.

In terms of plot, the early novels employ a technique—derived variously from Simon's literary masters—which consists of deferring information or temporarily interrupting the action to bring up elements of a side- or sub-plot, or in order to introduce, via a flashback or a supplementary narrative, information which explains an earlier dramatic episode whose cause, at the time, was obscure. Since Simon's early books are not much read, let me take an example from a better-known novel written under the influence of much the same literary forbears, Samuel Beckett's *Murphy*. Being a comic novel it tends to exaggerate these devices for humorous effect; but this makes it all the more effective as an illustration of the technique I am concerned with. The fifth chapter ends with Murphy returning to the flat he shares with his girlfriend to find her 'spreadeagled on her face on the bed—a shocking thing had happened'. The next chapter deals with something quite different (it consists of a digressive description of 'Murphy's mind'), and the seventh takes us back in time to a moment prior to that of the main events of chapter 5; it brings us up to date about the doings of the other principal characters in the story. It is only in chapter 8, some twenty pages after the announcement of the 'shocking thing', that we

learn what it was that prostrated Celia with grief. This kind of
recoupement is found in *Le Tricheur*, for instance when a character
receives a letter on p. 66 and we are finally informed of its
contents on p. 112. In the early novels, of course, interruption
is practised like this for dramatic effect, but in the mature
fiction the changes of scene—as, say, in the closing pages of *The
Grass*—are more readily accounted for in terms of the jumps
and modifications provoked by the mechanisms of association.

Another feature of Simon's plots—and all this of course
concerns only the work up to the early sixties, after which
date plot ceases to be a factor of any importance in his fiction—
is the gradual revelation by fits and starts of a story, for example
the theft of jewels in *The Wind*, or their loss on a railway track
in *The Grass*; in both novels the text returns frequently and
often unexpectedly to events like these which are of dramatic
interest and, in *The Wind* at least, of serious consequence.
Sometimes aspects of a story are told from more than one
point of view; either the narrative is continued from another
person's angle without much interruption in the progression
(as in *Gulliver*, when Bert's altercation with Max is first told
'straight' on p. 81, then continued by pub talk on p. 121), or
the same events are repeated in a different register of discourse.
Le Tricheur repeats a lot of material in this way, first describing
Louis's activities in the third-person, then repeating the story
as told by himself. *Le Sacre du printemps* shows some fairly
complex forward-backward references of this kind, such as
the meeting with Ceccaldi seen first by an omniscient narrator
(p. 140) and then by the hero (p. 159), or Bernard's childish
behaviour seen both from his own self-satisfied point of view
and from the much more critical angle supplied by his step-
father. There are also instances of anticipated narrative (of the
kind beginning 'later, he was to . . .') which subsequently
catches up with itself, as it were (see pp. 230 and 233). *The
Grass* likewise has events, like Louise's return to dinner in the
house after a rendezvous with her lover, which are seen first
from her point of view and then from her mother-in-law's

(pp. F133 and 202); and there is a fairly dramatic cut when we jump from the 'omniscient' account of a struggle between Pierre and Sabine over a clandestine bottle of brandy to Louise's description of the episode given to her lover some twenty-four hours later (p. F206). In *The Flanders Road*, likewise, we have events told first in the form Iglésia gives them, then in the shape Georges's imagination clothes them with. There is, moreover, as Claude Simon himself has pointed out in diagrammatic form, a hierarchy of events in the novel, the one enclosing the other, with the ambush in the centre, the horse race which De Reixach loses outside that, and his death forming the outer core of the onion (or, to use Simon's own analogy, the outer edge of an artesian basin).[24]

In the later novels the notion of reconstitution, which formed the basis of *The Wind*, comes to the fore as the major structural principle. In *The Battle of Pharsalus*, the publisher's blurb says, 'an observer himself observed seeks to reconstitute something which is ultimately revealed as being constituted solely by the quest itself in its progression, its hesitations and its meanders.' And in Simon's most ambitious exploration of the fictive process to date, *Triptyque*, three separate and distinct stories are told, not consecutively as in Flaubert's volume *Three Tales*, but concurrently, with little to indicate that the text has switched gear. The unprepared reader is all the more likely to be misled because the book is divided into three parts; but these are purely arbitrary divisions and bear no relation to the subject-matter. In fact, one might claim that after the early novels—say up to and including *Le Sacre du printemps*—in which the chapter-break retains its traditional dramatic value as a suspense creator or as a way of modulating to another level of the plot or to another point of view, the reason for which the prose is cut up in sections is mere convenience. The chief exception is *The Palace*, where each of the five parts (which are linked together by the last phrase of the one being repeated at the start of the next) corresponds to a different episode, or at least aspect, of the fiction, and where a clear principle of symmetry is at work in that the first chapter entitled 'Inventory' corresponds to the last, 'Lost and Found', and the second, 'The Rifle's Story', balances the fourth, 'In the Night' (for 2 and 4 both concern a murder, the one retold by the protagonist, the other suspected by an uncertain witness), while 'The Funeral of Patroclus' forms the nub of the book, and an ironic one, since the 'Patroclus' in question is merely an obscure republican general. In the case of *Triptyque* the divisions are made simply to divide the text into three parts and thus make the book resemble a triptych (as in painting) physically as well as metaphorically. As for the intercalated fragments of the stories, these do seem to get longer as we progress through the book, as if the whole mechanism were decelerating.

In all the later novels the reconstitution is provoked and pressed forward by generative elements. In *Histoire* the postcards fulfil this function, and *The Battle of Pharsalus* is at least partially generated by the photograph of Uncle Charles in the Dutchman's studio which perhaps lay among the family papers that the narrator of *Histoire* clears out of the chest he is selling to the antique dealer. Such a link between one novel and its successor would be fully characteristic of Simon's method. *Les Corps conducteurs*'s generators have been published in *Orion aveugle* (paintings by Poussin and Rauschenberg, photographs of the Amazon basin taken from the air and other sights and objects, cigar-box labels, and so on), and they turn this novel into a kind of scrapbook. Postcards come back into their own in *Triptyque*, the opening sentence of which reads 'The postcard represents an esplanade planted with palm-trees . . .' But this is not a particularly recent development in Simon's fiction: *The Grass* was to some extent at least generated by the biscuit tin, and there is a sense in which Louise 'becomes' the picture on this box of a young woman reclining in the grass.[25] When the generators are not external objects like these, the text develops according to the changing associations in the narrator's mind; in *Les Corps conducteurs*, for instance, there is fertile confusion between a woman's boa, a serpent, and the serpentine meanders of a great river seen from the air. And the text of *Triptyque* shunts off along this track or that solely according to the principle of association, though the nature of what is associated often seems rather remote. We usually know where we are, or rather which story we are in, by sounds which are reported and serve as a kind of signature; in the case of the tale set in a wooded river area in the country, it is a church bell, and the sequences dealing with a wedding in an industrial suburb are marked by references to the noises made by a railway junction. Similarly in *The Grass* Louise's consciousness jumps from her frenzied attempts to unbutton her lover's shirt to the grotesque struggle in the bathroom next to her own when Pierre catches Sabine tippling (p. F239), and in *The Flanders Road* the description of POWs in a meadow lying exhausted head to foot jumps straight to Georges engaged in cunnilingus with Corinne (pp. 192-3). Purely fortuitous verbal similarities (e.g. between *morts* [dead men] and *maures* [Moorish] in *Le Palace*, p. 43) can cause perturbations in the text; Jean Ricardou, in particular, has made much of puns and anagrams as a structural factor in Simon's prose. More obvious than Ricardou's sibylline exegetic is the fact that newpaper headlines provoke particular resonances in Simon's texts; as Sharon Spencer observes, 'everything that is printed in any novel automatically carries with it a group of associations, and these associations are capable of considerable multiplication'.[26] Perhaps Simon acquired his interest in newspaper headlines from the collage artists he admires, from Braque to Rauschenberg; but however that may be, there is no question about the powerful associative role such elements play in his work, from the insistent denunciation of fifth-column activity in the Barcelona papers in *The Palace* to the title SHE THROWS HERSELF OUT OF THE FOURTH FLOOR WINDOW which stirs such deep feelings of guilt in the narrator of *Histoire*, since it appears to activate a painful personal memory, one which lies buried in his consciousness.

To these talismans or fetishes in Simon's prose must be added those common objects, like watches in *Le Tricheur* or trains in *The Grass*, which serve as *leitmotif*, cropping up at intervals in the narration and offering discreet parallels or illustrations. For watches and trains—like wind, in *The Wind*—pace out duration, act as indefatigable reminders of what Simon refers to more than once as our gradual, remorseless progress towards death.

This sort of thing represents the symbolist side of Claude Simon's artistic make-up; but there is a strong realist vein which we ought not to overlook. The early books contain moments of sharp visual perception, as of the barber shaving his customer in *Le Tricheur*, dipping his fingers in the bowl, passing them carefully over the skin as he probes for uncut bristles (p. 192); but these passages still smack of artifice, of the need to 'fill out' a scene with convincing detail. By the time he wrote *The Grass* Simon was moving away from this sort of circumstantial realism, and tending towards a more poetic kind. Thus, like Warhol with the Empire State Building, he trains his 'camera' on the façade of the house and notes all that goes on there during an extended period: the maid shaking out a duster, Sabine emerging with a parasol, Pierre lumbering down the steps, and so on (p. F107). This eye for detail is active in the subsequent novels, noting in *The Flanders Road* the traces left by the trowel on hardened mortar (p. 184), in *The Palace* the greasy stain spreading on the satin of an upholstered sofa after a rifle has been leant against it (p. 113), in *Histoire* the odd resemblance between a piece of newspaper blown about in the breeze and an injured bird (p. 294), and the appearance and smell of natural things in *Triptyque*. Sometimes, as in the description of the writers' congress in *Les Corps conducteurs*, one suspects that the impassively bland manner of the narrator conceals a satirical purpose—conveying the situation without comment has the effect of ridiculing it in the reader's eyes.

This realism far surpasses in subtlety the well-intended but clumsy efforts to match life which we get in *Gulliver* and other early novels. *Gulliver* not only treats us to a wealth of circumstantial detail about the setting of the story, a dreary *Nacht-und-Nebel* kind of situation, it also attempts at the level of the plot to mirror life's mystery and untidiness by leaving a few loose ends and one or two matters unresolved. This almost phenomenological, behaviourist kind of writing, with its tough take-it-or-leave-it air, may have seemed authentic to Simon at the time, but now it reads as something modish, self-consciously literary, and hopelessly dated.

This novel, *Gulliver*, is clearly influenced by the *misérabiliste* school of French film-makers who produced films like *Le Jour se lève* and other works in which Jean Gabin or Michèle Morgan look mistily at the spectator from tawdry hotel bedrooms or bleak quaysides. Simon's debt to the cinema is of course immense throughout his career. His novels are full of analogies and metaphors of cinematographic origin; *The Grass* compares a sense of unreality with old films projected at the wrong speed and thus showing people behaving in comically jerky ways, or poorly synchronized movies in which sound and vision do not coincide, so that people speak out of harmony with their lips. And the last novel, *Triptyque*, speaks of 'un long travelling' following two running boys (p. 148). But more than this, most of Simon's books use techniques from film practice, particularly the cut and change of scene which allows the action to be abridged, pruned of inessential transitions, or for fresh characters to be brought into view immediately, without preparation. Reading one or two of the early novels, especially *Le Sacre du printemps*, I occasionally think what a good film it would make: the cutting script seems already to exist in embryo and the dialogues are already written out, so that the transition to *mise en scène* would be smoothly accomplished; even the short-focus work and the close-ups are specified in *The Wind* (cf. pp. F157, 159), and as I have already had occasion to stress, the flashback is a basic structural feature of both *Le Tricheur* and *Gulliver*.

More than this, Simon appears to build his later novels

according to a principle very like that of montage. He has himself said that *The Flanders Road* is 'composed essentially of a sequence of images', written in fragments which he later put together 'by means of connectives provided by associations or by contrasts of feelings, emotions, words or sounds'.[27] In order to keep these strands distinct, he has said elsewhere, he used different coloured pencils, mapping out his text as a director might the varied sequences which make up his film. *Histoire* is obviously constructed according to similar principles. The following passage is made up of three paragraphs; and each paragraph represents a different 'sequence':

. . . The ones (or the one, since you might have thought it was always the same one) always standing on the steps of churches of banks or the edges of sidewalks huddled in their shapeless and royal rags, one hand offering a package of pins or a box of matches the other pressing the baby to the heavy breast, the same peasant scarf tied under the chin, the tragic satiated infant throwing back its head eyelids half-closed over a pale vitreous line, its tiny fists not dimpled but crumpled raised to each side of its face, the open mouth exposing toothless gums still smeared with milk, then able to see the . . .

toothless cadaver's mouth chewing the white grainy pulp ground between the yellowish stumps then he swallowed, his Adam's apple rising and falling then examining the remains of the sandwich before biting into it again . . .

. . . the woman represented on the bill of a classic type nonetheless from Lorraine perhaps (since the background shows tall smoking chimneys drawbridges cranes), the breast thrusting through the unlaced opening of one of those jerkins Joan of Arc wears in pictures where she is shown herding her sheep, and behind her, standing, another woman of the same vigorous type holding a sheaf of wheat, a naked boy turned toward her both arms raised as though to help her carry her burden or, on the contrary, begging her to pick him up instead, the entire vision . . .

(Histoire, p. 171)

The paragraph immediately following these three is a fourth sequence; but thereafter the paragraphs no longer offer new material, and confine themselves instead to developing and varying these initial subjects, in this order: third, fourth, third, second, and so on. Of course this only continues for a few pages; the novel as a whole is far richer than four themes like these would permit. But while it lasts it bears a remarkably close resemblance to montage techniques as practised in the cinema. And it will be evident how much *Triptyque* owes to the film; the three stories are interwoven as if we were being moved from one studio set to another, or as if we were watching the screening of a movie in which sequences originating from three different types of film stock were spliced end to end in a regularly recurring order. This composite picture even seizes up on occasion, freezing the protagonists in postures that were intended to be momentary and provisional, but have now incongruously become permanent (p. 195).

A subsidiary feature of film art is suspense, and here again Simon has learned from the practice of movies. In *Le Sacre du printemps*, for instance, he cleverly conceals the existence of the ring and thus maintains doubt about it until the very end of the novel, the last words of which describe its discovery; in fact the whole rhetoric of the book is converging on this one point, so that the text closes on the two significant syllables, 'la bague', the ring. *The Wind* has its dramatic moments too, such as the visit Cécile pays Montès in his hotel room (p. F145) or the death of Rose (p. F174), but these are perhaps more in the form of *coups de théâtre* than of film suspense, the essence of which is not so much to spring surprises on us but to keep us tense with expectation, in an

agony of doubt as to whether it will go one way and of fear
that it might go the other. *Triptyque* has something of this
quality; several of the sequences are modelled on the aesthetic
of the thriller, and create suspense by shrewd and timely
cutting (see p. 126 as an example; when we return to this
sequence on p. 185 the bridegroom has been beaten up by his
pursuer, the actual assault being left out because, as in a good
film, it pays to leave some events to the imagination).

But Claude Simon himself would claim, I suspect, that his
fiction owes more to the visual arts than to the film. It was noted
at the conference on the new novel held in Cerisy-la-Salle in
1971 that Simon tends to visualize his intentions more than his
colleagues, and the novelist himself has stated that 'plastic
imperatives' must be allowed to predominate in the art of
fiction.[28] For this reason he intends his novels should give the
reader plenty to 'see'; and it is for this reason that his methods
have been compared to those of the pointillistes, and also of the
cubists.[29] But these are at best only metaphors for his activity;
painting and writing are such different media that analogies
made between them must be tenuous (the same is not true of
the film since this art, like the novel, narrates fictions in the
dimension of time). Simon has a trained eye for art, and
has in a sense 'dedicated' some of his novels to painters he
admires. Thus *Les Corps conducteurs* is written under the aegis
of Robert Rauschenberg, and *Triptyque* is an act of homage to
the great triptychs of Francis Bacon. It is just possible to see
influence in these cases; the *objets trouvés* aspects of Rauchen-
berg's art, the collage and sculptural qualities present in his
work, are roughly paralleled in the collage devices of *Les Corps
conducteurs*. Similarly *Triptyque*'s structure offers some analogies
with Bacon's three-panelled works, but they do not extend
very far, since as I have shown, the three sections into which
the novel is divided do not correspond to three aspects of a
single narrative, as tends to be the case with Bacon. It would,
in fact, be difficult to parallel in pictural form the structure of
Triptyque in which the three elements interweave continuously.

There is, however, one aspect of Simon's fiction which clearly owes something to the plastic arts, and that is the occasional tendency of his scenes to 'freeze' into static sculptural or graphic representation. An example of the first is the way the lovers become statuesque in *The Battle of Pharsalus*, petrified into immobility in the frenzied energy of their erotic activity; and examples of the second are the cartoons into which scenes dissolve in *The Palace* (p. 102) and *Triptyque* (pp. 21, 42). But the visual arts have no monopoly in this: the circus is also invoked in *Triptyque* (p. 183), and at the very end of the novel it is suggested that the whole book is like a 'last picture show' with the spectators filing out of the movie theatre. The point is that a work like this is more than the sum of its parts, which in themselves are mercurial and though often dramatic, ultimately quite trivial.

Perhaps the best way to conclude this survey of the different aspects of Simon's art of fiction is to juxtapose quotations from two quite different novels. In the first, *The Wind*, the teacher describes Montès's narrative manner:

it was only in snatches that he told me all this, and little by little, and not as a story at all, properly speaking, but only when some detail or other occurred to him, without anyone's knowing just why—if anyone ever knows just what produces not a recollection—always stored somewhere in the mind's lumber-room—but the furious and intolerable sensation itself, abolishing the time between, materialized in all its flesh and fury, jealous, imperious, obsessive

(*The Wind*, p. 185)

This can be read as a wry comment by Simon on his own methods, exaggerated of course, but as I hope to have shown, with an element of truth.

The second quotation ponders on the probable inanity of all

story-telling functions: 'perhaps it was as futile, as senseless, as unreal as to make hentracks on sheets of paper and to look for reality in words . . .' (*The Flanders Road*, p. 218). This reads rather like Flaubert when he complains in his letters to Louise Colet of the horrors of novel-writing. But Flaubert did not allow the black moods which assailed him in the small hours after a day's writing to deter him seriously from the unrelenting pursuit of his craft. And neither, for all the occasional expressions of scepticism uttered by his narrators, has Claude Simon.

A NOVELIST'S WORLD—NOTES

1 *Le Figaro Littéraire*, 23 March 1963, p. 20.
2 *French Fiction Today: A New Direction* (New Brunswick, N.J.: Rutgers University Press, 1972), p. 163. Put another way, where *Le Sacre* has two distinct characters, which John Sturrock defines as 'incarnations of the Wise Old Man and the idealistic young one' (*The French New Novel*, London: Oxford University Press, 1969, p. 93), *Le Palace* makes the latter simply an earlier phase in the development of the former, an *alter ego* from the past.
3 *Entretiens* (Claude Simon special issue) (Rodez: Subervie, 1972), facing p. 121.
4 *The New Novel from Queneau to Pinget* (New York: Farrar, Straus and Giroux, 1971), p. 311.
5 *The French New Novel*, p. 63.
6 *Entretiens*, p. 17.
7 *The Vision of Jean Genet* (London: Peter Owen, 1968), p. 189.
8 *The French New Novel*, p. 86.
9 *L'Express* (Paris), no. 632 (25 July 1963), p. 26.
10 Cf. 'Je continue ma route, moi aussi remâcheur de cadavres, remâcheur de passé que je dispute au rêve', *Le Tricheur*, p. 54.
11 'L'Enfer, le temps', *Nouvelle Revue Française*, IX (January 1961), p. 102.
12 *French Fiction Today*, p. 168.
13 *Entretiens*, pp. 16-17.

14 'La Fiction mot à mot' (Claude Simon's paper delivered to the *nouveau roman* conference held at Cerisy-la-Salle in Normandy in July 1971), in *Nouveau roman: hier, aujourd'hui* (Paris: 10/18, 1972), vol. II, p. 97.

15 *The French New Novel*, pp. 101-2.

16 'Participe présent et procédés narratifs chez Claude Simon', in *Un Nouveau roman?*, ed. J. H. Matthews (Paris: Minard, 1964), p. 200.

17 'Claude Simon: "Il n'y a pas d'art réaliste"' [interview], by Madeleine Chapsal, *Quinzaine Littéraire*, no. 41 (15-31 December 1967), pp. 4-5.

18 *French Fiction Today*, p. 156.

19 Stephen Ullmann, *Style in the French Novel* (Cambridge University Press, 1957), p. 105. Though Ullmann does not discuss Claude Simon, I find his method more fruitful than that employed, for example, by Dominique Lanceraux in an article entitled 'Modalités de la narration dans *La Route des Flandres*' (*Poétique*, no. 14, 1973, pp. 235-49) which reads to me like Brian Fitch updated to conform to the jargon of the school which currently dominates literary criticism and analysis in Paris.

20 *Entretiens*, p. 26.

21 *The French New Novel*, pp. 100-101.

22 In a letter to me dated 13 January 1968, Mr Simon writes: 'La ponctuation me pose, vous vous en doutez, de difficiles problèmes. De longs passages d'*Histoire* ne comportaient, primitivement, absolument aucun point. Cependant, en certains endroits, s'est posé la question de l'intelligibilité du texte. Aussi, en corrigeant, ai-je été amené à ponctuer, lorsque cela me semblait indispensable. Les points, dans les pages que vous me signalez [I had asked whether the full stops on pp. 44, 228, 290, 309 and 317 were intended] sont donc bien de moi. Ai-je eu tort? Sans doute, à la fois, oui et non. . .' And in the interview with Madeleine Chapsal referred to in note 17 above, he suggested that 'c'est souvent pour contrebalancer ce caractère affirmatif du passé simple que je suis amené à supprimer la ponctuation, ce qui confère aux choses dites un caractère d'irréalité' (p. 5). He would seem therefore to view the dropping of punctuation marks as working towards the same end as the abandonment of finite verbs in favour of present participles, namely to undermine the emphatic certainties of conventional prose. This restless experimentation continues: see his remarks on dropping 'comme', *Nouveau roman*, II, 91.

23 A remark made during an interview with Madeleine Chapsal in *L'Express*, no. 500 (12 January 1961), pp. 31-2.

24 Simon's own diagram is reproduced in 'La Fiction mot à mot' (the paper referred to in note 14 above) on p. 93, and the next three pages offer Simon's diagrammatic analogies for the plots of his subsequent novels. In the original edition of *La Route des Flandres*, the cut from the race to the battle at the heart of the book occurs at line 1, 42 ems in, on p. 155, and

the return from the battle to the race is effected at line 13, 29 ems in, on p. 166.

25 As Roudiez rightly perceives (*French Fiction Today*, p. 169).

26 *Space, Time and Structure in the Modern Novel* (New York University Press, 1971), p. 143. It probably needs no stressing that eroticism, in the form of sexual analogies, is a major factor in provoking associations in Simon's prose; but so powerful is the erotic impulse that sometimes the text shies away from the subject (cf. *La Route de Flandres*, p. 13). In other words, sexuality, like a candle-flame to a moth, both attracts and repels the movement of the prose. See also p. 184 below.

27 In *Premier Plan*, no. 18 (October 1961), pp. 32-3.

28 *Entretiens*, p. 26; and see *Nouveau roman: hier, aujourd'hui*, vol. I, pp. 31 and 33.

29 Tom Bishop, 'L'Image de la création chez Claude Simon', *Nouveau roman: hier, aujourd'hui*, vol. II, p. 63.

CROSS SECTIONS

1

In Another Country:
The Palace and *The Third Book About Achim*

It is not down in any map; true places never are
—Moby Dick

Among the literatures of postwar Europe, German writing occupies a special and difficult position. It has had to be created virtually from nothing, because the twelve-year period of Nazi rule between 1933 and 1945 constituted a hiatus; writers at home were silenced or brought into line with state policy in artistic matters, and those in exile, like Brecht and Thomas Mann, were cut off from their linguistic and cultural roots. It has also had to come to terms with the shame and trauma resulting from defeat and the ensuing revelations about genocide, slave labour, and other horrors perpetrated by the police state Hitler set up over most of the German *Sprachraum*. None of the writers who have achieved eminence since 1945 has been either able or willing to elude the necessary confrontation with the facts of his country's crimes and of its total and crushing defeat, or of the terrible poetic justice meted out by the devastating, pillaging and raping soldiery repaying eye for eye and tooth for tooth. Nor has it been possible to ignore the obscenity of the continued division of the country, of what Uwe Johnson refers to as *die Grenze*, the border that begins 'three miles off the [Baltic]

4

coast with leaping patrol boats', that continues overland as 'a ten-yard-wide ploughed control strip [and] pushes into the forest that has been cleared for just that purpose',[1] and that within eastern territory becomes the fortified wall that drives a deathly wedge between the two Berlins, and makes the western half of the city an anomalous enclave. As Robert R. Heitner writes, 'the serious novelist [in Germany today] is likely to be a literary historian and critic in addition to being a creative writer';[2] and a practising novelist, Gerd Gaiser, comments that in contemporary German letters 'there is no room left for naive geniuses . . . hardly any author publishing today is without advanced university training'.[3] This training, this apprenticeship in technique, is essential if the writer is to find the right language to come to terms with the realities of the German situation, of defeat, territorial division, and the separate and antagonistic development of rival economies and political systems perverting and twisting the common language into forms the other side ceases first to recognize and then to comprehend. Added to which, the contemporary German writer is faced with a situation of profound social alienation which leads him to look enviously on his colleagues in France, 'where', Gaiser claims, 'literature holds a central position in society and politics, and the writer traditionally participates in public affairs, indeed is regularly consulted about them'.[4] Even though the French situation is not as rosy as all that, it is certainly better than in Germany. In the communist East the dogmas of socialist realism hold sway and stifle restlessly creative talents; in the capitalist West, complacency and excessive comfort threaten to drown with brash vulgarity and an ostentatious display of material prosperity the nagging voice of the writer for whom on neither side of the internal frontier is all for the best in the best of all possible worlds, and who repudiates the smug propaganda of both régimes. No wonder Uwe Johnson told a journalist that he stands on neither side of the 'Wall', but on top of it. And finally, the German writer has spent much of the postwar period overcoming his cultural isolation: for, after the long years of Nazi censorship, Joyce, Hemingway, Faulkner and above all Kafka had to be rediscovered. If novelists like Uwe Johnson occasionally appear to have been excessively influenced by these forbears, it is quite understandable, and certainly pardonable.[5]

All these factors—the trauma of the defeat and subsequent political division of his country, the need to recreate the literary tradition, and the problem of relating to a self-satisfied and philistine society—are present in Johnson's work, which I find aesthetically the most accomplished to have come out of Germany in recent years. He constitutes, for me, the genuine avant-garde: beside him, Böll appears ponderous, Grass flashy, and Walser arch. And yet his work to date centres on one obsessive theme (the mutual incomprehension of the two Germanies), and certainly lacks the richness and complexity of the world we associate with his rivals. But, like Naipaul, he has produced a masterpiece by concentrating rather than diffusing his focus. The masterpiece—dominating head and shoulders his other work—is *The Third Book about Achim*. It is undoubtedly better than the novel by Claude Simon with which I wish to compare it, *The Palace*; but I think the confrontation is useful, since both books are concerned to undermine any attempt to 'fix' the real (*The Palace* with time distortion, *Achim* with space distortion), either to determine reality's true importance and accuracy, or to solidify the past moment in all its sharp vividness. For in both, the world is not grasped by language, but created by it: language not only delimits the world, as Wittgenstein rightly perceived, it also structures it. Both Johnson and Simon—like Nabokov and Borges among the other great neo-modernists—have seized upon this essential truth, and both explore it with dazzling virtuosity and invention. But before embarking on a close analysis of the two novels, I will offer a few comments on Johnson's other books, since the available criticism in English on the contemporary German novel has relatively little to say about him, which is curious in the light of Johnson's standing in his own country, where he was awarded the Georg Büchner Prize in 1971, and in the world literary community, which honoured him with the International Publishers' Prize for *The Third Book about Achim* in 1962. It may be that the alleged narrowness of his subject-matter has led English-speaking readers and critics to underestimate him, though he makes all but the insensitive feel acutely his own pain over the barbed wire entanglements which split his nation in two; or the turgid and stilted translations of some of his books may be to blame. Whatever the reason, he is certainly neglected in the English-speaking world.[6]

His first novel, *Speculations about Jakob* (1959), was published when he had just escaped from his native East Germany to the West, at the age of twenty-five. The novel opens, arrestingly enough, with the death of its hero, the railway signalman of the title, and consists of various 'speculations' offered to explain the mysterious circumstances surrounding the manner in which he was killed. But Jacob's death is never elucidated; the various contributions of those who knew him tend to befog rather than clarify the issues, and there is no omniscient authority in the shape of the author to sort it all out. And since it transpires that Jacob had been offered the opportunity of settling in the West, but had turned it down and returned to the Democratic Republic, his story foreshadows the theme of Johnson's next work, *The Third Book about Achim*.

This was preceded by a novella called 'Eine Reise wegwohin, 1960' (in England published by Cape paperbacks under the title *An Absence*), which explores at much shorter length one aspect of the subsequent novel, namely the trip which the journalist Karsch makes to East Germany to visit his ex-mistress (the title means literally 'a journey to somewhere or other'). In the course of that journey, which profoundly disorientates him so that, on his return, he feels a complete outsider in his native West, he makes a half-hearted attempt to write a third biography of the champion cyclist Achim who now lives with his former girlfriend. But the book about Achim is secondary in *An Absence* to the theme of alienation. As a Westerner Karsch feels ill at ease in the Democratic Republic: he finds his German misunderstood because although the language east of the divide is syntactically identical to his own there are appreciable lexical differences which have grown up over the years, and it is these which make communication difficult. When even a word like 'democratic' means one thing on this side, and quite another on that, Karsch's difficulties are understandable. But matters are no better back home: he receives threats and insults for his alleged sympathy with the communist régime; and he is lionized by the young for possessing an (equally imaginary) insight into a system they admire at a safe distance. So, unhappy and deeply disillusioned with Federal Republic politics, Karsch retires to Italy and neutral territory. He still continues to publish regularly in the West German papers, and to the outsider his trip seems not to have affected him much. But the reader, who has been the spectator of the collapse of all Karsch's certainties, knows better. Like Germany itself, he is broken inside. His 'Reise wegwohin' has been more a mythic than an actual journey, a journey into and beyond himself.

The only other work that has so far been translated into English is *Two Views* (in German, *Zwei Ansichten*, 1965), which appeared in this country before its predecessor *The Third Book about Achim*. It is a much slighter and less impressive work. A West German press photographer, Herr B., is the lover of Nurse D., who works in East Berlin. After the Wall goes up he arranges for her escape at considerable risk, although his feelings for her (and hers for him) are curiously tepid and ambiguous. She offers only to 'think over his proposal of marriage' and is much more immediately concerned to inspect the Western hospital which is so much better than the ones she is used to, and to get a job and a room on the unfamiliarly free market. Their story is narrated alternately from

B.'s and D.'s point of view, but always in the third person by a narrator, who reveals himself at the end:

> She told her hosts politely, a little constrainedly, about East Berlin. Later she made me promise. 'But you must make up everything you write!' she said. It is made up.[7]

This narrator thus claims responsibility for the 'two views', B.'s and D.'s, East and West. The views reflect in turn the isolation of two minds, and beyond that of course the separation of the two Germanies. But somehow this novel feels 'contrived', elaborated to a formula; it does not project the territorial division with anything like the poignancy of *The Third Book about Achim*. It is a more exciting story, of course: D.'s escape is a cliff-hanger, and the suspense is built up by the classic device of portraying the protagonist's own impatience and anxiety. In one particularly graphic moment, 'she enumerated the dead, the wounded, in the canal, in the barbed-wire entanglement, machine-gunned along the walls, in the sewer pipes stunned with gas . . .' (p. 148). But the book is rather sensational, and therefore tends to trivialize what the others convey with such intensely genuine anguish.

Nevertheless the novel is well in the lineage in so far as its title incorporates a notion common to them all. The word 'view' implies conjecture, speculation or hypothesis, and all Johnson's works ask the same questions: what is the truth? What is the reality behind the appearance? The answer invariably is that there are many possibilities for interpretation, that there are no absolute truth-values, that enquiry must remain open-ended and ambiguous, and any report cannot help but be elliptical, cryptic and allusive. Such indeed is the case with *The Third Book about Achim* which is, among other things, an account of how the third book about Achim failed to be written.

As in *An Absence*, Karsch visits East Germany at the urgent request of his former mistress Karin, a famous film actress who

is now living with Achim T., the cycling champion of the
Democratic Republic. Karsch, who appears to live modestly
in the Federal Republic, thus finds himself associating with
VIPs on the other side of the border. But why he goes east so
precipitately, without even advising his friends of his absence,
contrary to his usual practice, is never made clear. Perhaps,
thinks the narrator, 'when they separated they very likely said
to each other: I won't forget you. If anything goes wrong . . .
or something to that effect' (pp. 4-5). But if that can explain
Karsch's prompt response, it does not account for the request,
which is made by long-distance call at night. When he meets
Karin he wonders why she had asked him to come: 'her invitation had sounded casual, not particularly friendly, without any
explanation' (p. 6), and he even feels he is not the point at all. It
seems that Achim suggested the invitation: but why? To have
his biography written for the third time? But in that case he
miscalculates: Karsch is not going to produce the sort of book
Achim expects, and in fact the biography is never finished. It
turns up too much in Achim's past that would compromise
him if made public: his Nazi youth, his resentment of the
Soviet occupation troops (the 'glorious liberators' of later
years), his illegal purchase of a three-speed gear in West
Berlin with East German currency and above all his participation (voluntary or accidental?) in the uprising of 1953.
Damning evidence of this last and most serious episode (which
seems to have earned Achim a jail sentence) comes into
Karsch's hands in the form of a photograph showing Achim
marching at the head of a column of protesters. Karin is
greatly worried about this discovery, although she appears to
have left Achim and gone to live with one Herr Fleisg, a
prominent official in the State publishing organization. Achim
too feels he is in danger: 'They want to trap me,' he says
(p. 236). Other people seem to be involved in the intrigue,
notably an innocent-looking young girl whose boyfriend has
absconded to the West, and who may have 'planted' the
incriminating photograph which Karsch later finds in his

jacket pocket. She and her friends, who refrain from political comment when they meet Karsch socially, despite his attempts to draw them, are according to Karin 'testing' him. What for? To assist in escapes to the West? But this is set in 1960 and the Berlin Wall has not yet been built. To trap him into compromising himself? In other words, are they opponents of the régime or *agents provocateurs*? Karsch doesn't have time to find out. Quite independently of these events Karsch has given a lift in his car to a doubtful young man in a garage mechanic's overalls who asked to be dropped at a spot where no roads led off in any direction. The police later call on Karsch and question him about this incident. On their next visit they invite him to 'refrain from stopping again this side of the border'. He was leaving, at the request of Karin and Achim, in any case. When he gets home he finds a large number of letters to answer and receives a mysterious telephone call, consisting of (a tape?) 'a soft murmured conversation involving several people' (p. 246), perhaps the group he met in the East. The novel ends rather abruptly at that point, quite differently from the novella version of the story. Karsch fails to write the third book about Achim because it is not the outward and public person of Achim which interests him, but the 'formation of a personality against a background of social and political change that is bewildering in its impact on the individual';[8] but such a portrait, based on conjecture and the interpretation of scraps of evidence gleaned from a number of sources, would hardly be acceptable to Achim and certainly not to his political masters. They want, and he needs, a simple picture of a people's hero whose motivations are politically impeccable and whose life-story serves to inspire socialist youth to imitate his glorious achievements and uphold like him the purity of the marxist ideal against the capitalistic corruption of the decadent West. For although Karsch's book about Achim is no more 'true' in an absolute sense than any other account composed by human agency, it is considerably more accurate than the windy rhetoric of state propaganda, which is the sort of abuse of language that was then making it harder and harder for the two Germanies to conduct a dialogue.

But the main reason why Karsch cannot ultimately write his book about Achim, much as he and Achim want the biography to be completed, is not political in any but the widest sense. It is the same as the reason why he cannot penetrate the intrigues that enmesh him like a fly in a spider's web: and that is what Johnson calls, in lapidary phrase, 'the border: the difference: the distance' ('die Grenze: den Unterschied: die Entfernung'). This is because, as Malcolm Bradbury puts it, the line of itself 'involves a complexity of viewpoint and a crisis for language'.[9] The three facets of territorial division, the barrier itself, the differences it propagates, and the resulting mental and spiritual isolation of the two peoples on either side of the line, weave their *leitmotif* through the novel, beginning it, ending it, and sustaining it throughout. More than that, they of themselves necessarily generate the book, which is written ostensibly in response to the persistent questioning of the narrator by a friend or acquaintance (someone close enough to be addressed informally as 'du'). The narrator claims that 'the characters are invented', that 'the events do not refer to similar ones but to the border: the difference: the distance / and the attempt to describe it' (p. 246), that he started out with something simple and sober, like 'she telephoned him', but the moment he adds 'across the border' in a casual fashion, 'as though it were the most natural thing in the world', he is caught, he has to explain that 'in the Germany of the fifties there existed a territorial frontier', and perceives at once 'how awkward [that] second sentence looks after the first one' (p. 3); but his novel is begun. The interlocutor keeps prodding him with questions such as 'What was it like?' and 'Who is this Achim?', and the replies, longer or shorter as the case may be, constitute the only chapters into which the novel is divided (unlike *Two Views* which is neatly built in ten instalments, five for D. and five for

4*

B., or *The Palace*, which is made up of five interlinked sections).
The narrator implicates Karsch in the story-telling, too, as if
he is only Karsch's spokesman in some way: 'he thought you
wouldn't want to know about all this' (p. 162), he tells the
questioner at one point. And relations between interrogator
and speaker are not always harmonious: 'Enough of that!'
exclaims one, 'Don't complain' retorts the other, for instance
(p. 193), but complicity is usually more in evidence than
bickering (cf. 'you know the feeling', p. 243). In any case,
the purpose is utilitarian. This is how the narrator explains it:

> The gaps in these conversations are not meant to create
> pleasant suspense; they are due to the story. Because: if a
> man visits this country and understands nothing, every-
> thing must be considered separately, comparisons are
> impossible, he speaks the language but fails to com-
> municate, the currency is different, and so is the govern-
> ment: and he is supposed to reunify himself with that one
> of these days; what does the visitor do? He asks questions,
> he says more than is written here. This has been selected
> because that was why he stayed, and he might have
> realized from the blanks even what he didn't perceive:
> that he ought to try the unification.
> Moreover, this is not a story.
>   (*The Third Book about Achim*, pp. 95-6)

In other words, the two main themes of this novel—the
fictiveness of fiction, and the alien nature for the West German
of Eastern Germany—imply each other. Any attempt at
telling a true story is false, any attempt at telling a fiction may
have a certain explicit truth; just as the undertaking of a visit
across the inter-German frontier involves necessarily an
interrogation into the status and truth-value of reality. Just as
that reality is hard to grasp, so the fiction we are reading folds
back upon itself, doubts itself, expresses weariness, offers
purely provisional descriptions, parodies official rhetorics,

and so on, in a desperate attempt to voice scepticism and draw attention to its own fictiveness. Everything is thus progressively undermined; the feasibility of getting at the truth of the political situation is mocked for instance in this piece of comedy about righteous indignations in a twin-state system:

> The official city paper would report solely on West German rearmament, mention unfair court verdicts against real patriots and the daily deterioration of morals; Karsch was checking whether people were still leading a life back home: they were, but the West German papers were endlessly reporting on East German rearmament, unfair court verdicts against real patriots and the daily deterioration of morals.
>
> (p. 154)

And, more seriously, the narrator points out Karsch's own selectivity and bias. Karsch writes in detail in his draft biography of the day Achim crossed the border and spent money illegally on a set of gears, 'but he had omitted the afternoon in the thickly overgrown ditch beside the autobahn where Achim took a swim in the ice-cold muddy water with a girl,' as well as other things, because they 'had not fitted into his selection, or were too numerous, although they would have completed his description, and incompleteness is a lie?' (wonders the narrator). But 'Karsch didn't want everything about Achim, he only wanted to pick what distinguished him (in Karsch's opinion) from other people, from other bicycle riders, for that was the purpose of his choice among the different episodes of a life, that's what he wanted of the many truths. And what do you want with the truth?' (asks the narrator rhetorically).[10] Achim had reason to feel aggrieved since, as the narrator pertinently reminds us, 'they were his truths, after all' (p. 174), and Karsch had little right to treat them so cavalierly. Achim is happy that Karsch turns up some good stories about how he improved his bicycle and acquired a mechanic for his team, and he approves of the amount of hard technical information about the machine and about the body that rides it at the very limit of strength and endurance; but he cannot be pleased when Karsch points up the hesitations and ambivalence behind what Achim is now pleased to call, in deference to the masters who have allowed him fame and influence, 'My Development Toward Political Awareness' (p. 209). In the end the two men fail to understand each other: 'It's shabby to speak this way of us', says Achim, 'a guest doesn't do that' (p. 235). Their mutual incomprehension reflects in little the bafflement which Achim experiences during his short trip to the West to purchase what no one manufactures at home: a three-speed gear; in a remarkable passage, Johnson compares his feeling to that of being alone in a strange town on a Sunday, a sensation conveyed here as graphically as a similar one in Bergman's movie *Wild Strawberries* when Isak Borg in one of his nightmares dreams he is taking a stroll in an unfamiliar part of his home town which 'seemed strangely deserted, as if it were a holiday morning in the middle of summer'.[11] Filmgoers will recall that Borg there meets a man without a face, and soon afterwards, when a hearse spills its contents, finds his arm gripped by the corpse, which turns out to be himself. This is how Johnson conveys Achim's sense of alienation in West Berlin:

> If he had lost his way, or wanted to stay over there: the policemen wore different uniforms, a different cut in a different colour, crankily or cheerfully they were performing tasks of which a nineteen-year-old from a differently governed country could only have the vaguest notion. The inscriptions on administration buildings were incomprehensible to him, at the newsstands he read headlines about events he had never heard of, which he did not believe. He didn't know what the money here looked like, how it felt, he saw bank

buildings soar hugely towards the sky, but also apartment
buildings. Who might be running this country. Nothing
invited him. The people he passed in the streets lived
mysteriously for him, he couldn't guess whether they
worked in factories stores offices, as he was able to by
glancing at a casual pedestrian in his home town, they
drove their cars, walked with inexplicable purposefulness
to unimaginable places, moved their faces towards objects
and situations he didn't understand: they were all there,
he saw everything, he guessed nothing. Unknown persons
discussed unknown things in an unknown language, next
to him they lived in the balmy evening of a different
country, they lived with one another secure in what he
didn't know, he was as distant from them as the impression of Sunday morning from working days; there was
movement all around him that left him standing still, the
way Sunday stops and leaves one standing, alone and
helpless in lonely rooms. In this clean remoteness, in this
neat foreign country, Sundaylike alone and insecure.

                                        (p. 169)

The central phrase in this passage, 'Unknown persons
discussed unknown things in an unknown language', so
expressive of alienation, is more forcible in the original
German: 'Fremde sprachen über Fremdes in fremder Spra-
che.'[12] It also illustrates Johnson's gift for rhythm and
terseness of phrasing, which makes him as consummate a
craftsman in words as Claude Simon. They have, curiously,
other things in common, in fact of all the novelists discussed
in this book Johnson is, technically speaking, closest to Claude
Simon. They both share, for instance, a fondness for the
parenthesis, even for the parenthesis-within-a-parenthesis, as
a device for qualifying and sub-qualifying statements, or
amplifying or nuancing utterances.[13] Johnson's scepticism of
narrational accuracy is so extreme that at one point his narrator
offers variant versions (one in film-script form) of 'Karsch's

penultimate plans for bringing a certain order into the scraps
of paper on which he had prepared fragments of Achim's life'
(pp. 193ff.), because no single one strikes him as 'very
rewarding'.

In his attempt to 'describe it'—both Johnson and Simon
are obsessed with the question 'how was it?', 'wie war es
denn?', 'comment c'était alors?'—the narrator in *The Third
Book about Achim* offers through the cycle champion an illu-
minating insight into the condition of Germany during and
immediately after the war: the mother who died in a bombing
raid, the draughtsman father who opposed the Hitler dictatorship and appears to have sabotaged one modest portion of
the war effort by introducing an error into his drawings, and
who as a result could not confide even in his own son; these
and other incidents throw light on the essential background to
the situation in the late fifties, not least to the things that have
to be forgotten, suppressed, like the behaviour of the 'heroic
liberators' who had 'unanimously, one after the other, torn
the German women up between the legs' (p. 131). A palpable
feeling of the grotesque tragedy of things is conveyed by such
details as these, inserted in the narrator's answers to his
interlocutor's questions about Achim.

In *The Palace*, too, the past is resurrected, or rather the
attempt to do so is made. A man who had spent a crucial
period of his youth in civil war Barcelona—the late summer of
1936, to be precise—and who is identified by the narrator
merely as 'the student', returns to the city in 1951, and tries
to relive the three days or so which are so deeply engraved in
his memory, when he associated with the Republican forces
and in particular with three men, the 'schoolmaster', 'the
American' and 'the rifleman'. He recalls how the American,
whom he greatly admired and imitated, went away to the
front to join the American battalion, and how the rifleman
killed himself with his weapon in an underground public
lavatory, apparently by accident. All this, and much more,
comes back to the ex-student's consciousness when in 1951 he

orders a beer in a bar opposite the site of the 'palace', the luxury hotel of the title, which in 1936 was taken over by the Republicans as their headquarters, destroyed during the insurgents' capture of the city, and then rebuilt as a bank. As the older man contemplates the edifice opposite, and as he feels himself nauseated by the beer, his mind goes back into the past, and the hotel comes to life in his consciousness; beer even provides the link, since he leaps from the liquid swilling about in his stomach in the present to the 'bottles of beer on the long zinc-topped refectory table' in the mess nearly fifteen years before (*The Palace*, p. 33). Thus the conventional form of time is broken down, and the omnipresent use by Simon of the participle in '—ing' serves to facilitate the merger of 'now' and 'then'. Similarly, characters are not identified, or if they are, by only the commonest of names (Martinez, Alonso): more important in the narrator's consciousness, certainly more memorable, are such distinguishing and personal traits as the manner of handling a rifle, or of squatting on the edge of a refectory table. The method is often filmic: first the image is ambiguous, then it becomes clear, indeed usually appears extremely sharp in focus. One episode in particular is unforgettably graphic: the rifleman's account of how, a few years earlier, he carried out a political assassination in a Paris restaurant. The story is told in minute detail and in slow motion, as befits an incident which engaged all the protagonist's emotions. But the rest of the world went on at its normal pace, as is tellingly shown by the fact that although the assassin appeared (to himself) to have spent an eternity in the restaurant, dodging the waiters, selecting his victim, firing, escaping, in fact the crime took only a minute or two to commit. For as he leaps out of the restaurant, turns about with arms flaying wildly, in grotesque Chaplin-like fashion, he sees a man paying off a taxi, the same man, the same taxi that he had passed shortly before on his way to shoot his victim; in fact, the whole thing had in reality not lasted, or taken, more time than to glance at the amount registered on a meter, unbutton a coat, take the bank notes out of a pocket, wait until the driver had opened his own wallet, counted the coins, handed him one, and then straighten up and pocket the rest.

(*The Palace*, p. 108)

It is 'as if immobility . . . were somehow the complement, a paradoxical, obligatory element of speed' (pp. 99-100). Time is as relative in the world of Simon, in fact, as in the world of Uwe Johnson.

Both writers, indeed, treat time in very similar ways. Just as Simon's narrator switches us abruptly from 1951 to 1936 and back again several times in a few pages, so Johnson's speaker moves from Achim late at night worrying Karsch about Karin's whereabouts, to earlier in the day when he had been engaged in an important race:[14] the jumps are very like film cuts. The purpose in both cases is to undermine our assurance about linear chronology, because things occurring in a neat and stable order give a false impression of reality, which is, according to both novelists, unstable and untidy. For both writers, history thus offers only ironies. In Johnson we read how 'on every anniversary of the German surrender the leader of the East German team stepped up to the captain of the Soviet team with a bunch of red roses and embraced him and thanked him for having liberated them from an unjust dictatorship and for having set up a just one instead' (p. 196); in Simon the concept of 'revolution' is satirized by the novel's epigraph, which is taken from the definition in the Larousse dictionary: 'the locus of a moving body which, describing a closed curve, successively passes through the same points.' The mechanical sense of the term casts doubt on the political meaning: revolutions, it is implied, change nothing, progress nowhere, they only move eternally through the same crises. This ironic patterning runs through the whole of *The Palace*.

General Santiago's funeral (burlesquely contrasted with that of Patroclus in the *Iliad*) takes place while the student is in Barcelona; he notes later that the cortège followed a path now taken by city trams. Public transport replaces the hero's burial train; a bank stands where once men congregated in the hope of a different future. Likewise, Achim is the creature and puppet of a repressive régime which manipulates this son of the people, overlooks his political lapses of the past in order to employ him in the provision of bread and circuses in the present. Both novels, profoundly committed to their age, are thus equally profoundly sceptical of its political aspirations. Only objects have any permanency, despite being condemned to be 'periodically requisitioned by more or less provisional governments' (*The Palace*, p. 15). The circular flight of the pigeons, who open and close Simon's novel, reflects the circularity of this historical process.

Finally, at the centre of both works there is, as I pointed out in connection with *The Third Book about Achim*, a preoccupation with the fictive nature of all narration, however apparently objective. The book about Achim is crucified on the dilemma of what constitutes truth—the way Karsch sees it, or Achim? —and similarly Simon's student ponders why the rifleman tells his story. Perhaps, he thinks, because

> . . . he hopes that once it's told, once it's put in the form of words, it begins existing all by itself, without his needing to endure it any longer, that is, to deal only with himself, with his meagre strength, his puny coolie's carcass: as if he were trying to tear, to fling from himself that violence, that thing which had seized on, made use of him—which is why he said that it was only his hand, his arm, not him—(as in those games when the loser draws an unlucky card, which he must pass on to someone else before he loses for good), possessing him, consuming him . . .''.

(*The Palace*, pp. 85-6)

The same ambition to invest incidents with the permanence of words activates Karsch; but as both Johnson and Simon make implicitly clear, such an ambition is doomed to irremediable failure. Karsch, who returns from East Germany empty-handed, and the ex-student, whose return to Barcelona leads to no fresh insight, only to the futile resurrection of inchoate memory, are both brought face to face with the fact which constitutes the moral of both these books: it is impossible to tell the story of another person, even if that person, in the case of the student, is a former self. 'Achim knew what Karsch could only guess at', writes Johnson's narrator (p. 171), but by the same token Karsch knows other things of which Achim is ignorant. From our own viewpoint we misinterpret habitually: the student, incensed because he believes in the night that the American has fooled him and gone to bed with a girl, discovers next morning that the naked body he had glimpsed opposite was not in the American's room at all. Such misapprehensions are characteristic of all attempts to understand reality.

And just as we can never finally know another's life and modes of perception, so we can never truly know places. The Barcelona of 1936 has vanished for ever: and Karsch's journey eastwards is truly anywhere—and nowhere. Just as for the Jew of Malta's act of fornication, indeed, the past reality of Johnson's Karsch and of Simon's former student lies irredeemably 'in another country', where 'the wench is dead'.

SECTION 1—NOTES

1 *The Third Book about Achim*, tr. Ursule Molinaro, London: Cape, 1968, p. 3. This is the edition I shall be citing throughout this section, but with a few silent modifications to bring the English into closer relation with the German text.

2 *The Contemporary Novel in German: a Symposium*, ed. Robert R. Heitner, Austin: University of Texas Press, 1967, p. 5.

3 'The Present Quandary of German Novelists', in *The Contemporary Novel in German*, p. 81. Like other critics of the German novel today, I am greatly indebted to Gaiser's remarkable essay on the present state of fiction-writing in his country.

4 Gaiser, p. 85.

5 Kafka's influence is fairly marked in the opening paragraph of Johnson's 'Eine Reise wegwohin, 1960', in *Karsch, und andere Prosa* (Frankfurt am Main: Suhrkamp, 1964), p. 29, and Faulkner's in parts of *The Third Book about Achim* (cf. pp. 243-5). According to Gaiser, what postwar German novelists learned from Kafka was the art of understatement, while Hemingway provided an example of 'coolness'.

6 Among readily accessible English writing, there is a rather dismissive entry in *Penguin Companion to European Literature* (ed. A. K. Thorlby), and scant reference in *Critical Strategies: German Fiction in the Twentieth Century*, by Elizabeth Boa and J. H. Reid (London: Edward Arnold, 1972). In *The Modern German Novel* by H. M. Waidson (London: Oxford University Press, 1971) there is a short, factual entry on pp. 123-5; there is no separate essay on Johnson in Heitner's symposium; but Malcolm Bradbury has a few perceptive comments, to which I am indebted, in his essay on the contemporary novel in *The Twentieth-Century Mind: History, Ideas, and Literature in Britain*, ed. C. B. Cox and A. E. Dyson, vol. III (London: Oxford University Press, 1972), pp. 319-385.

7 *Two Views*, tr. Richard and Clara Winston (London: Cape, 1967), p. 183. In this translation B. is perversely named Dietbert and D. Beate.

8 Waidson, *The Modern German Novel*, p. 125.

9 Bradbury, in *The Twentieth-Century Mind*, p. 378. The richness of Johnson's language is difficult to render in English. The phrase 'die Grenze: den Unterschied: die Entfernung' has not only the literal meaning of 'the border: the difference: the distance', but a metaphorical connotation which might be rendered 'the borderline: the difference: the remoteness (or gap)'. In other words, the notorious *Zonengrenze* between the two Germanies is not only a political and geographical reality but also a metaphor of all divisions and discrepancies of mind, and Johnson's subtle linguistic ambiguities (in the Empsonian sense) reflect both orders of truth.

10 *The Third Book about Achim*, pp. 171-2.

11 Ingmar Bergman, *Wild Strawberries*, tr. Lars Malmström and David Kushner (London: Lorrimer, 1970), p. 24.

12 *Das Dritte Buch über Achim*, Frankfurt am Main: Fischer, 1971, p. 155.

13 Cf. *The Third Book about Achim*, p. 135 (p. 124 in the Fischer edition), and *The Palace*, p. 122.

14 Cp. *The Palace*, pp. 234-6 with *The Third Book about Achim*, pp. 150-151.

2

Fragmentary Descriptions of Disasters:
The Flanders Road and *August 1914*

For our time is a very shadow that passeth away . . .
—Wisdom, ii. 5

I

The contemporary Russian literary scene is of course rather particular in that it is overhung by the spectre of censorship which, at varying degrees of intensity, has affected artistic creation since Pushkin was harried by Tsarist officials in the early part of the nineteenth century. But whereas the Tsars were largely concerned to curb dissent, or at least its overt expression, in a fairly negative way, the Soviet authorities offer the writer their own positive creed to which he is expected to adhere. There is no intrinsic reason why this creed—socialist realism—should of itself have an inhibiting effect on writing, indeed critics like Georg Lukács convince us that it can give rise to work of a high order once it is properly understood and applied. The trouble is that since the early thirties a bastardized and trivialized version of the doctrine has received official sanction, to the detriment of writing which the outside world is able to take seriously as art in the broadest sense of the term. The two postwar Soviet writers who have created a real impact in the West (not always, it must be said, for purely literary reasons) are also prominent among those who have found themselves in open disagreement with the régime, and it is hard to see how it could have turned out otherwise. The two I refer to are, of course, Boris Pasternak and Alexander Solzhenitsyn. Both from a profoundly patriotic conviction have disdained the obvious solution: to go into exile; but neither is able to be read by his fellow-countrymen. There is a tragic irony about this, since both share the traditionally Russian romantic view of the writer as being committed to his people, its history and its language, and as having a sacred role to play in preserving the heritage of the past and in extending its potential in the present. Both are in a real sense 'cultural nationalists', intensely and dedicatedly Russian, and as the very reverse of an aesthetic cosmopolitan like Nabokov, are determined to 'warn in time', as Solzhenitsyn has put it, 'against threatening moral and social dangers' which beset their country.[1] Both share, indeed, a fair measure of the messianism one associates with Russia's greatest novelists, Tolstoy and Dostoyevsky, and it is understandable that their literary methods do not, as I shall try to show, diverge greatly from those of such illustrious forbears. There is no reason why they should particularly, since Pasternak and Solzhenitsyn see their vocation in fairly traditional terms: 'the downgrading of political forms and the insistence on the power of art and spiritual renewal'.[2] But that is hardly something which is likely to enable them to stay within the confines of official orthodoxy in cultural matters. In fact, as Lukács argues, Solzhenitsyn has succeeded in 'really breaking through the ideological bulwarks of the Stalinist tradition',[3] a fact which has not endeared him to the political masters of his country. Art of this order raises questions, stirs sluggish consciences, provokes thought, and no autocratic and paternalistic régime can be expected to tolerate that.

Deplorable as it is that a writer of Solzhenitsyn's calibre should be silenced in his own nation, we in the West should not allow the dubious political circumstances surrounding the publication of his novels to blind us to their intrinsic aesthetic merits and importance. As T. R. Fyvel put it, reporting on the Formentor Prize conference of 1964 when, in the final vote, Nathalie Sarraute won against Solzhenitsyn: 'just as Sarraute by her technical innovations [has] widened the scope of the French novel, so Solzhenitsyn, by his daring in describing Soviet prison camps combined with deliberate understatement and deliberate lack of overt anger, [has] widened the scope for the current Soviet novel',[4] or at least will have done as soon as he is allowed to be read by his fellow-citizens, for whom his mature and greatest works, especially *August 1914*, must for the nonce remain a dead letter. Lukács puts it more emphatically, and also more mystically, when he claims that Solzhenitsyn points the way to a rejuvenated socialist realism which will be able to explore a radical new reality beyond the reach of bourgeois modernists.

II

Whether this is the case or not, it is an undeniable fact that the two most characteristic and significant novels to have come out of Russia since World War II are *Doctor Zhivago* and *August 1914*. It so happens, though it is clearly no accident, that both are historical novels, and that they are both about defeat of one kind or another. It happens, too, though once again hardly by accident, that the novel by Claude Simon I wish to compare *August 1914* with is also about a defeat, the French débâcle of May 1940. In fact, different as Simon's book—*The Flanders Road*, first published in 1960—is from Solzhenitsyn's, they have in common the fact that they are both, self-avowedly, 'fragmentary' descriptions of a particular national disaster. Simon intended originally to adopt precisely this expression as a subtitle, and Solzhenitsyn's heroes too give 'fragmentary and disjointed descriptions' of the inferno into which military incompetence has thrown them.[5] It could hardly be otherwise, since the contemporary writer has willy-nilly lost the confidence with which Tolstoy, for example, engaged in the magnificent reconstruction of the defeat at Austerlitz. Tolstoy's account in *War and Peace* has a tidiness about it slightly at odds with the chaos of the event itself, but even there, as Solzhenitsyn points out, the disorder was geographically speaking on a relatively small scale: 'to cover those forty-five miles—which in Kutuzov's time [would have] been a mere three miles—the only means remained the same old horses' hooves, whose stride had not increased by an inch since Kutuzov's day' (p. 300). Solzhenitsyn's Tannenberg, the battle which proved such a disastrous calamity for the Russian armed forces in August 1914, is on so much vaster a scale than Tolstoy's Austerlitz of over one hundred years earlier, that the novelist must—if only through modesty at his own lesser talents—decline to attempt any emulation. That such military collapses are never purely strategic Tolstoy, Solzhenitsyn and Simon are at one in demonstrating: routs of this magnitude involve, often in far-reaching ways, the lives of many people, some of whom may appear at first to be rather remote from the scene of conflict. In Tolstoy we have of course Natasha, Andrei and Pierre whose lives, loves and personal difficulties are held in the foreground while great battles rage first afar off and then increasingly closer. To make convergence between the microcosm and the macrocosm possible, Tolstoy (closely imitated not only, as we would expect, by Pasternak and Solzhenitsyn, but even by Simon) establishes an elaborate system of coincidence. In the thick of battle his characters will tend to run into someone who happens to be precisely the person the novelist needs for a purpose not necessarily connected with the main war plot. This applies not only to moments in *War and Peace* like the fortuitous arrival of the wounded Prince Andrei at the house Natasha's people occupy in Moscow, but also to apparently accidental meetings in *Doctor Zhivago* like that between Yuri and Strelnikov at Varykino after Lara's departure, or to the manner in which Colonel Vorotyntsev comes across Ensign Lenartovich in the forest during the retreat in *August 1914*, or to the way Claude

Simon's hero Georges finds himself conveniently incarcerated
with his dead captain's orderly and former jockey Iglésia in
The Flanders Road. Such a device, for all its artificiality, does if
used sparingly create the illusion of reality. By taking war
as one's subject, a confusing enough phenomenon in all
conscience, one needs to create a limited number of sufficiently rounded characters whom the reader can readily
indentify with and recognize on every appearance, otherwise
the war is not meaningful as imaginative experience, a palpable
thing suffered and engaged in by living people, but appears
rather as it is presented in official histories or demonstrated on
staff maps. This was, incidentally, precisely what Raymond
Williams reproached *August 1914* with when it was first
published,[6] but the criticism no more applies to Solzhenitsyn
than it does to Tolstoy, Pasternak or Simon, although there is
probably more actual military history in *August 1914* even than
there is in *War and Peace*. But it is necessary: a battle of such
epic proportions as Tannenberg needs after all to be described
in some detail if the apparently unexpected and even absurd
nature of the disaster is to be satisfactorily explained.

On the other hand, I think one needs to stress the differences
that exist between Pasternak and Solzhenitsyn. As John Wain
perceptively points out, Pasternak is a symbolist novelist;[7] as
Lukács points out equally perceptively, Solzhenitsyn is not.
Pasternak is not much interested in realism at all, socialist or
otherwise. His coincidences are even more extraordinary
than Tolstoy's. He devotes a lot of space to the dreams and the
visions of his characters, who are all larger-than-life and
vested with an often bewildering symbolic function. In fact I
think Pasternak has few connections with the Tolstoyan
tradition of mimetic realism and far more with the visionary
strain in Russian literature which is most clearly exemplified
by Dostoyevsky. *Doctor Zhivago*, like some of Dostoyevsky's
novels, is curiously imprecise about some things, and oddly
evasive about others. Some events are never satisfactorily
explained, others are never followed up to a satisfactory

conclusion. Not all the imagery, by any means, is clear in intention, either: there remain several mysterious elements of indeterminate significance, like the 'iced rowanberries' that attain some prominence in the symbolic framework of the book. And as occasionally in Dostoyevsky, there is not always a sense of continuity in the action: characters tend to come forward according to a logic more of dreams than of strict realism, and their every appearance is rather *sui generis*. There is also a slightly hectic, even feverish quality about some of the episodes which is very reminiscent of Dostoyevsky, and emotional experiences, such as the final brief idyll at Varykino, have a Dostoyevskian intensity about them. Even the unforgettable details—such as the trains strung out in the snow along the Siberian railroad, with an immobilized train every few miles, seemingly halted for eternity—have a truly Dostoyevskian sharpened vividness. And of course Yuri Zhivago partakes of the nature of that classic figure in Russian literature, the 'superfluous man'. There's a lot of the Oblomov about him; he has much of the comic indecisiveness of Goncharov's hero, who, like Yuri, marries his landlady or her daughter. Like Oblomov, too, he has a lot of the Hamlet in his makeup: one of his poems in the anthology printed at the end of the novel is entitled 'Hamlet', in which the speaker asks for 'this cup to pass from him'.

Solzhenitsyn, on the contrary, is not in the least a symbolist. He is very concrete and down-to-earth, like Tolstoy, whereas Pasternak, as Edmund Wilson has pointed out, is putting us 'under the spell of what is really a legend, a fable' rather than a realist novel, a book whose main theme is 'death and resurrection'.[8] Solzhenitsyn, on the other hand, shares the earthy simplicities of the younger Tolstoy. He even goes in for Tolstoyan similes, though not usually of Tolstoy's Homeric proportions; Solzhenitsyn's do not extend over half a page, but they do have a homely quality which is reminiscent of some of Tolstoy's. Here is a typical example:

Just as a jar of sunflower-seed oil, shaken until it is cloudy, needs to stand a while for the dregs to settle to the bottom and for the rest to regain its sunny, transparent colour with a few bubbles floating on the top, so Samsonov longed for some peace and quiet to clarify his mind.

(*August 1914*, p. 329)

Pasternak tends to disdain explanations of this sort. The disaster he is concerned with stretches from before the First World War to the middle of the Second, and then in the very last section looks beyond it to a kind of hopeful future. Its harbinger is 'a book of Yuri's writings' compiled by his half-brother Yevgraf, who crops up at various points in the story but remains throughout a rather shadowy figure. He is, as Edmund Wilson has shown, both a guardian angel and the angel of death who foretells resurrection; he is also, as his name ('writer') implies, Yuri's creative genius, the nature of whose power remains unexplained. This good jinnee pops up indestructibly to bring succour to Yuri or his people; whatever purges are raging, whatever disasters are taking place, Yevgraf rides the storm, like a petrel. He is not intended, and does not function, as a realistic character at all.

But whatever the literary affiliations of these three novelists —Pasternak's with the visionary and 'dreamer' strain in Russian writing, Solzhenitsyn's with its more realistic tendency (though the two are not of course mutually exclusive), and Simon's, as I showed in the first chapter, with the high achievements of Anglo-American modernism—whatever analogies we perceive between their works and the major figures of the past, all three are concerned, in the present, with the depiction of disaster. It is the different ways in which they treat disaster that is the most interesting thing about them when they are considered together. Pasternak portrays, in terms of image and symbol, the years of civil war in post-revolutionary Russia, the breakdown of law and order, and the country's degeneration into anarchy. He tells of the colossal human losses, and the immense suffering to individuals, whose happiness is destroyed and whose lives are broken. This is how he describes, with laconic reserve concealing great emotion, the fate of one of the leading characters in the novel, Yuri's loved one, Lara:

> One day Lara went out and did not come back. She must have been arrested in the street, as so often happened in those days, and she died or vanished somewhere, forgotten as a nameless number on a list which later was mislaid, in one of the innumerable mixed or women's concentration camps in the north.
>
> (*Doctor Zhivago*, Collins 1958, p. 449)

Solzhenitsyn's novel, though longer, covers a much shorter span in time. War has already been declared when the book opens, but it has not made much impact on the more distant Russian provinces, and it ends a few weeks later with the Russian seizure of the city of Lvov on the Austrian front; it starts in high summer and harvest, and ends with the cold rains of autumn setting in. Solzhenitsyn begins, too, as Tolstoy does, with particular characters, individual people living deep in the country, and then he moves us via the Russian headquarters to the war zone in East Prussia. The Russian army, of course, was a slow and cumbrous force which took a long time to mobilize, and it should not have entered the war in an active manner as soon as it did. But Russia's French allies were hard pressed at the battle of the Marne, and appealed to the Russians to exert pressure on Germany's eastern borders and divert part of the German war effort in their direction. So against all logic and the wisest counsels the Russians decided to advance into German territory. Since they had expected to fight a defensive war on this front, no storage depots had been built near the frontier. The troops had therefore to carry all their supplies with them, over vast expanses of trackless territory, before they even reached the border. This error was soon compounded by others. The first army advanced northwards, more or less parallel with the Baltic coast, while the second struck south-wards into the sandy area of lakes and pine forests in central East Prussia. After a while the northern army was halted and kept in idleness by Headquarters, while the southern army, by forced marches, penetrated ever more deeply into enemy territory, literally ploughing its way through hot, dry, sandy country in the blazing heat of August. And because it kept being given contradictory orders, it tended to fan out, one detachment being sent to the right, the other left, and this was exacerbated by the necessity of moving round the large natural obstacles constituted by the Prussian lakes. So this very powerful army, superior in numbers and even in equipment to anything the Germans could field, soon found itself spread out over a vast area with impossibly distended supply lines to the rear. Then again, the Germans had retreated before them, with little or no attempt at a burnt earth policy, and left an uncannily deserted terrain. Russian soldiers would enter a house from which the inhabitants had recently fled, and would find the family's clothes still hanging on the hook behind the bathroom door. The effect the Germans created by just walking out in this way and leaving everything as it stood was eerie, and understandably upset the Russian troops. It was rather like the *Marie Céleste* mystery for them. The Germans were in fact allowing this otherwise invincible army to get bogged down, and then they initiated a pincer movement to enclose it. If this did not go quite as smoothly as it might have done it was, as Solzhenitsyn points out, because the Germans themselves made one or two mistakes. For one thing, they found it difficult to believe the Russians could be as careless and inefficient as they were. For instance, when the telegraph broke down and couriers could not be despatched across such distances, the Russians had recourse to the wireless, and they broadcast crucial orders to the troops: but these instructions were transmitted uncoded. The Germans could not believe their ears, and wasted time because they suspected a trap. Also they could not grasp that when the Russians dodged pointlessly about the country this was not in pursuance of a shrewd master plan, but a result of the most monumental incompetence occasioned by the fact that generals many miles to the rear had no idea what the terrain was like at the front and so despatched contradictory orders. The Germans therefore did not always take fullest advantage of their opportunities. Also there were some very courageous stands made by certain detachments in the Russian army, which Solzhenitsyn describes rather as Tolstoy does Russian resistance around the Raevsky redoubt at Borodino in 1812. But if the Germans were occasionally held up by properly led detachments which stood their ground, they were not prevented from carrying out the pincer movement which resulted in the almost total annihilation of the Second Army, while the First Army received no coherent instructions to come to its assistance. There were twenty thousand dead and seventy thousand prisoners, and at the intense shame of having presided willy-nilly over such a calamity the commander of the Second Army, General Samsonov, committed suicide. The Tannenberg defeat was of such proportions that the Russians never fully recovered from its traumatic effects, and it constituted one of the contributory causes of the Bolshevik revolution; this is to be the subject of a subsequent volume in a series of novels of which, Solzhenitsyn tells us, *August 1914* is only the first. This is indeed evident, since in the early chapters characters are introduced who have little to do with later events in the book. Their roles will no doubt become clear as successive volumes appear. Meanwhile we have in this novel one of the most moving and most effective descriptions of military defeat in the whole of contemporary literature.

Claude Simon in *The Flanders Road* is also describing a military disaster. Like Tannenberg, the battle he is concerned with—the battle of the Meuse in May 1940—was the occasion of a similarly traumatic collapse for the French troops. One can see why. As Simon describes it, some of the French cavalry divisions were fighting on horseback against armour, a preposterous state of affairs. At the same time, the French army, for political reasons stretching back into the prewar period, had lost much of its will to resist, and such rearguard actions as were effective turned out to have little strategic significance. Whereas Pasternak tells his story more or less straight, with an omniscient narrator following the hero's fortunes over a lengthy period of time, and whereas Solzhenitsyn, for all his newspaper or film style interludes à la Dos Passos, also gives his account in fairly straightforward chronological order, Simon does not narrate *The Flanders Road* in an orthodox manner at all. Basically what happens is that the hero Georges (who also appears of course in *The Grass*, the novel published two years before this one) is captured, along with his captain's orderly Iglésia, and interned in a POW camp in Germany after the fall of France where he and Iglésia make friends with a Jewish comrade, Blum, who dies a year or so later. These three survivors have one habitual subject of conversation: the young woman who married their officer in 1936; her name is Corinne (she recurs as a relation of the narrator in later novels, notably *Histoire*) and the captain's name is De Reixach (pronounced—it is a Catalan name—Rayshak). He is a distant relation of Georges, whose mother is a De Reixach, and he becomes confused in Georges's mind with a common ancestor, a French Revolutionary general who died in mysterious circumstances. When the war is over Georges seeks out Corinne, who in the meantime has remarried, and he becomes her lover. In the course of the night he spends with her he tries, through his sexual knowledge of her, to acquire an understanding in depth of the past and in particular to penetrate the mystery of her husband's death. For De Reixach, despite warnings, had led his men into a German ambush, and had himself died under fire. Georges has grounds for suspecting that this death in action was veiled suicide. Did he know, as

Georges learns from Iglésia in the camp, that his wife was having an affair with, of all people, his jockey? He could hardly have been ignorant of the fact, although he never betrayed any awareness of it. Was it part of his aristocratic code not only to keep silent about such a shaming matter, but even to obliterate the ignominy by committing suicide? Perhaps—since an officer does not take his own life except, like Samsonov, when he is defeated militarily—De Reixach does the next best thing, and rides into a German machine-gun trap. Whether this incident constituted a normal casualty in action, or something else, is thus the central question of the book. Georges returns after the war and the years of captivity to try and find out why and how this event occurred, but his pursuit is a vain one because the past is truly dead and there is no way of resurrecting it. As the hours of the night with Corinne go by he realizes that he is getting nowhere. The woman herself is angry with him because all his reminiscences of army life make her feel she is being treated like 'a soldiers' tart', as she puts it. She loses her temper, hits him with her bag, and walks out on him, leaving him no wiser than he was before. So the novel in a sense, like its hero, comprehends nothing and achieves nothing, and yet in the process it manages to tell us a great deal, conveying with extraordinary vividness the atmosphere of Flanders in 1940. We experience precisely what it felt like to ride into battle in warm spring weather, what it was like to come up against superior forces, mechanized divisions, and what it was like to collapse: the rout, the disorder, soldiers throwing away their weapons in their panic, civilians abandoning their possessions in their haste to escape. There are the inevitable suitcases burst open by the roadside, and the bodies of horses already swelling in the heat (both Simon and Solzhenitsyn seize on this particularly potent image of débâcle—'how hugely', Solzhenitsyn comments, 'horses swell when they are dead,' p. 551). Of all the many remarkable descriptions of rout in *The Flanders Road* the following, in which Georges tries to render it clear to himself and to Blum, is one of the most affectingly simple:

> Maybe it wasn't only the fact of that battle, a simple defeat: not just what he saw there, the panic, the cowardice, the runaways throwing down their arms, screaming treason as usual and cursing their leaders to justify their panic, and gradually the shots coming at longer intervals, then isolated, without response, without conviction, the battle fading, dying of its own accord in the late-afternoon languor. We saw that, we knew that: the slowing down, the gradual immobilization. Like the wheel of the country fair lottery, the dry crackle of the metal (or bone) tongue on the shiny circle of stoppers gradually decomposing so to speak, the clicking that made only a single continuous rattle separating, dissociating, rarefying, those last hours when the battle seems to continue only by virtue of the momentum it has built up, to slow down, start up again, break out in absurd and incoherent starts, only to collapse again while you begin to hear the birds singing, realizing suddenly that they have never stopped singing . . .
>
> (*The Flanders Road*, p. 167)

Although he is ostensibly describing what must have been the experience of his revolutionary ancestor, Georges is clearly reporting on his own, on the incidents that are so deeply burned into his consciousness that what happened one early summer day on a road in Flanders haunts and obsesses him for years afterwards.

III

Fragmentary and individual though Simon's and Solzhenitsyn's descriptions of their respective national disasters undoubtedly are—and for all his apparent, and rather illusory, 'documentariness', Solzhenitsyn, like Simon, requires a central

5

narrative consciousness and supplies it in the shape of Colonel Vorotyntsev—there are solid achievements. Both books establish the sensuous concreteness of things, beginning with Solzhenitsyn's opening passage dwelling upon the appearance of the Caucasus range seen from a distance, a quite remarkable piece of landscape description sharply observed and sensitively written:

> All the time, from village to village, the road kept the ridge directly in front of them, an ever-present goal with its snowy expanses, its bare crags and its shadows hinting at ravines. But with every half-hour it seemed to melt slightly at the base and detach itself from the earth, until it appeared to be no longer fixed but with its upper two-thirds hanging in the sky. It became shrouded in vapour, the gashes and ribs and mountainous features seemed blended into vast, cloud-like white masses which were then riven into vaporous fragments indistinguishable from real clouds. After a while they too were wiped away and the range vanished altogether as if it had been a celestial mirage, leaving the travellers surrounded by a greyish sky and a pale heat-haze. They had driven without changing direction for half a day and had covered more than thirty miles by mid-afternoon; now it appeared as though they were no longer faced by a gigantic mountain range but were instead hemmed in by rounded foothills: the Camel, the Bull, the bare-topped Snake and the thickly wooded Iron Hill.
>
> (*August 1914*, p. 7)

Those who compare *August 1914* unfavourably with obviously lesser works of didactic and moralizing intent by Solzhenitsyn like *The First Circle* and *Cancer Ward*, and who find it ponderously naturalistic and anecdotal, might like to weigh the findings of two critics from very different theoretical backgrounds. Firstly, Georg Lukács, who feels that Solzhenitsyn 'stands in marked contrast to all the trends within naturalism' in that 'the detail in [his] work has a peculiar function which grows out of his material' (pp. 19-20); and secondly, Malcolm Bradbury, who sees in Solzhenitsyn's fiction 'deeper acts of imagination, real complexities of realist technique'[9]. To construct a novel of this length, relying heavily on the historical record, Solzhenitsyn (who is well aware that 'no one would dare to write a fictional account of such unrelieved blackness' (p. 399) because of the incredible nature of the story), has recourse to a number of devices that are not just tricks. The fictionalized account is interspersed with historical summaries of a more objective kind printed in smaller type, and these sometimes provide interesting alternative versions of events narrated in the 'imaginative' passages (a good example is when Vorotyntsev's men put Von François's searchlight out of action by rifle fire, pp. 542 and 549). This sort of thing simultaneously backs up and slightly ironizes the fictional version, and certainly draws attention self-consciously to its fictiveness. Then there are the 'screen' sequences, when an incident is presented in film script form, or the newspaper sections, where patriotic propaganda rubs shoulders with advertisements for patent medicines. Solzhenitsyn is here clearly experimenting with various techniques to fill out dimensions of reality which straightforward novelistic narration of a traditional kind—which of course he also uses extensively—cannot conveniently encompass. Certainly such sections provide a graphic vividness that establishes the feeling of war mentality. Solzhenitsyn also at one point narrates the same incident—Vorotyntsev's earlier encounter with Von François—twice, first from Vorotyntsev's point of view, then from Von François's (pp. 382 and 387), in an attempt to give the impression of perspective, of complex multiplicities in the situation.

Simon too has an exceptionally graphic manner, arrived at by a dense prose form involving continual parentheses. This makes his descriptive passages very long, because of the amplificatory digressions, and therefore difficult to quote. But here is one which illustrates the point rather well. Georges, Blum and Iglésia are cooking makeshift pancakes from flour which Georges has acquired by bartering his watch, a deal which made the food of 'a price which no proprietor of a three-star restaurant would have dared ask for a serving of caviar'. Simon continues:

> . . . all three wearing, then, instead of their cavalrymen coats that had been taken away from them, overcoats of Czech or Polish soldiers received in exchange (soldiers dead perhaps, or perhaps—the coats—the spoils of war seized from untouched stockpiles in the Warsaw or Prague quartermaster stores), and of course not fitting, Georges' with sleeves that came just below the elbow and Iglésia, more of a scarecrow, a clown than ever, swimming (his delicate jockey's skeleton vanishing in a huge overcoat from which the carnival nose and the fingertips were all that emerged:) three ghosts three grotesque and unreal shadows with their fleshless faces, their eyes burning with hunger, their shaved skulls, their absurd clothes, leaning over a wretched clandestine fire in that ghostly setting of the barracks aligned on that sandy plain, with here and there on the horizon groves of pines and a motionless reddish sun, and other vague silhouettes wandering, approaching, circling angrily (abjectly) around them with envious, vulpine and feverish glances . . .
>
> (*The Flanders Road*, pp. 128-9)

Since Simon's narrative stance is much closer than Solzhenitsyn's to the mode of operation of the untutored consciousness, there is more repetition of the same material in *The Flanders Road* than in *August 1914*, and more abrupt 'cuts' in cinema style from one 'sequence' to another, the cut provoked, of course, by associations occurring within the mind and arising directly out of the material it is handling. (An example of such a natural transition is that between the ill-starred horse race in which De Reixach engages and the last ride he makes under fire.) For *The Flanders Road*, unlike *August 1914*, is not a chronicle, but the elaborated and highly extended record of an impression of a particularly intense kind: the vision of an officer falling to enemy bullets. This incident is not only explored from every angle in the present, its analogue in the past—the obscure death of the common eighteenth-century ancestor—is probed in almost equally imaginative detail. It is all, of course, ultimately in vain: the narrator laments 'the days gone for ever that would never come again never what had I looked for in her hoped for pursued upon her body in her body . . .' (p. 203).[10] It is this admission of failure at reconstruction (a failure that is relative since, as I have shown, a palpable feeling for realities does come across) that makes *The Flanders Road* such a particular achievement. Whether it is a greater achievement than *August 1914* is not a very meaningful question since the aims of the two writers are so different. (Simon, Lukács would say, comes at the end of an evolution of modernist experiment in fiction, while Solzhenitsyn is the harbinger of a new dawn in socialist realist writing.) What is curious, and ultimately rather encouraging, is the way that both use their different treatment of a similar theme—the collapse of an army—to suggest something noble and dignified in man in spite of his blunders: the will to understand and thereby master the blind fates which seem to play with him. For man is more than just a plaything of those fates. The corps which in *August 1914* maintained their dignity in the midst of general rout, the prisoners in *The Flanders Road* who retained compassion and the gift of self-sacrifice, these people are at one with Yuri Zhivago and his Lara, for whom, writes Pasternak (p. 355), 'the moments when passion visited their doomed human existence like a breath of timelessness were moments of revelation, of greater understanding of life and of themselves.'

SECTION 2—NOTES

1 As quoted by J. G. Garrard in his article 'Art for Man's Sake: Alexander Solzhenitsyn' in *Books Abroad*, xlvii, 1 (Winter, 1973), pp. 49-53 [50]. The fact that Solzhenitsyn has been expelled from his own country (an event which occurred after this chapter was written) does not affect his mission. His books will continue to be read clandestinely, at least, by the intelligentsia.

2 Garrard, 'Art for Man's Sake', p. 53.

3 *Solzhenitsyn* by Georg Lukács (London: Merlin Press, 1970), p. 10. Subsequent references to Lukács are to this study.

4 'Literary Frontiers', *The Listener*, 14 May 1964, p. 803

5 *August 1914*, translated by Michael Glenny (London: The Bodley Head, 1972), p. 305. Subsequent references are to this edition.

6 In his review in *The Guardian*, 21 September 1972.

7 'The Meaning of *Doctor Zhivago*', *Critical Quarterly*, x (1968), pp. 113-37.

8 *The Bit Between My Teeth* (London: W. H. Allen, n.d. [1965?]), pp. 440, 425. Wilson also contends that Pasternak's novel 'is studded with the symbolism of the Orthodox Church' (p. 441). It is of note that Garrard says the same thing about *August 1914* (*Books Abroad*, xlvi, 1972, p. 411).

9 'The Novel', in *The Twentieth-Century Mind*, ed. C. B. Cox and A. E. Dyson, vol. III (London: Oxford University Press, 1972), p. 380. One of such 'complexities' might be the attitude in *August 1914* towards Vorotyntsev, who is by no means the straightforward author's spokesman British critics have seen, but rather another individual character, subject—for all his special status—to much the same ironies as others in the novel.

10 As Leon S. Roudiez points out, there are at least three disasters recorded in *The Flanders Road*: one, Reixach's marriage; two, 'esthetically a mere objective correlative', the collapse of the French army; and three, Georges's erotic disaster with Corinne. (*French Fiction Today*, Rutgers University Press, 1972, p. 167.) Less convincingly, to my mind, Roudiez argues that 'the captain is as much the central character of the fiction as Georges is' (pp. 166-7). De Reixach remains a deliberately shadowy figure in the novel, which is hardly about him at all, but rather about the true nature of reality, and how difficult it is to penetrate.

3

Women in Crisis:
The Grass and *The Middle Age of Mrs Eliot*

At least let me seek for the words, she decided, and
with them I may discover my emotions
—The Middle Age of Mrs Eliot

There are a number of coincidences linking the destinies, otherwise so different, of Claude Simon and Angus Wilson. On the eve of the First World War both men were born of folk more 'gentle' than 'common' in terms of the society of that period: Claude Simon's father was a cavalry officer, and about his own father Angus Wilson has written that 'if he had ever known employment one might have spoken of him as in retirement; it was among retired professional people that [my parents] found their social circle'.[1] Both novelists embarked on their career relatively late, after doing other things: Simon tried to become a painter, Wilson worked for many years as a civil servant. Both have tried, unsuccessfully, to make a parallel career as dramatists: Simon's play *La Séparation*, based naturally enough on the most 'theatrical' of his novels, *The Grass*, failed in Paris in 1963, and Wilson's *The Mulberry Bush* fared little better at the Royal Court in 1956, since when neither writer has felt inclined to recidivate. And, more significantly, both novelists draw to some extent on their own autobiography to provide them with a factual basis for the two fictions which I propose to examine in greatest detail, *The Grass* and *The Middle Age of Mrs Eliot*. Angus Wilson's trip to the Far East in

1957 is relived by Meg Eliot in the novel, and 'Srem Panh' is an amalgam of his experiences at Karachi airport, where he heard someone crying in the lavatory and wondered how he himself would feel if he discovered, with the same painful abruptness as Meg does, that his own life was in ruins and that he had lost everything, and at Bangkok, where in fact he had a good time;[2] the name Srem Panh itself of course looks and sounds more Cambodian than Thai, whereas the country is called 'Badai'. These fairly complex fictionalizations—like the association, which Wilson has drawn attention to, between his attitude towards David's nursery and towards a friend's garden on the edge of Ashdown Forest[3]—resemble Claude Simon's practice. The dipsomaniac mother, Sabine, resembles the uncle who brought Simon up after his father's death and who in his declining years took to drinking alone at night to distract himself from his loneliness, against which, during the day time, he was able to preserve an attitude of considerable dignity.[4] Likewise, Marie's diary in *The Grass* is directly transcribed from documents in the family's possession; and in particular the photograph, which reveals to Louise that Marie could have experienced a normal married life had she wished, since there had been a suitor, is based on a photograph which has been published and shows Simon's relations chatting in a garden in a somewhat similar grouping.[5] The experiences of Marie herself, and especially her epic journey across France in the heat and chaos of the 1940 débâcle, are modelled closely on those of Simon's own aunt (one side of his family comes from Franche-Comté, as Marie herself does). And, as a last but most curious coincidence of all, let us note that both novels appeared in the same year, 1958, and both have come to be seen as the first of the truly mature accomplishments of their respective authors.

But, these similarities apart, the world of Claude Simon and the world of Angus Wilson are rather different. Wilson derives very clearly, according to Malcolm Bradbury,[6] from the dual tradition of English fiction—the social-panoramic novel of

Dickens, and the liberal novel as exemplified by E. M. Forster
—and such affinity as he feels with European fiction seems
slightly off-centre in current terms, being rather with 'all those
French bores' whom Richardson influenced, or with Zola, who
'showed him that his proposed method of composition was
right',[7] rather than with the obvious giants. Simon on the
other hand, with characteristic French lack of diffidence,
places himself firmly under the aegis of the great moderns:
Dostoyevsky, Conrad, Proust, Joyce and Faulkner. The
differences in literary technique, which are so immediately
apparent when you open a book by either novelist, can to a
large extent be explained in terms of the radical dissimilarity
in the traditions to which they subscribe. This is not to fall for
the easy trap, into which other critics have stumbled, of noting
either with praise or blame that Simon is an 'experimental
novelist' (whatever that may mean, since Zola too wrote about
le roman expérimental), and Wilson a 'traditional' novelist. The
fact is that they are both traditional novelists in so far as they
have chosen to derive from traditions in which they consciously
see themselves functioning, different as those traditions are;
and they are both experimental novelists in so far as they
experiment with, adapt and modify the forms they have
inherited from their respective traditions. Simon is, of course,
more radically innovatory than Wilson, but then he is bound
to be, since his tradition is itself radical. Starting as he does
from Dickens, Trollope and Forster, Angus Wilson is naturally
less strikingly avant-garde, even in his most recent novels,
than Simon was as early as *The Wind* (1957), because Simon
begins where Virginia Woolf (for whom until recently Angus
Wilson had scant sympathy) and William Faulkner leave off. It
may perhaps simply be a case (to quote one of Valéry's most
eloquent lines, much cited by Simon himself), of '*Achille
immobile à grands pas*', or 'Achilles motionless in his giant
stride'. In any case, Wilson's novel is the more self-consciously
literary: Meg Eliot naturally reads George Eliot, as well as Henry
James, L. P. Hartley, and a host of minor eighteenth-century

5*

figures. And she is something of a Maggie Tulliver herself (*Mrs Eliot*, p. 67). But though Wilson's novels are placed under the aegis of Dickens in particular, they cannot hope to recapture his tension, excitement and melodrama. It must be admitted, I think, that Simon's novel is the more satisfying of the two, if only because it does not strike one as such an uneasy compromise between a very modern consciousness of human character and interplay, on the one hand, and a rather well-tried fictional form—especially as regards dialogue—on the other. In other words, I feel that Claude Simon has matched form to content and married them into an amalgam more successfully than Wilson has. Wilson's novel gives the impression of sometimes creaking at the joints, whereas Simon's is much more of an entity, a unified whole. I will try to make clear how in what follows.

I

Both novels have a clearly defined central character, and in both cases this is a woman. Meg Eliot is the middle-aged wife of a leading company lawyer, Louise the rather younger wife of a failure: because Georges, her husband, has succeeded neither in his father's calling as a professor, nor in his grandfather's, as a farmer. Both women (who, it is not irrelevant in their destiny to note, are childless) experience, in the course of the novels, a crisis in their lives. For Meg this occurs the moment Bill is killed in a far eastern capital, grotesquely, by accident, simply because he throws himself in the way of the bullet fired by a disgruntled student at the local minister of education, a man whom Bill has instinctively admired as they sat together in the airport restaurant awaiting their respective flights. The assassination takes place while Meg is making up her face in the ladies' room—the sort of terrifyingly ridiculous, meaningless fate we all dread for ourselves in nightmares. As soon as she emerges, all uncomprehending, Meg faces a new, hostile and totally alien life: a life without Bill. 'Leftover life to kill', indeed; how she comes to terms with these totally unexpected circumstances is the subject of this moving and powerful story.

For Louise, on the other hand, things are not so unpleasantly dramatic. Georges's aunt Marie has had a stroke, and is dying in one of the upstairs rooms of the large country house which the young couple share with Sabine and Pierre, Louise's in-laws. Marie's agony lasts ten days. Louise, who has planned to elope with her lover and live in nearby Pau, has a profound change of heart during this period, so that, as the novel ends and Marie is on the brink of eternity, it is clear to Louise that she will not leave after all. How this change of mind—an entirely plausible if not particularly rational decision—occurs, is the principal subject of Simon's novel.

After Bill's death, and the intense first phase of her grief, Meg Eliot begins the painful process of adjustment to her new life. She bravely decides not to cling to her old set: she is now single, they are married; and they are well-off, while she is poor, thanks to Bill's compulsive gambling, undertaken, she now realizes, because she drove him too hard. She sells the Westminster house and her lovingly collected porcelain; she is quickly disillusioned by professionals who tell her that her erstwhile hobbies—antiques and social work—could not possibly become a career, and takes up a secretarial course instead. By the end of the novel it is clear that she has become a first-class personal secretary, and holds the key, in middle age, to a new life, totally different from the old. Then she was a wife, a dazzling, gregarious hostess, a parasite; now she is a widow, a self-sufficient loner, and an employee. In her middle age Mrs Eliot has come of age: this is one of the most impressive and invigorating metamorphoses of character in modern fiction; for a similarly moving transformation in a heroine, one has to go back to Gwendolen Harleth and Isabel Archer. As with these women, it is impossible not to end up a little in love with Meg Eliot when you have finished reading her book.

Such a degree of emotional involvement with the heroine is

neither possible nor sought after in *The Grass*. We see everything from Louise's point of view, even when there is,
ostensibly at least, an independent narrator (I will come back
to this crucial aspect later). As a result, we are not beguiled,
as we are by Wilson's omniscient narrator (in this respect so
similar to George Eliot in *Daniel Deronda* and Henry James in
The Portrait of a Lady), into letting ourselves be seduced by the
heroine of this novel. Louise is unhappy in her home. Her
worthless husband Georges is deeply in debt through poker
playing, and he does not seem to be guiltless either over the
disappearance of an emerald belonging to his mother, or over
the apparent protuberance in the housemaid's abdomen. Her
mother-in-law is a painted and dyed old woman who refuses to
grow old gracefully, and who feeds her alcoholism on the
neurotic obsession that despite all evidence to the contrary,
her husband Pierre has been unfaithful to her in the past with
innumerable women—cousins, maids, students, whores—and
that he continues his priapic bonanza undaunted by his
grotesque obesity. The only person who seems to have any
feeling for Louise is Georges's dying aunt. When Louise
married, Marie gave her a ring, not worth a fraction of the
ring her husband, or rather her bourgeois mother-in-law, had
given her on the same occasion, because 'she would have
considered it a sign of decline if I had worn something worth
less than five hundred thousand francs on my finger' (*The
Grass*, p. 12). Marie gives Louise this ring, which she intends
to keep when she leaves although she will be returning all the
other jewellery the family has bestowed upon her, for the
simple reason, Louise tells her lover, that 'I was Georges's
wife, and I might have been a whore, a duchess, or a shoplifter,
she would have loved me the same way, and without asking for
a thing in return' (*The Grass*, p. 13). This totally disinterested
gift sets up paradoxically a web of obligations which will prove
far more binding than those of Louise's marriage vows or
duties to her adoptive family, especially when it is reinforced
by a quite unexpected death-bed legacy. This is the rusty old

biscuit tin which the sick-nurse, interpreting the paralysed woman's barely articulate sounds and gestures, tells Louise is for her to take and keep. At first Louise does not want the gift, feels anger at the old lady for placing her in the position of having to accept it. But she is mesmerized by the box, and cannot stop herself opening it. The contents are paltry: knick-knacks and oddments, a few in gold, others in silver, the rest in silver-gilt; the accumulated junk of a lifetime, a military medal without its ribbon, a broken pair of embroidery scissors, a handful of buttons: nothing worth having. But the poignancy of the gift, its very tawdriness, brings tears to Louise's eyes, tears of love, grief and rage, all at once. Then she contemplates something else: six notebooks covering the years 1922 to 1952, fastened together 'by one of those reddish-grey, tongued rubber rings usually used to seal jars of preserved food' (p. 99). Her resistance reaches its peak and as suddenly subsides: 'then Louise capitulated, made up her mind, broke open the rubber ring' (p. 101). That moment, like the fatal shot at Srem Panh airport, changes Louise's whole life in the same way as the other event transforms Meg Eliot's, and if not perhaps as dramatically, just as irrevocably. From this point onwards it will gradually become clear to Louise that she will not leave, that her lover will have to go without her and set up house in Pau alone.

And yet Marie's diaries are the reverse of confessional. The most significant events from a personal point of view—such as the last illness of her sister Eugénie—are entered with far less detail than minor debits and credits for snow clearance and sales of wood. It is 'all on the same level', the narrator says, 'not tragedy, screams, the accidental, the spectacular, but what constitutes, so to speak, the very warp of existence, as if . . . some secret knowledge, that rigorous experience which needs neither books nor eloquence, had led the hand through all these pages, had taught it not to make distinctions between the fact—the obligation—of stocking the woodshed, of wearing a dress, or of dying . . .' (pp. 103-4). Later, having

seen her lover twice in the interval and renewed her promise
to run off with him, 'her voice harsh, violent, still full of that
gasping rage' (p. 107), Louise stumbles upon the photograph,
'finally pushing away the notebooks with a gesture of rage, of
despair, and then the photograph fell out of one of them,
looking—the proof on bromide paper badly fixed, yellowed,
with brownish reflections—like a dead leaf . . .' (pp. 184-5).
Louise recognizes Marie with ease, but she takes a little boy
'with his knickers, his shaved head, his starched collar, his
looped tie, his shoe-buttoned feet hanging under his chair' to
be Georges at first. Realizing her mistake, she turns the print
over and sees the date: August 1896. The small boy is Georges's
father Pierre. But there is another male in the picture, looking
'like a young professor or more likely a school-teacher on
vacation', and Louise bringing the picture to life imagines

> . . . perhaps a little later the two figures—the bronze
> dress and the knickers—slipping between the ragged
> branches of the evanescent orchard . . . and the dog
> leaping around them and they talking together about the
> child, he resting his hand as he walked on the round head
> that barely reached his waist, and she leading him to the
> best plum tree, and both of them shaking the tree,
> laughing—or rather the plum tree shaken, the rustling of
> the leaves, with nothing showing except a patch of a
> dress, a hand, an arm?—and nothing more (or perhaps—
> almost in a whisper because of the child still walking
> beside them—making his proposal, asking permission to
> come back, and she saying Yes while looking into his eyes,
> her own eyes clear, calm then lowering them to the
> child, saying: 'Our father would like him to become a
> teacher . . .' and not submission, not passive filial
> obedience, not resignation, but that same serene, stiff,
> smiling and virginal conviction (or belief—but in what?)
> consisting, too, of a material as indestructible as bronze,
> and saying to him Yes, comprehending, calculating,

perhaps thinking: 'All right. I'll wait.'), and nothing
more, among the almost vanished branches of the orchard
(and perhaps not even that much), and then something
which must have kept the period of waiting from coming
to an end . . .

(*The Grass*, pp. 192-3)

At this point Louise realizes that she had all along been
unconsciously aware that something like that had happened,
that Marie was one of that army of women who never married,
not out of choice or lack of inclination, but out of loyalty to a
weaker member of the family, in this case a younger brother
in whom the father's hopes were vested. The father, we
discover, was an unlettered peasant in whom respect for
learning amounted almost to superstition. He had seen his
daughters become junior school teachers (*institutrices*), but,
characteristically, he entertained a higher ambition for his
male heir: that he should go to the immensely prestigious
Ecole Normale Supérieure in Paris and become a *professeur*,
something like a cross, in our terms, between a sixth-form
master and a university lecturer. Pierre more than fulfils his
father's dream. But, unbeknown to everyone, his sister
sacrifices her own chance of happiness to help him through
the difficult early years of his career, deliberately foregoing the
hope of having children of her own, and mending and patching
her clothes so often that 'a single dress represented (collars,
sleeves, blouse, waist, skirt) an ingenious combination of at
least four others, like those arms, those heraldic blazons
whose worth is calculated by the number of quarterings . . .'
(p.37). It is therefore doubly cruel that her sister-in-law, the
well-heeled and once doll-like student whom Pierre married,
should despise her for her childlessness, attack her for her
atheism (Marie, typical of *instituteurs* sprung from peasant
stock, is a radical, a republican and a freethinker) and show
more concern for how they would fit her coffin into the
family vault than how to atone for her blighted existence.

Cruel, and yet grotesque in an almost Wilsonian fashion: Sabine is a pathetic painted ruin, Marie even in her paralysis, with her wig removed, maintains a dignity such as she preserved even in the midst of the rout of the French in 1940 when, not a hair out of place, she arrived after days and nights in a cattle truck with her handkerchief still immaculate, and with only a little dust in the creases of her shoes.

All this becomes clear to Louise as she contemplates the photograph. But so what? she wonders. The answer comes soon afterwards. She goes to meet her lover, but she feels encased in glass (Sylvia Plath's image of the bell-jar is prefigured here). Her lover tells her all is arranged for their departure the next day. Desperately, frenziedly, she lets him make love to her: but it is not out of love for him. He senses something strange about her mood; when he leaves her she reaffirms her intention of leaving with him, but it is clear to both of them that he will not come and she will not go. As she lies on the ground she listens to the 'imperceptible and delicate murmur, the tiny, delicate rustling of the crushed blades of grass, flattened, rising one after the other, beginning to raise themselves by brief and invisible jerks' (p. 206). Later that night, in the house, she listens to the leaves dripping after the rain, and to the Pau train returning and the metal bridge rumbling, and then to the last splattering of drops on the leaves, the tree shaking itself, 'shuddering, all its leaves scattering a sudden and final shower, then a few last drops, then a long silence afterwards, then another drop—then nothing more.' That is the end of the novel. Vivian Mercier writes: 'If the inexperienced reader complains afterwards that *The Grass* has a beginning but no ending, one can only refer him to the epigraph.' This is a remark of Pasternak's: 'No one makes history, no one sees it happen, no one sees the grass grow.' The reader, Mercier explains, has 'shared in the making of history, the growing of the grass, but history never comes to an end and the grass never stops growing'.[8] The novel ends, in fact, as it begins, with Louise and her lover meeting in the little wood below the house, listening to the evening train rumbling by; but in the interval Marie has got nearer to death, and Louise has changed her mind. That is exactly like the grass: we do not notice anything happening until one day we recognize just how long it has grown.

II

So it is clear what a magnificent 'portrait of a lady' *The Grass* is. Louise, like Meg Eliot, is one of the most convincing women in contemporary fiction (curious, one feels, that some of the best women characters—Emma Bovary, Anna Karenina, Isabel Archer, Ursula Brangwen—have all been created by men). What more perceptive stroke than this one? 'The next moment finding herself . . . in the bathroom, standing in front of the mirror again, taking off her make-up for good now, quickly spreading over her face (as if it had been someone else's, staring at it, frozen, impassive, wooden) the sweetish-smelling cold cream, while through the thin partition she could hear Sabine's voice . . .' (pp. 138-9). Claude Simon, like Angus Wilson, is a master of the vignette, the *aperçu*, the sharp observation that sums up so accurately the real nature of a person. I cannot imagine many other writers who could fix more perfectly in words the rather crisp gestures women have when they smear *démaquillant* on their faces, the way they draw their features in doing so, the particular odour of the cream they use. Loving, precise scrutiny lies behind a short passage such as this, like the one in which Angus Wilson describes Meg Eliot's tragicomic hysteria in the airport toilet on upsetting her handbag in her haste to 'find her Cologne-soaked tissue pads' with which she wishes to freshen herself up before the next stage of their flight—a journey she is fated not to undertake (p. 77).

Inevitably, in Simon's novel, the other figures are shadowier than the female protagonist: Georges, in particular, is a vaguely defined character, and the lover even more so; apart from the fact that he is an oil engineer, and drives a grey Simca, we learn nothing else about him, not even his first name. But this is to be expected: the people with whom Louise is emotionally most intimately involved are bound to seem remote to the reader, since everything is seen from her point of view, and she is not likely to dwell as much on the particularities of people she knows well as she is on those of people, like Sabine, who are the object of her slightly disgusted fascination. In Angus Wilson's novel, on the other hand, it must be counted as a weakness that Bill Eliot and Gordon Paget, for example, are shadowy figures, hardly convincing as characters. This is serious, since they play an important part in the lives of the major characters in the book—Bill is Meg's great love, and Gordon is David's—and since the novel is narrated throughout from an 'omniscient' point of view, the concentration of focus operating in the Simon novel on one character cannot explain or justify corresponding fuzziness in Wilson's case. In *The Grass* the narrator—clearly a surrogate of the author himself—slips in and out of the heroine's consciousness, like 'an anonymous being, a voice (at once memory and witness) who presents her in the third person but most of the time precisely as she would describe or recall herself', writes Jean-Luc Seylaz. 'This "she",' he goes on, 'is usually a disguised "I" . . . the novel thus oscillates between traditional narrative style and the transcription of the content of consciousness.'[9] This anonymous voice never intervenes but blends so closely with the persona of the protagonist that we have the impression that 'it is the character who watches herself observing, hears herself speaking, and reflects her own thoughts or feelings'.[10]

In Wilson's case, on the other hand, it is not so easy to be positive that the thing comes off. The difficulty with *The Middle Age of Mrs Eliot*, as several critics have noted, is the ambiguity of the narrative point of view. In the first two of the three books the third-person narration is firmly centred on Meg's life before and after Bill's murder. But at the end of Book II she suffers a breakdown, and is moved to her brother's in Sussex. From this moment onwards there is a shift of emphasis to David, with the consequence that Meg's actions seem unpredictable, even irrational, because we do not have the reasons shown up from the inside. It is only towards the end that Meg explains herself. She refuses, she says, to compromise herself and destroy David, which is what will happen if she continues to stay at Andredaswood and to make his life so unhealthily cosy for him. So, after the evening which he is later to look back upon as the happiest in his life, because of the warmth of mental and spiritual intimacy he has achieved with Meg, she leaves, and it is clear she will never come back (as clear as it is that Louise will never abandon Georges). But it is not so clear whether or not she is being selfish, whether at heart she is not a meddler in other people's lives, a destroyer who disrupts their peace—often precariously and laboriously built up—before passing on to wreak fresh havoc elsewhere. After all, she did this to Jill when she interfered in her friend's relationship with her daughter and son-in-law. The narrator says as much in the closing pages of Book II, where it is evident that Meg has badly, even cruelly blundered. There is no such implied condemnation at the end of the novel, though David is quite heartlessly ditched. It is not usual to make someone transfer his affections from a dead friend to yourself, lead him to cut his links with all his old associates in your favour (poor Else is given the not-so-polite brush-off, it should be remembered), and then abruptly, without warning, at the zenith of his new-found happiness, to leave him in the lurch, to pick up the pieces of his shattered life in the bitterness of abandonment. To say that this is all for his own good, as Wilson does in *The Wild Garden* (pp. 35, 134), is at best a rationalization, at worst a heartless sophistry. No wonder critics remarked on the ambiguity of Wilson's attitude to David; Wilson admits himself that he did not get his own feelings about David (modelled to some extent on a school and university friend) quite straight. But nor did he get Meg into proper moral focus either, and no wonder, since

'Meg', he confesses, 'is in large part modelled on myself'
(*The Wild Garden*, p. 102). Malcolm Bradbury seems to approve
of this sort of thing when he writes of the 'curious and
difficult patternings of authorial involvement and distance
Wilson creates'. But the compliment, if it is one, sounds
rather backhanded. Halio puts it more bluntly when he says,
rightly I'm sure, that 'a shift [of viewpoint] of this kind two-
thirds through a novel is always dangerous and at best awkward'
(p. 59). Wilson probably felt impelled to make this shift in
order, Halio suggests, to give symmetry to the book (Meg,
who dominates Book I where David hardly appears, is dis-
tanced in Book III where David provides the central focus).
But whether the reasons were conscious and aesthetic or
unconscious and psychological on Wilson's part, I am sure the
shift not only is ineffective, but also explains perhaps why our
interest flags in two places in the book: just after Bill has been
killed, and during Meg's long illness and convalescence in
Sussex. It revives just at the end: how dearly we should like
to know more about Meg's career! The point is, surely, that
the strength of this novel lies in its portrayal of Meg; had it
focused on her much more consistently throughout, it would
have been a very fine novel indeed. This is precisely where
Simon scores: he sticks to Louise, to what she sees, hears,
smells, touches, remembers, feels; and he never strays from
this point of view.

This is the crucial difference for me between the two books,
and the cardinal factor in Simon's resounding success compared with Wilson's impressive failure. Other differences—
such as moral ambiguities in *Mrs Eliot* as compared with the
more positive features of *The Grass*—seem to me to follow
from this. And the rest—contrasts of style, manner, tone—is
purely secondary. Though I do think that Simon's dialogue,
because it is fragmentary and as perceived by the mind (what is
called the 'implacable and absurd concatenation of all language', *The Grass*, p. 129), is more effective than the rather
stagey 'set' talk of Wilson's characters; contrast these

passages, for example. In the first, Georges and Louise are quarrelling over his gambling:

> Then the dialogue again, the two alternating voices not mingling now, but somehow confronting each other, a kind of give and take, like an exchange of blows:
> 'Louise
> 'What
> 'Stop
> 'Stop what
> 'Listen do you want me to stay
> 'Whatever you want
> 'Do you want me to stay
> 'Whatever you want
> 'You'd rather have me go out wouldn't you
> 'Why
> 'What are you going to do
> 'Go to bed and read why
> 'Listen Louise
> 'What
> 'Nothing
> 'Poor Georges
> 'Oh my God.' Staring at her with that sullen, outraged expression, their eyes meeting for the second time, clinging, motionless, for an instant, then Louise turning away . . .
>
> (*The Grass*, pp. 133-4)

And in the second passage, Meg and Bill are chatting (the journalistic term seems somehow appropriate) in the aircraft carrying them eastwards:

> 'Meg,' he said, 'this travelling's worn you out.' He called to the steward for two brandies. 'You haven't slept, my dear, that's the trouble. But we'll be in Singapore not long after midnight.'

She drank the brandy slowly and then forced herself to try to bridge the gap. 'How long does it go on for?' she asked.

'The desert? Oh, pretty well till we get to Karachi, I think. Why? Does it get you down?'

She laughed hysterically. 'Yes,' she replied. 'Just that. I'm down there *and* it's got me.'

For a moment she feared that he would laugh, but he said, very seriously, 'I see. Of course, I'm familiar with it already from the boat but . . . Do you feel lost in the immensity?' He could not keep a certain puzzled irony out of his voice as he spoke the cliché.

'No, Bill,' she cried. 'Please be fair. It isn't just adolescent egotism. I've come to terms years ago with the vast spaces of the sky and all that. At least as far as I'm able, which isn't probably much. But this is different. I literally have been down there for what seems hours now. I'm terrified of it but I can't take my eyes off it.'

He said again, 'You're overtired.'

And she answered quite angrily. 'I've been that before now, as you know. Even made myself ill with it. And don't tell me it's agoraphobia because I've known that too and it isn't.'

'Well, hardly in an aeroplane,' he said and smiled, but she looked at him and his tone altered. 'Listen,' he said, 'these things change or can do so. Even something as apparently primeval as that desert. In fifty, a hundred years new technical processes may have altered the whole of that.'

'Then I should have come hereafter,' she said.

He took her hand and began to talk to her about the desert lands.

(*Mrs Eliot*, pp. 67-8)

Even through a rather stilted translation, Simon's dialogue comes much closer, it seems to me, to the way a couple really

talk when they are alone together. It is also less obviously
dated (not always intentionally, Wilson can sound like
Rattigan or Coward in their heyday), and less literary in the
bad sense, because Simon neither sustains the authorial
running commentary which accompanies the Eliots' exchanges,
nor indulges in a wink to the reader on familiar phrases like
'come hereafter' with their proverbial and Shakespearian
overtones.

I also agree with Bernard Bergonzi that because, perhaps,
Wilson began his literary career as a short-story writer, his
novels tend to contain brilliant episodes not welded into a
whole, and his 'successes remain local'.[11] In *Mrs Eliot* certain
sections are of unforgettable brilliance—the farewell party in
Book I, the scene in Jill's flat which ends Book II, for instance
—but the link passages can be rather tedious, like the flight to
Srem Panh with its bravura section about the desert at dawn.
The Grass also contains some striking moments, such as the
recollection of Marie's arrival in 1940, but these are much
more part of the warp and woof of the novel, and could
certainly not be detached from it to form an independent
short story as so many of Wilson's best passages can be. I do
not share Bradbury's view that 'Wilson is genuinely a writer
of scale'. I think he tires too easily on the long hauls, as is
shown by what Bergonzi calls the 'palpable weariness' in the
last part of *No Laughing Matter* (1967). On the other hand, I
do not agree with Bergonzi that Wilson's failing lies in the
alleged 'obtrusiveness' of the thematic elements in his novels.
Much nearer the mark is B. S. Johnson's observation, which
Bergonzi quotes, that there is a conflict in Wilson's work
between the form, which is based on the methods of Dickens
(especially the humour: cf. Shuffler, the Trade Union official,
in *Mrs Eliot*, p. 349), and the content, which is concerned with
some very difficult and ambiguous contemporary moral
dilemmas (it does not worry me, as it appears to worry
Bergonzi, that to foreign writers inured to oppression such
dilemmas 'are likely to seem a little fine drawn'; the problems

Wilson's characters face, even if not so dramatic as Solzhenitsyn's, are quite as genuine). Wilson is concerned, as he himself
says, with 'the existence side by side of constant intellectual
self-inquiry and emotional blindness' (*The Wild Garden*, p. 43).
The trouble is that his elaborate, rather Shavian set pieces do
not convey this nearly as effectively as a less traditional form
might.

The problem, basically, is one of realism. Replying to
criticism from Frank Kermode, Wilson says that he does not,
in fact, 'care for exact realism' (*The Wild Garden*, p. 137), but
produces a novel from the fusion, in his imagination, of
realism and fantasy. I wonder if he is right. One can see
elements of fantasy, in varying degrees, in the novels of Iris
Murdoch, Muriel Spark and William Golding. But Wilson, on
the contrary, is widely praised for the deadly accuracy of his
satirical portraits of those imbued with what Bergonzi calls
'the *Observer* ethos'; to me it is probably their very accuracy
that makes them so embarrassing to read, because so rapidly
dated. The novelist of manners—which is what all are agreed
Wilson to be, and he certainly invites us to judge his work
according to the standards of the *mœurs* authors of the past—
suffers from the fact that manners are not only severely
localized (could the mid-westerner seize all the nuances about
life in British new towns portrayed in *Late Call*, for instance?)
but liable, today more than at any time in the past, to change
very quickly (if the students figuring in the last episode of *No
Laughing Matter* ever lived, they certainly no longer do so).
The alleged fantasy, indeed, is kept well within bounds;
basically Angus Wilson is a master of the sketch, of the novella,
of the playlet; he has a remarkable gift for observing contemporary *mores*, and a distinct talent for characterization,
particularly of women. Sylvia Calvert is the best feature of that
otherwise weak novel *Late Call*; Clara Matthews ('the Coun-
tess') is memorable in *No Laughing Matter*; and Meg Eliot is
one of the finest women characters in post-war fiction. But
this, unfortunately, is not enough, by itself, to make him a

novelist of the stature of Claude Simon. For Simon too can create fully rounded and accurately situated women characters, and since his realism is not of the external, 'Dickensian' variety, but more in the internalized mode developed by Faulkner and Virginia Woolf, the portrait of Louise emerges much more organically from within the fabric of the novel than is the case with Meg Eliot. The style of *The Grass* itself, its tensions and dynamic, produces by accumulation of detail and nuance an impression in depth of the person of the main character, of her strengths and of her limitations. Meg Eliot, on the other hand, is at once blurred and sharply-focused; we think we know her every feature because the omniscient author so carefully describes her, but before long we realize she is in fact rather hazy, since with a scrutiny which is technically as close as George Eliot's goes a moral focus which is a good deal less sharp. This is a pity, because Angus Wilson is one of the most talented of contemporary British writers, and *The Middle Age of Mrs Eliot* is in my opinion his finest achievement. If from what I have been saying it follows that few, if any, British novelists writing now possess either the same technical mastery or the same intensity of vision as Claude Simon, I am willing to defend such a conclusion. In order to find English writers of Simon's stature we have to go, I believe, outside the British Isles proper, since the greatest fiction in our language now originates beyond these shores, as I hope to show in the next section. What Angus Wilson has created in *The Middle Age of Mrs Eliot* is a smoothly-functioning fictive engine, in which every part operates impeccably: the ironies, the nostalgias, the intrafictional echoes are all carefully adjusted to their proper place, and the central portrait is a consummate achievement. But as with Iris Murdoch's *The Sandcastle*, the reader has no sense that *The Middle Age of Mrs Eliot* is other than a generously elaborated artefact. There is much intelligence, but little evidence in the novel of an organic impulsion to creativity. These and others like them are, paradoxically, the 'cerebral' novels of the present time.

SECTION 3—NOTES

1 *The Wild Garden, Or Speaking of Writing* (London: Secker and Warburg, 1963), p. 13.

2 *Angus Wilson*, by Jay L. Halio (Edinburgh and London: Oliver and Boyd, 1964), p. 11. References to Halio in what follows are to this book.

3 *The Wild Garden*, pp. 100-102.

4 *La Corde raide*, pp. 21-7.

5 See *The New Novel From Queneau to Pinget*, by Vivian Mercier (New York: Farrar, Straus and Giroux, 1971), p. 311, and for the photograph, the Claude Simon issue of *Entretiens* (Rodez: Subervie, 1972), facing p. 120.

6 'The Novel', in *The Twentieth-Century Mind: History, Ideas, and Literature in Britain*, edited by C. B. Cox and A. E. Dyson, Vol. III: 1945-1965 (London: Oxford University Press, 1972), p. 345. References to Bradbury in what follows are to this article; but since then, he has published in *Possibilities: Essays on the State of the Novel* (London: Oxford University Press, 1973) a most perceptive, and persuasive, chapter on 'The Fiction of Pastiche: The Comic Mode of Angus Wilson' (pp. 211-30), in which he argues for a positive, if precarious, balance of registers in Wilson's novels. It is a brilliant and, for me, all-but-convincing thesis.

7 *The Middle Age of Mrs Eliot* (from here on abbreviated as *Mrs Eliot*), Harmondsworth: Penguin Books, 1969 reprint, p. 170, and Halio, p. 10.

8 Mercier, *The New Novel*, p. 300. Richard Howard's rendering of the French form of Pasternak's dictum differs slightly from the formulation in the standard English translation of *Doctor Zhivago* by Max Hayward and Manya Harari (London: Collins, 1958, p. 406).

9 My paraphrase of Jean-Luc Seylaz's remarks on p. 231 of his essay 'Du Vent à *La Route des Flandres*: la conquête d'une forme romanesque', in *Un Nouveau Roman? recherches et tradition*, edited by J. H. Matthews (Paris: Minard, 1964).

10 *La Crise du roman français et le nouveau réalisme*, by Pierre A. G. Astier (Paris: Debresse, 1968), pp. 208-9, my translation.

11 *The Situation of the Novel* (Harmondsworth: Penguin Books, 1972), p. 188 (the whole section on Angus Wilson goes from pp. 177 to 189). I cannot quite accept Walter Allen's argument in *Tradition and Dream* (London: Phoenix House, 1964), p. 273, that Wilson is best at the short story because the 'private nightmare', especially of family conflict, which his novels project, is as unbearable to read about for long as it is to endure in real life. Sustained horror can be accepted, from Beckett or from Burroughs, when it is not so naturalistic as it is with Wilson. I

think Allen should have stressed that this kind of naturalism, after a while, becomes profoundly inauthentic—and it is this the reader cannot take, rather than its so-called excesses. Similarly I respect, but feel unable to share, Valerie A. Shaw's advocacy as expressed in her article '*The Middle Age of Mrs Eliot* and *Late Call*: Angus Wilson's Traditionalism' (*Critical Quarterly*, xii, 1970, pp. 9-27). She cannot surely be right in thinking that Wilson is seeking to establish that 'a coffee-table book on the garden flowers of Africa may be a more valid expression of vitality than either the objectivity at which David's research aims or Meg's earlier subjective confusion of the traditional novel with life' (p. 18); but the fact that Miss Shaw is able to read the book in this way reveals that its ironies are not fully or coherently worked out.

4

Families and Their Fortunes:
Histoire and *A House for Mr Biswas*

> The writing of a long novel is an
> anachronistic act: it was relevant
> only to a society and a set of
> social conditions which no longer
> exist . . . The novel should now try
> simply to be Funny, Brutalist and
> Short
> —B. S. Johnson

In spite of this warning by someone who, before his premature
death, was one of its leading British practitioners, the contemporary novel does not always eschew a length which makes
possible the elaborate and detailed construction of a fictive
world of the kind we associate with the classic novel of the
more leisured nineteenth-century masters. V. S. Naipaul's
book *A House for Mr Biswas* runs to nearly six hundred pages,
Simon's *Histoire* to four hundred. In Naipaul's case methods of
a deceptively traditional kind are used to build up the history
of a man in the context of the sort of extended family structure
associated with the Hindu community in Trinidad; in Simon's
book, which cannot fail at first sight to appear disconcertingly
avant-gardist, another man's life story is set in the framework
of European family relationships. Both works cover a considerable period of time, at least half a century. Simon's achieves a
strong impression of extended duration by using techniques of

association which provoke flash-backs and flash-forwards in the narrative; Naipaul by means of a prologue, an epilogue, and what amounts to an extended flash-back in the two central sections of the novel, with the occasional flash-forward to remind us of what is to come.[1] Neither novel concerns itself very much with narratorial suspense of the *Bleak House* variety, and few rabbits if any are pulled out of the hat. Both are chronicles, in fact, and do not try to spring any surprises on the reader. Naipaul adopts a traditional third-person narrative stance to tell the story of Mohun Biswas and his houses; Simon uses a more complicated doubling-up of narrative focus as part of his fictional strategy in recounting the affairs of his unnamed protagonist's family.[2] But what emerges from both novels, transcending differences of technique and literary tradition, is the picture in depth of two distinct worlds, both conjured up with sharp vividness and presented with warmth, humour and compassion. Both serve as homages to the society in which each novelist grew up. In Naipaul's case, of course, this was colonial Trinidad, in Simon's, south-western France in the early decades of the century. And in so far as both worlds are now dead and gone, 'murdered' by the passage of time, neither of the two writers can avoid a note of elegy, of lament for what is destroyed, however unhappy, imperfect or deficient it may have been. And both novelists construct their funeral oration around a central, concrete image. For Claude Simon this is the collection of postcards belonging to the narrator's family, discovered when an antique chest is sold to pay off some debts; it is these postcards which generate the narrative, literally provoke it into being by their presence, by their very existence as real things, authentic documents selected from among the author's own family papers.[3] This is how the narrator presents them to us, in inventory-type style:

The third drawer filled almost completely by the parallel dog-eared rows of postcards: sometimes whole series tied by faded ribbons but mostly loose (doubtless originally

grouped and tied by dates, by years, then perhaps untied
again, looked at later and put back loose, the whole group
arranged in columns squeezed perpendicularly into the
drawer, like playing cards in a croupier's dealing-box, a
grayish beige mass, the upper edges of the colored ones
sometimes showing: azure or opaline lines spotted here and
there by the bright hue of a stamp pasted over the edge as
was probably the fashion in those days and then able to read
in a semicircle INDIA POSTAGE & REVENUE, then
only the lower part of the nose, the beard and, along a
line suggesting the arch of a woman's slipper, the severed
neck of the bald king suspended in something which
compared to the sky (that is to space, to transparency, to
air) would be more or less what ground-glass is to a
windowpane: as if under the effect of the heat the oxygen,
the cobalt the ceruleum had finally turned into a pulpy
compact substance halfway between sand and glass, or
perhaps glass becoming sand again, the last vestiges of
blue pushed back behind a thick ochre layer in suspension,
crunching under the teeth, covering everything: the
camel, its nomad load of tents, baskets, sacks, leather
bottles, ropes, the faceless forms crouching or standing,
widows in their black, dusty veils:

Aden: A Caravan at rest

and on the back:

"Aden 18/9/07
Henri"
Hôtel de l'Europe—Turkish Shop

and on the other side the caramel-pink bald skull the
complement of the beard, and the symbolic crown,
separating the words ONE and ANNA

(Histoire, pp. 211-12)

The importance of these postcards arises not merely from
their authenticity; they possess for Simon's narrator a strong

emotive charge, as most of them were sent by his father to his mother during the couple's protracted engagement; thus they antedate his own conception, and pace out, as it were, the weeks and months that led up to it.

The central object in Naipaul's book is the house in Sikkim Street, St James, Port of Spain, which the hero manages to buy on credit towards the end of a life spent in the houses of others; not unnaturally, Mohun Biswas is obsessed by home ownership. The novel is principally 'about' the houses he progressively inhabits, from the mud hut in which he was born to the rambling concrete fortress-like mansion in which his in-laws the Tulsi clan live, and from the Bonne Esperance Grocery store to the estate at Shorthills, until finally he can afford to install his family in a home of their own. The trials, difficulties, tribulations and happinesses large and small which he encounters on the way are the subject of Naipaul's affectionately ironic chronicle, of a book which is at once detached and personal, fictive and autobiographical, like Simon's. For somewhere near the centre of *Histoire* looms the figure of an elderly woman, quite clearly modelled on the author's own mother. This makes the book to some extent an act of filial piety. Likewise with *A House for Mr Biswas*: 'a lot of my work', Naipaul has declared, 'especially my early work, I meant to be dedicated to [my father]' towards whom, he says, he has 'always felt protective'.[4] The fact that Naipaul's family 'never lived in any house for more than about three and a half years', that his father was a journalist, that he died when his son was away at university in England, that before his death they wrote a lot to each other, and that their 'little group within the clan' was always impoverished: all this is faithfully reflected in *A House for Mr Biswas*. Or, more precisely, refracted. Mohun is clearly based on Naipaul's father, also a 'defeated man', and the son Anand is a surrogate of the author himself. In fact, the narrational point of view, which for most of the novel is focused on Biswas senior, becomes shared towards the end with his son, the winner of scholarships, of whom the

signwriter-turned-journalist father is so legitimately proud.
The refractions which are permitted by keeping the author's
surrogate himself in the background until old enough to come
forward, are not dissimilar from those created by Simon,
whose narrator closes the story on the threshold of his own
existence, imagining himself as a developing foetus in his
mother's womb:

> taking refuge in the shop of some kind of merchant prob-
> ably the one who had sold her the postcard a Mr S. S.
> Ohashi with yellow skin watching her writing on a corner
> of a table or the counter the lady bending over, her
> mysterious bust of white flesh swathed in lace that bosom
> which already perhaps was bearing me in its shadowy
> tabernacle a kind of gelatinous tadpole coiled around
> itself with its two enormous eyes its silkworm head its
> toothless mouth its cartilaginous insect's forehead,
> me? . . .
>
> (*Histoire*, p. 341)

The novel works backwards, as it were, from this point, at
least structurally; the narrator is attempting continually to
define himself, and seems to be succeeding at this moment of
interrogation which seals his narrative. But as far as time is
concerned, the novel works forward to this point: the postcards define a relationship which culminates in the narrator's
conception. Much else which occurred after this event is of
course narrated. The action in the present, the sale of the
chest, probably does not extend beyond a single day; but the
associations provoked by the happenings of this day, the
memories its events give rise to, provide the materials from
which the novel is built, so that what we end up with is a vast
panorama both in space—because the postcards were posted
from all over the world—and in time (more than the narrator's
lifespan).

The time-scheme in *A House for Mr Biswas* is no less complex, though its shifts are perhaps more clearly signalled. Sometimes the flash-forward is a matter only of an hour or two, as in the bracketed portion of the following passage:

> 'You feeling better, Mai?' Mr Biswas asked, stacking some biscuits on a chipped enamel plate. He spoke very cheerfully.
>
> The hall was hushed.
>
> 'Yes, son,' Mrs Tulsi said. 'I am feeling better.'
>
> And it was Mr Biswas's turn to be astonished.
>
> ('I was wrong about your mother,' he told Shama before he left that morning. 'She is not a old hen at all. Nor a old cow.'
>
> 'I glad you learning gratitude,' Shama said.
>
> 'She is a she-fox. A old she-fox. What they call that? You know what I mean, man. You remember your *Macdougall's Grammar*. Abbot, abbess. Stag, roe. Hart, hind. Fox, what?'
>
> 'I not going to tell you.'
>
> 'I going to find out. In the meantime, remember the name change. She is the old she-fox.')
>
> He remained on the staircase landing, sinking lower and lower through the torn seat of a cane-bottomed chair in front of the stained, battered, disused and useless piano, sipping his tea, cracking biscuits and dropping the pieces into the tea.
>
> (*A House for Mr Biswas*, Penguin ed., pp. 128-9)

The interval here is only that between breakfast and departure for work the same morning. A more substantial flash-forward occurs when Mohun returns to his mother's dwelling after his expulsion from pundit Jairam's house. The narrator comments at this point:

> He did not see at the time how absurd and touching her behaviour was: welcoming him back to a hut that didn't

belong to her, giving him food that wasn't hers. But the memory remained, and nearly thirty years later, when he was a member of a small literary group in Port of Spain, he wrote and read out a simple poem in blank verse about this meeting. The disappointment, his surliness, all the unpleasantness was ignored, and the circumstances improved to allegory: the journey, the welcome, the food, the shelter.

(p.57)

Much later, after his mother's death, the episode is narrated again, in its proper place, and in the following manner:

To do honour he had no gifts. He had no words to say what he wanted to say, the poet's words, which held more than the sum of their meanings. But awake one night, looking at the sky through the window, he got out of bed, worked his way to the light switch, turned it on, got paper and pencil, and began to write. He addressed his mother. He did not think of rhythm; he used no cheating abstract words. He wrote of coming up to the brow of the hill, seeing the black, forked earth, the marks of the spade, the indentations of the fork prongs. He wrote of a journey he had made a long time before. He was tired; she made him rest. He was hungry; she gave him food. He had nowhere to go; she welcomed him. The writing excited, relieved him.

(p. 484)

Among the supplementary details supplied on this occasion is the emotion with which, to the acute embarrassment of himself and his hearers, Mohun reads this story from which he believes he has freed himself. (This leads, incidentally, to one of the finest passages in the whole book: 'He stared down at his lap, as if angry, as if he had been completely alone. He said nothing for the rest of the evening, and in his shame and

confusion drank much. When he went home the widows
were singing softly, the children were asleep, and he shamed
Shama by being noisily sick in the outdoor lavatory,' p. 485).

By repeat-narration of this kind we are continually reminded
of the continuities of this story and the world it reflects.
Another device to create a similar effect is the singling-out of
objects and the brief sketching-in of their history, like the
fourposter which 'went from The Chase to Green Vale to
Port of Spain to the house at Shorthills and, finally, to the
house in Sikkim Street, where it nearly filled one of the two
bedrooms on the upper floor' (p. 145). But the most striking
feature of the time-scheme in the novel is the prologue,
which mentions the circumstances of Mr Biswas's death in a
house he is at last able to call his own—'how terrible it would
have been, at this time, to be without it . . . to have lived and
died as one had been born, unnecessary and unaccommodated'—
and this prologue is followed immediately by a leap nearly
fifty years back in time to the birth of the protagonist,
comically still called 'Mr' though a babe in arms.

Histoire also conjures up time in all its inexorable reality.
Old photographs present an 'elegant and perfumed crowd of
dead men and dead women', dead not when the picture was
taken, of course, but since. For

> it was all over now present immobilized everything here
> in the same moment forever the images the moments the
> voices the fragments of time of the multiple sumptuous
> inexhaustible world scattered on a dying woman's bed
>
> (*Histoire*, p. 326)

Everything in this novel stresses decay and dissolution, with
'the invisible army of termites continuing its invisible labour
attacking now the final remains, the carapaces, the fabrics,
everything crumbling, peeling, dissolving until the whole
salon, the guests, the musicians, the pictures, the lights, blur
and disappear . . .' (p. 71). Only a Proustian type of recall

system can restore something of the reality of dead things like these. This is how Naipaul's narrator describes such a possibility, in words that are surprisingly close to a statement Simon makes in an autobiographical essay which has never been translated and which I am sure Naipaul has never even heard of.[5] Naipaul's version of this notion is placed near the end of *Mr Biswas*:

> Occasionally a nerve of memory would be touched—a puddle reflecting the blue sky after rain, a pack of thumbed cards, the fumbling with a shoelace, the smell of a new car, the sound of a stiff wind through trees, the smells and colours of a toyshop, the taste of milk and prunes—and a fragment of forgotten experience would be dislodged, isolated, puzzling. In a northern land, in a time of new separations and yearnings, in a library grown suddenly dark, the hailstones beating against the windows, the marbled endpaper of a dusty leatherbound book would disturb: and it would be the hot noisy week before Christmas in the Tulsi Store: the marbled patterns of oldfashioned balloons powdered with a rubbery dust in a shallow white box that was not to be touched. So later, and very slowly, in securer times of different stresses, when the memories had lost the power to hurt, with pain or joy, they would fall into place and give back the past.
>
> (*A House for Mr Biswas*, p. 581)

Simon, of course, is more pessimistic, and lays most stress on the forces tending towards chaos and destruction of the rationally ordered world. He quotes Rilke admiringly in his epigraph: 'It submerges us. We organize it. It falls to pieces. We organize it again and fall to pieces ourselves.' We arrange the chaos—in other words—but only to return to it, like old films cut and crudely respliced, 'erosion scissors and glue replacing the tedious narration of the director in order to restore to the action its lightning-like discontinuity' (p. 29).

To scatter the neatly-arranged pack of cards is the only way the novelist has of conveying reality in its genuine untidiness, and making the 'years change places out of order'. In both *Histoire* and *Mr Biswas* this reshuffling takes place; in both the order of narration is much more that of the mind moving freely according to its associations and much less that of the history-style of narrative practised by older masters. This, Naipaul explained to Ronald Bryden, is because 'societies everywhere have been fractured by all kinds of change: technological, social, political', and as a result 'the traditional novel is just no longer possible . . . today, every man's experience of dislocation is so private that unless a writer absolutely matches that particular man's experience the writer seems very private and obscure'.[6] This last assertion is not strictly speaking entailed by what Naipaul says just before it, and is not in any case borne out by his own work. His novel, though by no means traditional in form, and though imbued with a sense of 'dislocation', is not the least 'private' if this means inaccessible to the average sympathetic reader. On the contrary: it offers one of the richest literary experiences available in fiction written since the last war in the English language. For Naipaul stands head and shoulders above most of his contemporaries. This not just because his literary techniques are sophisticated: other English-language writers are just as deft. It is also because, like Claude Simon, he employs these skills to achieve in the contemporary climate what the novel at its finest has always been able to achieve in the specific conditions from which it arose, and that is to create and project in depth an authentic world which is at once original, specific and individual: a world the reader can recognize and penetrate even if, culturally and ethnically speaking, it is remote from his own.

The world of V. S. Naipaul is one of the globe's many 'forgotten diasporas' (Bryden's term), that of Indian indentured labourers shipped to work the Caribbean sugar plantations after the emancipation of the African slaves. Though lowly in

job status, such people were often high-caste Hindus; and
Mr Biswas, in fact, is a Brahmin. Those old men who still
recalled India boasted of their intention of returning, 'but
when the opportunity came, many refused, afraid of the
unknown, afraid to leave the familiar temporariness' (p. 194).
As for those who, like Mohun Biswas and his children, have
been born in Trinidad and increasingly speak English in
preference to Hindi, the 'dull green land which the sun
scorched every day' (p. 78) is their only home. But, curiously
like Russian emigrés in Paris, they shake their heads over the
Indians back in the subcontinent and grow grave as they
realize 'their responsibilities as the last representatives of
Hindu culture' (p. 540). This is because, as Mr Biswas explains
to a doctor who has embraced Christianity in order to escape
from his caste, no one can evade what he is. And yet, again like
Russian exiles, they lead a somewhat unreal, rootless existence:
their language, their rituals and their customs seem grotesquely incongruous in the relaxed and slovenly atmosphere of
the islands. Theirs is an artificial society, like all societies
produced by migration, societies 'doomed to remain half-
made'.[6] Although this attitude of Naipaul's has been attacked
by his fellow-countrymen as 'contemptuous', it quite obviously is not that. It is simply clear-sighted, and in so far as
honesty implies respect and love, it is also affectionate. He can
certainly stand up for his people against the absurdities of a
culture which the reigning system imposes upon them:
'childhood, as a time of gaiety and irresponsibility, was for
these exhibition pupils', he writes, 'only one of the myths of
English Composition' (p. 382), with no factual basis at all as
far as their own everyday lives were concerned. He presents
Mr Biswas as a peculiar kind of déraciné, writing short stories
that are a cheap imitation of degraded models like Warwick
Deeping. 'Sometimes his hero had a Hindi name,' the narrator
tells us; 'then he was short and unattractive and poor, and
surrounded by ugliness.' But sometimes, in an act of cultural
self-betrayal, 'his hero had a Western name; he was then

faceless, but tall and broad-shouldered' (p. 344). Discreetly, implicitly, Naipaul treats this particular diaspora and its cultural ravages, its bastardization of values, as a metaphor for all human uprootedness, what he has called, in a brilliant phrase from his journalism, 'the overcrowded barracoon' (a barracoon being an enclosure for slaves). Hence the power of the central symbol of this novel: a house for Mr Biswas. To stand on land of one's own, to have a house which one doesn't share with hordes of others, to be king in one's own castle, however humble or jerry-built: this is Mohun's primitive, possibly scandalous, but entirely comprehensible ambition. The rootless—and we are all uprooted in one way or another now—are bound to respond to such an urge, as the effectiveness of political slogans like 'a property-owning democracy' proves. Hence, too, the power of episodes such as the moment in the novel when Biswas's wife Shama smashes up the doll's house he has bought for his daughter Shiva. Shama has no alternative; she must appease the jealous resentment of the other members of the Tulsi clan, a hostility which has resulted in mother and daughter being ostracized. Mr Biswas's rage, when he hears of this, knows no bounds. But in a sense he has brought this punishment upon himself, for presuming to assert, in this rather childish way, his urge to possess his own home and live independently of the clan. Blinded by this ambition, he offends against one of the family codes: when one gives to one child, one gives to all. Mohun's western-style individualism, which is continually making him fall foul of the Tulsis, has tripped him up once again, and the only result is to make himself and his wife and children unhappy and isolated within the extended family group. Perhaps those who exalt such tribal structures, at the expense of the maligned 'nuclear family', would care to ponder the subtle tyrannies they impose, which the novelist exposes.

What is clear, though never spelt out by Naipaul, is that Mohun Biswas is too intelligent, too much infected with 'advanced' ideas, to fit comfortably in such a framework. The

other Tulsi brothers-in-law are content to live more or less as
undignified parasites on the matriarchal bounty. Not so Mohun;
he rebels, but his poverty condemns his rebellion to remain
ineffective. He cannot—and he knows and resents the fact—
support his family by his own unaided efforts. He is a per-
manently defeated man, a tragicomic Walter Mitty. His only
consolation is his developing relationship with his son:

> Anand understood. Father and son, each saw the other
> as weak and vulnerable, and each felt a responsibility for
> the other, a responsibility which, in times of particular
> pain, was disguised by exaggerated authority on the one
> side, exaggerated respect on the other.
>
> (p. 374)

A similar lucid compassion informs Simon's treatment of
his hero. Within a successful clan the narrator, like Mohun
Biswas, is a failure. He is an economic failure in that he has to
mortgage his property and sell heirlooms in order to pay his
debts, and a failure in his private life in so far as it is strongly
hinted that his wife Hélène committed suicide as a result of his
infidelity with a younger girl. His relations possess villas by
the sea and can 'buy or sell in the course of a morning enough
land to build a whole neighbourhood' (*Histoire*, pp. 260-1).
The narrator lives alone, abandoned and hard-up in the
ancestral home in Perpignan until the day when he has to
clear the chest of drawers in order to sell it. This simple
action proves to be an extremely complex one, since in
stumbling upon the postcards the narrator is led to reconstruct in its dazzling disorder the world of his deceased
relations, the world into which he was born, but which now is
truly dead. In doing so he inevitably engages in an act of
homage to them all, and to his mother above all: firstly, the
virginal girl who received laconic postcards from her fiancé
and saucier ones from less inhibited young men, as well as
chaste and demure missives from a Spanish pen-friend; later

the young wife travelling with her husband in exotic colonial places; and finally the emaciated crone receiving the gallantries of decrepit old men at her musical evenings. This woman in her diverse metamorphoses threads her way through the novel, appearing lengthily and more than a dozen times, and so providing one of its guiding *leitmotifs*. The narrator's father was killed in the First World War and so is scarcely mentioned except as the shadowy author of so many postcards, but Uncle Charles, who brought the narrator up in his own home, is a prominent figure. He coached the narrator in Latin, and he had an affair with an artist's model; his infidelity becomes confused with the narrator's, and the guilt becomes as it were transferred, especially when it becomes too painful to bear by virtue of the effect it had on the narrator's marriage. Uncle Charles's peccadillo becomes, in fact, a convenient alibi, which the narrator can switch to when more personal associations come too close for comfort. Simon thereby creates psychological realism as acute as Naipaul's, radically different though their methods are. In both cases we end up with a sharp feeling for place and milieu: the run-down family in Trinidad, the scattered clan in south-west France, and the dead and dying relations who live on in the memory, to haunt the survivors with a nameless sense of guilt.

Both writers thus wrestle with the problem of what is public, and suitable for fiction, and what is private, and treatable, if at all, only as essay-journalism. Simon has made only one attempt at the autobiographical essay, the unsatisfactory book he published in 1947 under the title *La Corde raide* ('The Tightrope'), but Naipaul has written quite a lot of 'higher journalism' (Anthony Powell's phrase, not mine), and he tries to reserve it for experiences, like his visit in 1962 to the India of his ancestors, which are too 'particular' for fiction. He is surely right. Any attempt to fictionalize an experience of that order would have been as embarrassing as Mohun Biswas's poem about his mother, or his jejune short stories imitated from Warwick Deeping. But to fictionalize

6*

the relationship between the author and his ethnic family, as Naipaul clearly has done in *A House for Mr Biswas*, is a quite different matter. He has made this story a universal one, like *Histoire*, which may sound paradoxical since the community of which he treats is itself a relatively small and certainly a forgotten one. How many people in this country, before Naipaul became a successful 'British' writer, even knew there was a Hindu culture still actively flourishing in the West Indies? But the story possesses universality because the problems of the relationship between father and son, between second-generation migrants and those who still remember the old country, and between an imported culture and an alien environment—all of which are treated in this novel—are not restricted to Trinidadian Indians. The love and the pain in *A House for Mr Biswas* can be felt in works as different as *The Europeans* by Henry James, Joyce's *Portrait of the Artist*, and Nabokov's *Ada*, with all of which it has analogies. Like James on Anglo-American differences, like Joyce on the anguish of writing in a language that, ethnically speaking, is not one's own, like Nabokov on the pains of exile from a homeland to which one can never return because since one's departure it has simply disappeared, Naipaul offers the anglicized Hindu of Trinidad as a paradigm of the countless millions who have, through the centuries, been forced by persecution or poverty to sever their roots and live among strangers. His achievement, and it is a very considerable one, is to have made one feel both the generality of the problem and its specificity: there is in his novel both a Kafkaesque sense of widespread alienation, and a Dickensian concreteness, rendered through precision of detail and accuracy of dialogue. We can feel the humid heat of the island, its dust and flies and smells, just as we can hear its authentic accents in an exchange like this, between Mohun and the 'senior' brother-in-law Seth:

'Mohun, I hear you have a case.'
'Case? Oh, *case*! Small one. Tiny tiny. Baby case, really.'

'You are a funny sort of paddler [an ironic reference to Biswas's boast that he would "paddle his own canoe"]. Get your summons yet?'

'Waiting for it.' [. . .]

'Well, don't worry.' Seth got up. 'These people just want to see whether your dollar-notes look any different from theirs. I settle it up. Wouldn't do anybody any good for your case to come up.'

(pp. 224-5)

The speech of these people is characteristic, extremely vivid in its ellipses, such as the dropping of articles and the verb 'to be', and its use of words like 'vex' which have an old-fashioned ring in standard English. Such dialect contrasts strongly with the superbly rich, polished and poetic qualities of Naipaul's own prose, where language is handled with deftness and fluency; it is a rather formal and restrained style, quite unlike Simon's unorthodox baroque syntax, but equally evocative, just as complex and leisured in its gradual accumulation of significant and telling detail, just as apparently neutral but equally impassioned underneath. Both writers could in fact declare, as Naipaul did to Ronald Bryden, 'I'm really writing one big book' because all their work is really one, organic, and complete in itself.

Curiously, the one classical writer Naipaul reminds me of is someone he does not mention much. He does refer to Dickens (Anand hates a mixture of brandy and water prescribed for his health by Mrs Tulsi, but 'drank it for its literary associations' since he had read of it in Dickens) and he does allude to Maupassant, especially to the sardonic tale of the imitation necklace, the cruel humour of which Mr Biswas fails to grasp since for him, as for poor Matilda, debt is a 'fearful thing' (pp. 521 and 564). But I have not come across him mentioning Flaubert, yet how like Flaubert he can sometimes be; the same apparent detachment, the same non-committal air, the same discreet compassion, the same dead-pan humour. How like *Bouvard and Pécuchet* is the leisured, episodic, apparently disconnected manner in which Mr Biswas's story is told! The various jobs, the different dwelling-places that make up his life history are rather similar to the successive fads and interests of the two retired copy-clerks in Flaubert's comic masterpiece. And the sentence which closes the third chapter of Part I, 'Shama was pregnant when they moved', might almost be an unconscious translation of a very similar sentence in *Madame Bovary*, which likewise ends a section (the first part, in this case), and closes one phase of a life before opening another which will be different and yet the same: 'Quand on partit de Tostes, au mois de mars, Mme Bovary était enceinte.' Both sentences are subtly phrased, both placed strategically in the narrative, and in both the information is at once banal and significant, of little interest to the wider world but of crucial importance in the lives of the protagonists. Emma Bovary's daughter will survive her, and be sent to work in a spinning-mill; Mr Biswas's will survive him too, after returning from abroad to nurse him in his last days and take a job 'at a bigger salary than Mr Biswas could ever have got'. Surely there is something of Emma in Mohun? Both are dreamers, both at odds with their time, and both die frustrated, defeated and unfulfilled. And neither is treated entirely seriously by their narrator. Flaubert's dry and sometimes sardonic wit can be heard frequently in Naipaul: *Collins Clear-Type Shakespeare* is dubbed 'a work of fatiguing illegibility', for example, and in his articles for the now respectable *Sentinel* Mr Biswas is required, in Naipaul's words, always 'to praise, to look always beyond the facts to the official figures' (pp. 161 and 375). Like Flaubert's, Naipaul's quips are subtle.

Simon's jocularities are also devious. The pompous Lambert of the later years, the self-righteous political militant, contrasts sharply with the smutty-minded choirboy of earlier days, although both boy and man display a similar gratuitous rudeness to those they feel inferior to. Such ironies are picked up by the reader who follows the sinuosities of the narrative, and they relieve the pervading note of sadness, of decay and corruption, which is the dominant theme of this sombre novel. Its atmosphere, as I have already suggested, is heavier than in *A House for Mr Biswas*. But we should make no mistake about it: both books are profoundly sad; they both concern failures; they are both about pieties, but they both recognize that ultimately all piety is vain since nothing, ultimately, can escape what Claude Simon, in a beautiful and sombre phrase, has called 'the incoherent, casual, impersonal and destructive work of time' (*The Flanders Road*, p. 231). The depredations continue apace, and we cannot stop them. All we can do, if we are lucky, is record them. And that is what in their different ways, starting out from individual memories, both *Histoire* and *A House for Mr Biswas* seek to do.

SECTION 4—NOTES

1 These time-schemes might be represented diagrammatically in the following way:

Histoire (achronological)

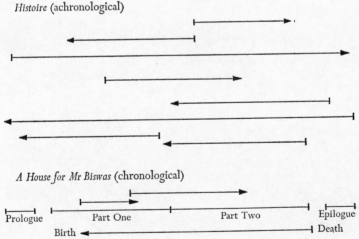

A House for Mr Biswas (chronological)

2 See 'Claude Simon: the narrator and his double' by Anthony Cheal Pugh (*Twentieth Century Studies*, December 1971, pp. 30-40) for a clear and detailed exposition of the way 'dédoublement' operates in Simon's narratives.

3 See *The New Novel* by Vivian Mercier, p. 311.

4 'The novelist V.S. Naipaul talks to Nigel Bingham about his childhood in Trinidad', *The Listener*, 7 September 1972.

5   Maintenant tout cela est fini, et depuis si longtemps, et tant d'événements se sont passés depuis, qu'il n'en reste plus, comme au fond d'un tiroir qu'on rouvre après des années, exhalant un mélancolique parfum désséché, qu'une suite confuse d'images et de figures, pleines de violence et de lumière, véhémentes, muettes, dans la pesanteur assourdie du silence, un film gesticulant, sans sous-titres, sans même le secours de l'accompagnement d'un grêle et fantômatique piano.

                                                        (*La Corde raide*, p. 47)

6 *The Listener*, 22 March 1973.

5

Eros and Thanatos:
The Battle of Pharsalus and *The Leopard*

*La vie humaine ne peut suivre sans
trembler—sans tricher—le mouvement
qui l'entraîne à la mort*
—Georges Bataille

I

Before he died the Sicilian prince Giuseppe Tomasi di Lampedusa completed *The Leopard*, his first and only novel, which was published in Milan in 1958 and appeared in English translation two years later. The romantic circumstances of its production—the typescript by the amateur, aristocratic and wealthy author recognized as a novel of outstanding merit and importance by the writer Giorgio Bassani, who established the text and saw it through publication—together with the piquancy of its posthumous status, virtually guaranteed it best-seller status, and a prestigious film version by Visconti followed. Now that the commercially orchestrated fanfares have died down we are in a better position to judge *The Leopard*'s true, as opposed to its proclaimed, merits and value, and, perhaps rather surprisingly, they turn out to be considerable. This is not to say that it is entirely without blemish or defect. There is a certain amateur quality about the writing— eyes flash in rosy-hued faces, girls' mouths are strawberries set in a complexion of fresh cream, for instance—and there are silly moments when the author's unfortunate habit of archness comes to the fore (Freud, Marx and Eisenstein are three figures coyly referred to, with scant relevance). But the occasionally fatuous passage is eclipsed by writing of this quality, by similes of which Claude Simon could feel proud:

> Those days were the preparation for a marriage which, even erotically, was no success; a preparation, however, in a way sufficient to itself, exquisite and brief; like those overtures which outlive forgotten operas they belong to and hint in delicate veiled gaiety at all the arias which later in the opera are to be developed undeftly, and fail.[1]

Lampedusa's metaphors, when they succeed, have an intense yet ironic quality like the character of Tancredi, the beloved nephew of the novel's hero Fabrizio: 'The two lovers', writes Lampedusa epically, 'embarked for Cythera on a ship made of dark and sunny rooms, of apartments sumptuous and squalid, empty or crammed with remains of heterogeneous furniture' (p. 128). And there is a delightfully dry sense of humour: Bellini and Verdi are excellent topics of conversation at ticklish moments since, we are told, they provide 'perennial curative unctions for national wounds'; and a northern visitor, dyspeptic through oily Sicilian cookery, is also terrified of the island's legendary 'knife in the guts' which are 'still dear to him however upset'. This wit, of a rather Stendhalian kind, assorts well enough with a gift for aphorism which is more Flaubertian. 'The pleasure of shouting "I told you so"', he tells us, is 'the strongest any human being can enjoy'; that characteristically Sicilian institution, the 'man of honour', is dryly categorized as 'one of those violent cretins capable of any havoc'; and we are assured that 'love's eternity lasts but a year or two, not fifty'.

We are therefore not surprised to find that Lampedusa is a narrator of the unselfconsciously traditional kind, the sort who uses the first person plural in speaking of himself and blithely

omits matters which it would be 'boring to narrate' in any
detail, and who makes no bones about looking beyond this
chronicle of the Risorgimento period to events of his own
day, even the future in so far as the year 1960 is mentioned
(Lampedusa died in 1957, and these anachronisms may reveal
unease on the part of the author at using old methods). We are
not surprised, either, to come across the rather heavy symbolism associated with this sort of direct narration: as when
the Prince toasts his revolutionary nephew on the eve of
Garibaldi's triumph and sees the engraved initials F.D., a
souvenir of Bourbon royal munificence, fade from sight as he
empties his glass of the golden colour of the wine. Such ironies
are rather laboured, like the overneat way the first chapter
begins and ends on the office of the Rosary, or the fairly
artificial manner in which Father Pirrone, the family chaplain,
is sent by the author on a visit to his own humble folk so that
we can be given an insight into how the other half lived in the
1860s. And though the heading of the last chapter in the
English translation, 'Relics', is certainly not Lampedusa's,
and the Italian chapter-summary ('fine delle reliquie—fine di
tutto') may not be his either but the editor's, the idea is
surely his, and it is not particularly subtle. Since it is set nearly
thirty years after the death of the Prince, the central, magnificent creation of this novel, the last chapter is bound to be
an anticlimax; but it is also lacking in finesse, which is worse,
and it was a particularly unfortunate piece of bathos to
symbolize the final disappearance of the Prince by describing,
in the closing sentences of the book, how the embalmed
remains of his great dane Bendicò are thrown on the rubbish
heap, and as they fall are seen to raise a paw in imitation of the
armorial leopard.

Nevertheless, there are some fine moments in this novel.
Little things, like the birds shaking off the dew as they bestir
themselves at dawn, or the priest, having injudiciously clicked
his tongue in surprise at a remark he should not have shown he
was impressed by, attempting vainly 'to rhyme the improvident

sound by making his chair and shoes squeak and by crackling
the leaves of his breviary'; and bigger achievements, like the
description of Sicily as a 'lovely faithless land which now, after
a vain revolt, had surrendered to him again, as always to his
family, its carnal delights and golden crops'; and above all the
portrait of the hero, the Prince of Salina. This is an affectionate,
even loving presentation of a man of great parts: intelligent
(with something of an international reputation as an astrono-
mer), handsome (a successful womanizer) and immensely
imposing (an aristocrat and a gentleman through and through,
sensitive to every nuance of behaviour and dress).

The novel in which he appears is equally conscious of its
good breeding. It sets itself in a tradition which includes
Dickens, George Eliot, George Sand and Flaubert, although,
perhaps understandably, the greatest influence—Stendhal—is
nowhere mentioned. It is, all in all, a leisurely novel of
character and manners in the best nineteenth-century tradition;
it plays no games with the reader, its rhetoric is of the comfortably familiar kind, and it tells with great skill and deftness
the story of a sceptical, liberal aristocrat who happens to have
been on familiar terms with the author's own ancestors. The
reviewer of a recent book on Sicilian history, *Princes under the
Volcano* by Raleigh Trevelyan, commented that throughout it
we can see history compared with *The Leopard*, and vice-versa.[2]
So it is a historical novel in the strictest sense, and part of a
noble and even august tradition. And unlike Claude Simon's
book 'about' the battle of Pharsalus, it is genuinely concerned
with the Risorgimento in Sicily and its impact on the neo-
feudal aristocracy in the person of Prince Fabrizio, and it tells
it straight, in chronological order, as it happened. It creates a
sense of space, accurate and atmospheric: Sicily burned by the
summer sun, panting for the autumn rains, is there, palpably,
before us, and its glare makes our eyes smart, too. It offers an
intense awareness of time, of period, as precise as it is nostal-
gic. And it presents that rare thing in modern fiction, a 'great
character' with all that implies in terms of magisterial

creation and fake verisimilitude at one and the same moment, of descriptions as true as they are false, of perspective granted by the author rather than participation on the reader's part.

The Battle of Pharsalus is very different, as defiantly neo-modernist as *The Leopard* is neo-romantic. Its universe, like that of the painters about whom the central character is reading, is not continuous but consists of juxtaposed fragments. It begins in the writer's study with the attempt, as the blurb puts it, 'to reconstruct something which ultimately turns out to be constructed only by this very attempt', that is by the fictive act itself. In *Finnegans Wake* style, as we have seen, the closing sentence, the last words the putative author sets down, are also the first sentence with which the novel opens: 'Yellow and then black in the wink of an eye then yellow again.' Next we witness the unfolding of the book's themes, all of which, as in music, are introduced in the first few pages and then developed, orchestrated and varied in interwoven patterns the length of the novel. There are several. The title is supported by one of them: a visit to the ancient battlefield in Greece where Caesar defeated Pompey in 48 BC. On that mythic journey the travellers see graffiti gouged into the plaster on a farmhouse wall, and a rusty, abandoned McCormick reaper-binder; both these objects provoke lengthy descriptions and developments. Then there is the uncle—Uncle Charles—from *Histoire*, and his amatory difficulties with the artist's model (this theme tends to be triggered off by the suggestive word 'kimono'); and the 1940 battles on the Meuse, commemorated in *The Flanders Road*. There are chunks of Latin, some worthy like Caesar's account of the civil war, others more scabrous, like the ass's adventures from Apuleius. Some material, particularly of an erotic kind, is repeated verbatim, as if the mind, like Krapp in Samuel Beckett's play listening to his tape, goes back over the salacious with especial predilection. And there is, of course, no one story, but a conglomeration of different stories, all threaded inextricably one with another, and all tending towards a demonstration of the tragic quality of time, of ancient and modern battles superimposed and blurred into one massive statement of a non-didactic and undemonstrative kind.

Both novels, in fact, expound a similar theme: that time destroys all things, especially human love, and that death and sex are intimately related. The ephemeral nature of carnality, the threatening beauty of eroticism, and the climax of the sexual act seen as a prefiguration of the last spasm: these are the *leitmotifs* which weave through these fictions, structurally so different, thematically so close.

II

In one of his more recent works, *Orion aveugle*, Claude Simon gives considerable prominence to an etching Picasso made in 1968 which takes up once again one of the painter's favourite, even obsessive motifs: the artist and his model. These are shown locked in a lascivious and provocative embrace of great formal beauty, and it is in the light of that work, so close to the novelist's preoccupations, that I want to examine one of the most persistent themes of Simon's later fiction, especially *The Battle of Pharsalus*, and of Lampedusa's novel *The Leopard*.

Indeed, in reading these two books the critic cannot fail to respond to the power of this motif which they share, and which gives rise to a question in his mind: do they seek a totality, a way of looking at human experience in order to discover a basic and fundamental harmony between the various impulses in the human psyche? This was the case, for example, with Freud's correspondent Lou Andréas-Salomé. According to Dominique Fernandez this early convert to psychoanalysis 'found a way of reconciling the intellect and the sexual instinct and of explaining the source of both artistic creation and the exaltation of love'.[3] Following this up the French novelist, critic and thinker Georges Bataille claimed in his turn to have 'sacrificed everything to the search for a point of view which would demonstrate the basic unity of the human mind'.[4]

Can the same thing be discerned in Simon and Lampedusa? Are they moving towards the totality envisaged by Andréas-Salomé and Bataille, which is so perfectly expressed in Picasso's etching of the eternal myth of the painter, his palette still held in his hand, about to possess a beautiful woman who is swooning with ecstasy and whose unfinished portrait stands on the easel, its execution temporarily interrupted to permit the gratification of an urge in which aesthetic adoration yields to the erotic enjoyment that is its very basis and justification? Is that how Simon and Lampedusa see the connection between eroticism and creation? Other writers, like Apollinaire and Lawrence Durrell, certainly present things that way. Or is the situation rather different? Is there disjunction, are eroticism and creation ultimately irreconcilable, even radically opposed? Does fictive creation tend to disrupt the terms of Rimbaud's fine image of the genesis of poetry, 'la mer allée avec le soleil', the sun's alliance with the sea? In trying to see what answers are offered to these questions in the work of Simon and Lampedusa, let us begin with some facts about them.

Women play an essential, if frequently ambiguous role in both *The Leopard* and *The Battle of Pharsalus*. It is no accident that Simon published in 1966 a text entitled *Femmes* to illustrations by a painter he greatly admires, Joan Miró: like Miró's abstract designs Simon's women are always enigmatic and sometimes indecipherable. It is possible nevertheless to sketch a rough typology of his female characters. There are a few gentle, mature women like Bernard's mother in *Le Sacre du printemps*, like Hélène her namesake who is fleetingly glimpsed in *Histoire*, and like Louise in *The Grass*; but they are in the minority, and rather shyly contemplated as if based on a familiar real-life model which stands too close for comfort to the author's private experience.

More numerous are the stiff, gauche, innocent girls who become embroiled in the lives of the inadequate heroes of

Simon's novels, usually to their cost. There is Belle, in *Le Tricheur*, who elopes with the future murderer Louis; and there is Vera, the pretty Russian in *La Corde raide*, of whom Simon affectionately recalls:

> But she didn't know how to kiss, just as she didn't know how to make love, stiffly and hiding her face in her arms, as when she gave herself, with a brusque movement, late in the night. There were no sheets on her bed, and to put the light out you had to unscrew the bulb from its socket . . . We remained standing a long time in front of each other when the time came for me to leave. She gripped the lapels of my jacket with both hands and cried. I was very upset myself.
>
> (*La Corde raide*, pp. 16-17)

The metamorphoses of Vera, offering a tantalizing beauty, abrupt manners and a touching vulnerability, are manifold in Simon's work. She is met again as Eliane in *Gulliver*, the mistress of the handsome but rather despicable Max whose 'last chance' she realizes herself to be, and as Edith in *Le Sacre du printemps*, driven to petty theft in order to pay for an abortion. She is reincarnated as Cécile in *The Wind* with her 'hard and delicate boy's features', and something brusque and impulsive about her bearing, more usually associated with male adolescents; this Cécile, having failed to arouse any interest in the sublime fool Montès with whom she has fallen irrationally in love, gives herself—to the young dummy her family wishes her to marry—in one of the dreariest scenes of coupling in Simon's fiction, the girl weeping with fierce rage, the boy grasping that he has been cheated, that the virginity sacrificed on that hotel bed has been offered in contempt to him because he was not the one for whom it had been intended. The same girl crops up again in *Histoire*, to be 'deflowered among the sylvan flowers' (p. 289), and in *The Battle of Pharsalus* where she embarrasses the narrator with her 'abrupt gestures' which 'are those of an adolescent who has grown too fast' (p. 88). She can even be seen in *The Grass* under the aspect of the maiden aunt Marie, who had never held a man in her arms, we are told, and never given birth. Not all are viewed as sympathetically: the young lady who visits the narrator and meets his decrepit uncle is unable to conceal her distaste and is condemned for her 'hypocritical desires and ephemeral civilities', considered somehow typical of young women in general (*La Corde raide*, p. 27). Foolish virgins, virgins painfully deflowered, these young and not-so-young girls all represent avatars of one single figure which haunts Simon's pages.

The third kind of female character—after the gentle matrons and the aggressive maidens—is the voluptuous devouring creature, full of experience, with something of the harlot, even the nymphomaniac about her, like the woman who in the manner of a new Pasiphae takes her pleasure with the donkey in Apuleius's bawdy Latin novel *The Golden Ass*, a fragment from the tenth book of which is quoted in translation in *The Battle of Pharsalus*:

how with legs so heavy and so long might I bestride a body so delicate how with my hard hooves embrace limbs so white so tender made of milk and honey and the little lips empurpled by a dew of ambrosia how could the kisses from a mouth as wide as mine monstrous with its misshapen rocky teeth and then finally how could a woman even lusting to her fingertips ever receive so enormous a member and she meanwhile pouring out endearments her furious kisses her soft moans her eyes devoured me I'm holding you she said in a paroxysm I'm holding my little pigeon my sparrow and then how wrong my suppositions were and my stupid fears she proved it to me for embracing me ever more closely it was the whole thing yes the whole thing she took in and even each time that I pulled it out to make it easier for her she pushed herself

closer and seizing my cock in both hands she thrust it in
with an even deeper embrace so that by Hercules! I
might even have believed that to complete her pleasure I
still lacked something ah! that the mother of the Minotaur
and her bellowing lover . . .

(pp. 61–2)

This is, evidently, the face of a woman overflowing with desire,
terrifying and bewitching at one and the same time. The crude
simplicities of the Latin work are absent of course from
Simon's, but the impression of frightening lust remains. It is of
such a woman that Bernard entertains fantasies, when he
contrasts her type with that of the frigid mother who, he
believes, conceived him in the arms of a husband she did not
love:

At least a bastard can claim to be a love-child and dream
of his unknown father, of that night, of the savage and
secret embrace during which he was conceived, of her
desire, of her opening, receiving, a mad, lost, foolish
girl, stammering, moaning . . .

(*Le Sacre du printemps*, p. 15)

Another representative of the same type is Rose, the good-
hearted waitress of uncertain morals whose death is indirectly
brought about by Montès in *The Wind*, and other more shadowy
figures in the same novel: the maid whom Cécile's heavily
pregnant sister discovers in frenzied copulation, or the estate
manager's daughter whom Montès's father 'dishonours' with
his attentions. The same woman, now called Sabine, has so
often 'groaned and fornicated in spirit' in *The Grass*, or is
heard sobbing gently with love in the night of *The Palace*. This
is how Georges Bataille describes what happens to a woman
like this when seized by the demon of eroticism:

In the hands of her assailant she is dispossessed of her

being. Along with her modesty she loses that firm barrier which separates her from others and makes her impenetrable. Suddenly she exposes herself to the violence of erotic play unleashed in her reproductive organs, and opens herself to the impersonal frenzy which overwhelms her from without.

It is this same woman, her sex an abyss, who will yield to the tempest of masculine violence and be sucked with her male companion into the eddy of madness where she will discover, after Baudelaire, that 'the supreme, the unique pleasure of love lies in the certainty of committing Evil'. It is in this light that the reader can best appreciate the significance of the references in Simon's work to cunnilingus and fellatio, described in terms of precise and intense sensuality, and to that Simonian harlot *par excellence*, the Corinne of *The Flanders Road*, of whom it is said that her unpolluted, unpollutable flesh had ceased to be virgin long ago, which perhaps explains why 'she was the one who spread her thighs, straddled, riding (or rather who had been ridden by) the same houri the same panting choking hackney' (p. 218), when she makes love with her husband's jockey.

But beyond the concrete, particular female in Simon's work—and this sort shares as her natural habitat too the '*ciclone amoroso*' raging around the sensual figure of Lampedusa's Angelica—it is her sex which fascinates, haunts and ultimately obsesses Simon's narrator, who could say with André Pieyre de Mandiargues, 'le sexe de la femme est présent partout'. This part of the female anatomy carries many synonyms, as if one or two terms were not enough to conjure this most troubling—even troublesome—of all organs. Sometimes it is a wound in the centre of her body, as with Louise as she lies in the grass after her lover's final departure and makes no attempt to cover 'the narrow, pale mauve mouth looking like a delicate bruised petal, a permanent, eternal and incurable injury'. Sometimes it is a 'bushy cavern' (*Femmes*), sometimes a

'smooth and tender and dazzling and hairy and secret crease in
the flesh' (*The Flanders Road*, p. 14), sometimes a mussel, a
'shellfish tasting of salt' (*Histoire*, p. 102), and sometimes,
quite simply, a mouth, 'oval, moist, split in two and surrounded by hair' (*The Battle of Pharsalus*, p. 4). Elsewhere
numerous substitute images designate insistently feminine
eroticism. Sometimes these are animate, like the 'Pompadour-
grey' pigeons of *The Palace* 'with their bulging breasts, their
iridescent coppery throats, their horny, taloned, coral feet,
advancing jerkily across the dusty gravel of the esplanade'
(p. 249); or they can be inanimate, like 'the sheets of newspaper crumpled into a ball and tossed into the bushes . . . no
sooner fallen than opening, distending with a sudden and
brief jerk, like a last start, a last breath, then no longer
moving' (*The Palace*, p. 250), as with the body after the coital
spasms have died down.

If woman's sex is receptive, welcoming and even on
occasion sinisterly stifling like an octopus, inspiring fear as
much as lust, the male organ is naturally more enterprising
and aggressive. It is described as a battering ram with a
cyclopean, blind brow in *Gulliver*, as a butteris in *The Grass*, a
bobbin in *The Flanders Road* and *Les Corps conducteurs*, and as a
pestle in *The Battle of Pharsalus*—in every case as a tool of some
kind. Notice how caressingly it is featured in *The Battle of
Pharsalus*:

> At the tip of the stiffened and erect member, the light-
> ochre foreskin half reveals the glans, surrounding it with a
> crown out of which emerges the ogival tip, pink and
> perforated in the centre, like a blind eye.
>
> (p. 147)

But this member, despite its pride and arrogance, is vulnerable
and subject to disgrace, like the old man's in *Histoire*. As it
waits for the fate which attends all things at the hands of
destructive time, the penis is seen to have analogies with the

animal world (in *The Flanders Road* it is called a fish), the
vegetable (in *The Grass* it is compared to compost plunging its
roots into the body), and even the mineral, in an image of
swollen water-drops which Flaubert would have recognized:

> then nothing more than a single drop swelling, stretching
> into the shape of a tear, distending, coming loose,
> dripping . . .
>
> (*Histoire*, p. 31)

These images—powerfully evocative and disturbing ones—
of the organs of human reproduction, go hand in hand with
ever more precise descriptions of the sexual act itself. As
early as *The Flanders Road* we come across this throbbing
passage imitating skilfully the panting rhythms of an activity
presented in openly erotic terms:

> I rolled on top of her crushing her with my weight but I
> was trembling too much feverish groping for her flesh
> for the entrance for the opening of her flesh among that
> tangled bushy moisture my clumsy finger trying to
> divide them blind but too hurried trembling too much
> then she put it in herself one of her hands sliding between
> our two bellies separating the lips with her middle and
> ring fingers in a V while her other arm seemed to crawl
> down her body like an animal like an invertebrate swan's
> neck creeping along Leda's thigh (or some other bird
> symbolizing the shameless the vainglorious yes the
> peacock on the net curtain falling back its tail spangled
> with eyes swaying oscillating mysterious) and finally
> slipping around passing under her buttock reaching me
> wrist bent back placing her palm bent back flat against me
> as though to push me back then taking it introducing it
> thrusting it in burying it engulfing it breathing heavily
> she raised her arms again the right arm around my neck
> the left pressing the small of my back where her feet were
> locked around me, breathing faster and faster now her

breath cut off each time I fell back drove against her
crushed her under my weight pulling away and driving
against her she rebounding towards me and once it came
out but this time she put it back very quickly with only
one hand not letting my neck go, now she was panting
moaning not loud but continuously her voice changed
different from the way I knew it as if it were someone
else a stranger childish disarmed moaning revealing
something frightened plaintive lost I said Do I love you?
I drove against her the spasm shaking her choking still she
managed to say:

No

I said again You don't think I love you, driving against
her again my loins my belly driving against her thrusting
again deep within her choking for a moment she was
unable to speak but finally she managed to say again:

No

and I: You don't think I love you Really you don't
think I love you Then do I love you now Do I love you tell
me! driving against her harder each time leaving her
neither time nor strength to answer her throat her lungs
releasing only an inarticulate sound but her head rolling
wildly from right to left on the pillow against the dark
blur of her hair meaning No No No No

(*The Flanders Road*, pp. 194-5)

I have quoted this long passage in full not because it is necessarily more explicit than others—*The Battle of Pharsalus*
contains more clinical descriptions—but because its great
plastic beauty will serve as a touchstone in the discussion
which follows. It is sufficient for the present to note with what
poetic intensity the Simonian narrator handles this subject,
and with what power he projects the erotic urge, which as
Bachelard and Bataille have demonstrated, must be assimilated
on the human plane to the forces at once destructive and
fecundating of the natural world, the sea, the rain, the wind.

It is no coincidence that this last element gives its title, and serves as a central image, in the novel which Simon published in 1957 and which was the first to indicate his immense potential as a creator of poetic fiction.

Indeed, sensuality in Simon's world is not restricted to the ephemeral friction of epidermises, but infects much else that he writes about. The same applies to Lampedusa, whose expression may be less frank but whose awareness of eroticism is just as acute. In Simon, as we have seen, painting and priapism are as closely linked as they are in the work of Picasso: the frolics of the lovers in *The Battle of Pharsalus* are presented as if they were the theme of an engraving, or a piece of monumental sculpture, into which indeed they freeze by the end of the novel. Here is an example of this habit of 'objectifying' the sexual act:

> The man's member, entirely withdrawn now, is repre-
> sented schematically, curving upwards, narrower at its
> base than at the tip, the glans represented by a more or
> less equilateral triangle pointed near its vertex . . . The
> woman's body is drawn with a smooth contour: a line
> starts at the armpit, curves slightly to indicate the
> inflection of the waist, then, with a single sweep, forms
> the hip, the buttock, the underside of the bent thigh and
> stops at the hollow of the knee.
>
> (p. 176)

And in the same novel the celebrated Roman battle is compared to music hall with its 'battalions of show girls raising and lowering their legs one after the other so that long ripples seem to run along the row of naked thighs, frozen smiles and plumed coiffures' (p. 77). The erotic aspect of all-in wrestling is similarly emphasized with its 'vaguely obscene couplings' (p. 95). In these examples the narrator brings out the obscene side or scabrous aspect of an activity, like war or wrestling, which is usually considered to belong to a different order:

everywhere the violence of eroticism is highlighted, even its potential for black humour, as when a jealous lover is shown listening to the sounds of lovemaking and beating so hard on the couple's door that he breaks some bones in his hand, or when Apuleius's ass shows concern that his enormous penis will injure the matron who shows such taste for his attentions. For 'essentially', as Bataille so rightly puts it, 'the domain of eroticism is the domain of violence, of violation, without which sexual love could not have lent its vocabulary to descriptions of ecstasy by religious mystics.'

This leads naturally to one of Bataille's key notions, and one that throws a great deal of light on the thinking of Simon and Lampedusa: the violation of taboos. If there is no sense of transgression, no fear of shame, there can, in such a world, be no erotic pleasure. There must be horror of pleasure for there to be pleasure in horror: in eroticism, says Bataille, 'the alternating play of taboo and transgression is to be seen at its most acute.' The awareness of culpability, of shame, the certitude of having 'transgressed a prohibition' (*The Battle of Pharsalus*, p. 95) are always present in the mind both of Simon's narrators and of the Prince of Salina. Rejected by Corinne who accuses him, soon after their lovemaking described in the long extract above, of treating her like 'a soldiers' tart', the narrator in *The Flanders Road* cannot, despite his consciousness of innocence of this particular reproach, help feeling profoundly blameworthy *vis-à-vis* the same young woman whom we have seen committing casual adultery.

This sense of guilt, which the Prince feels every time he returns from an assignation, or provokes his coy wife to invoke Jesus and Mary 'at the critical moment' of their embrace, is shared by the narrator of *Histoire*, who feels obscurely responsible not only for his own lapses (which may have led to his wife's suicide), but for those of Uncle Charles, who was badly involved with Van Velden's model, too. Such guilt can only be explained by the consciousness these characters have of the close relationship which exists between sex

and death, and which Bataille, commenting on Saint Teresa's
cry of ecstasy 'I die through not dying!' has elucidated with
his usual mastery:

> It cannot be denied that an essential element in sexual
> excitation is the feeling of losing hold, of keeling over.
> Love is only love if, *like death*, it represents a movement in
> ourselves of rapid destruction, sliding quickly towards
> tragedy, and only stopping in death: so true is it that
> between death, and the 'little death' or the loss of
> balance which intoxicates, the distance is infinitesimal.
> This longing to lose balance which is active in every
> human being differs from death in that it is ambiguous:
> it is, without doubt, a death wish, but it is at the same
> time a desire to live, at the limits of the possible and the
> impossible, with an ever-increasing intensity.

Claude Simon puts it in very similar terms when he writes in
La Corde raide of 'the same furious insurrection, the same
desire for an impossible transcendence, the same revolt
against the fragility of the most perishable incarnations' (p. 43).
And over Fabrizio's Sicily hangs a smell of both sage and
carrion, of luxuriant vegetation brought on by the rains and
death inflicted by the broiling sun; and in the ballrooms of the
aristocracy young bodies clasp, 'destined to die'. But most
significant of all is the visit of the phantom of the young woman
in brown travelling dress who raises her veil, 'chaste but
ready for possession', offering herself to the Prince in the very
instant of his death, so that the 'petite mort' and the large one
dissolve into each other.

Indeed Simon explicitly, and Lampedusa implicitly, associate the paroxysm that terminates every embrace with the
last spasm of death, and yet the 'short death, the sudden
annulment' can give man the illusion of having momentarily
overcome the long one. Thus the two capital experiences of
the human body—coitus and agony—are so closely related

that it is hardly surprising to read the narrator of *Histoire* referring to those lovers at Herculanum who were engulfed during copulation and so remain petrified for all eternity in postures of embrace, thereby fulfilling the dream of all couples, that they shall not survive the experience of intensest joy. For if they do, they must awake to what Fabrizio sees as the realities of love: 'flames for a year, ashes for thirty,' a sentiment Claude Simon probably shares, if the paucity of successful physical relationships in his novels is anything to go by. But the most striking illustration from his novels of the proximity of love and death is the way description of erotic play merges with that of the fratricidal struggle fought out two thousand years ago on a stony hillock in Thessaly:

now he leaps forward and almost at once receives a sword thrust in the mouth the point emerging through the back of the neck *not death but the awareness of your death* I didn't yet know

bending over her his thatch of yellow hair brushing the tips of her breasts she arched her body supported only on her shoulders and the apricot soles of her feet flat on the bed loins raised legs in the position of acrobats what is it called making a bridge

now the short piece of arrow or broken javelin sticking out of his back casts a shadow which lengthens crosses the shoulder blade extends diagonally to join the dark area in which his head and his arms vanish the raking light indicating that it is late in the lingering everlasting afternoon the sun

the cavalry is driven back the archers and slingers are cut to pieces

now she puts her arms around his shoulders

in the confusion voices scream Mount! Mount! With a rustling sound the pigeon passed in front of the sun wings spread Yellow then the shape of a crossbow black then yellow again blinding sand under my eyelids

one of my arms slipped under her shoulders the other
holding her underneath it trickled between her buttocks
my finger slid into

(*The Battle of Pharsalus*, pp. 82-3)

The wrestling of two bodies, indeed, be it for love or for
death (sometimes both at once, as in *The Leopard* where a
peasant girl is got with child as a way of taking revenge for an
injury inflicted by her father) is a controlling metaphor in the
work of both Simon and Lampedusa. The narrator of *The
Flanders Road* seeks, through his impenetration of Corinne
described in the passage quoted earlier, to elucidate the
mystery of the De Reixachs, of the ancestor killed by a bullet
in vague historical circumstances, and of the descendant mown
down by a German machine-gun at the battle of the Meuse.
But the search is in vain, for if, as Ronsard wrote, 'l'amour et
la mort n'est qu'une mesme chose,' love can never explain
death or illumine its darkness.

In view of all this, and in considering works which set
birth in the context of death and vice-versa, and over which
hangs a reek of corpses, as in *Histoire*, like the 'sense of death
looming darkly over the palaces' of Fabrizio's Sicily, is it
apposite to speak of that 'approbation of life even unto death'
which constitutes for Georges Bataille the essence of eroticism? An approbation which, despite all the reservations
which have to be made about the darker side of his neo-
romanticism, lies at the heart of the novels of D. H. Lawrence.
As he writes in *The Rainbow*:

This was what their love had become, a sensuality violent
and extreme as death. They had no conscious intimacy,
no tenderness of love. It was all the lust and the infinite,
maddening intoxication of the senses, a passion of death.

(Ch. 8)

Lawrence's lovers are plunged in the delirious ecstasy of

7

'Absolute Beauty' in which pleasure becomes so intense and extreme that it borders on pain. Such a view remains however profoundly optimistic, since with Lawrence one can normally expect to discover and realize oneself through erotic experience pursued with such frenzied determination that it is hardly distinguishable from a quasi-religious mysticism. His characters do of course suffer from what Bataille calls their 'discontinuity', since they are aware of being individuals 'dying in the isolation of an unintelligible adventure', and of experiencing nostalgia for their lost continuity. But unlike Simon's characters, or Lampedusa's, they are able, under certain conditions, to fulfil and transcend themselves in eroticism. If I read Lampedusa and Simon correctly, this kind of approbation is absent. It is impossible to forget the continual references in *The Leopard* to the ephemerality of sensual desire, to images like that of the kisses Angelica and Tancredi exchange in rhythm with the notes of 'disillusioned gaiety' tinkling out of the ancient music-box, a witness like so much in the rambling palace of 'hells redeemed by love' and 'forgotten paradises profaned by love itself'. Nor is it possible to overlook this symbol, this terrifyingly beautiful moment in *The Battle of Pharsalus*, when the orgasm is associated directly with the act of homicide, the woman in ecstasy under her lover and the legionary falling under the thrust of his adversary blending into one:

> pilum striking entering and coming out of the wound over and over the swelling of its triangular tip stretching the lips the blood rushing out burning She flooded me began gasping and crying stammering words disconnected phrases jerking her hips violently.

(p. 24)

For Simon's eroticism—like Lampedusa's but unlike Lawrence's, Durrell's or even Robbe-Grillet's—is hardly ever optimistic.[5] The only exception I can think of is a passage near the end of *The Grass*, where the countryside appears in a rather Lawrentian manner to raise itself, rhythmically and gracefully, to meet the fertilizing rain in an act of 'secret and interminable nuptial'. Somewhat similar moments occur in *The Leopard*, as when Tancredi feels that in kissing Angelica he is 'taking possession of Sicily once more'; but as in Simon they merely serve to emphasize the transience of human beings compared with the permanence of nature. In both writers eroticism is a thing of despair, linked intimately, as in the work of the Marquis de Sade and his romantic successors, with the idea of death. The visceral, abundant, organic world of Simon and Lampedusa is indeed haunted by this tragic awareness that man, imprisoned in duration, subject to the incoherent dilapidations wrought by time, to the 'illusory and soothing inundation' we read of in *Le Tricheur*, tries desperately, but ultimately in vain, to free himself of chronology through the medium of erotic transcendence. But one glimmer of hope, at least, survives: that of artistic creation. Painting and priapism, sex and scription form one in these splendidly baroque novels. Perhaps, like Samuel Beckett, a very different writer, Simon and Lampedusa have succeeded in wresting, from the nothingness to which all human activities tend, that sole and unique consolation left to us: the contemplation of the work of art which seals as it magnificently repudiates our irremediable and ineluctable failure to overcome time.

SECTION 5—NOTES

1 All quotations are taken from the translation of Archibald Colquhoun published by Fontana Books (Collins), but occasional reference is made to the original Italian *Il Gattopardo*, published by Feltrinelli.

2 'Yorkshire in Sicily' by John Vincent, *The Listener*, 7 December 1972, pp. 793-4.

3 *Nouvel Observateur*, 11 January 1971.
4 Quotations from *L'Erotisme* by Georges Bataille (Paris: Editions de Minuit, 1957) are here translated by myself.
5 Certainly, it is not in *Triptyque*, which describes 'blind, imperious and ephemeral couplings' (p. 207); sex in this novel is desperate. At the same time the whole of language seems to be eroticized (see the association between fish and penis on p. 15).

CONCLUSION
Humanism, Tragedy and the Contemporary Avant-Garde

Or poserai per sempre,
Stanco mio cor . . .
Posa per sempre. Assai
Palpitasti . . .

—Leopardi

I

In February 1972, BBC Radio 3 devoted an edition of 'Arts Commentary' to an attempt at answering such questions as 'Why do new works of fiction and criticism take so long to cross the Channel? Why is so little current fiction translated from French? Is there in fact little in common between contemporary movements in literature here and in France?' The discussion was introduced by the British novelist Julian Mitchell, who was joined by two cosmopolitan-minded critics, Christine Brooke-Rose (herself the author of 'experimental' novels like *Between*, published in 1968), and Gabriel Josipovici, whose important study *The World and the Book* appeared shortly before. The questions before the panel were timely and pertinent: why is the so-called *nouveau roman*, and even more the movement know in France as *la nouvelle critique*, so little understood, even so little known, in the English-speaking world?

There is no easy answer to this problem, though the facts can be stated clearly enough. Let me cite a concrete example.

To read, on the one hand, Malcolm Bradbury's recent collection of 'essays on the state of the novel', *Possibilities* (Oxford University Press, 1973), and on the other the most characteristic work of a leading critic of the French new novel, Jean Ricardou's *Pour une théorie du nouveau roman* (Seuil, 1971), is to plunge schizophrenically into a world where one continually needs to remind oneself that the two men are discussing the same subject, the novel, its present state, its past history, its techniques, and its future poetics. Both critics figure among the most authoritative spokesmen in their respective countries and yet, if Bradbury were translated into French, Ricardou would be well-nigh incapable of understanding him, and vice-versa. The two discourses are conducted on planes and registers so totally distinct as to be mutually incompatible. That this is not simply a matter of language is shown by the fact that a British critic who writes in English but within the French critical idiom, Stephen Heath, has been unfairly, though not inaccurately, accused of expressing himself in 'Frenglish'. The reproach was made by John Weightman, a leading British authority on the avant-garde, in his *Observer* review of Heath's book *The Nouveau Roman: A Study in the Practice of Writing* (1972). Heath, a former pupil of Raymond Williams at Cambridge, is currently studying under Roland Barthes in Paris. It would be fair to say, I think, that he has avoided the potential schizophrenia such a dual formation might lead to by unreservedly falling in with the French. As a result, his French criticism (he has contributed a study on *Finnegans Wake* to the journal *Tel Quel*) is completely fluent in its handling of the dominant Paris idiom, whereas his English work reads much of the time like a rather laboured translation from the French, as Weightman had little difficulty in demonstrating through his quotations. Bradbury's language, of course, is as fluently at ease within the registers of contemporary British critical discourse as is Heath's on the other side. The consequence, sadly, is that these two eminently professional and gifted writers have nothing to say to each other, despite a shared cultural background, the British university system, from which they both derive.

Now, such a dichotomy need not in itself be too serious. It used to be the case in philosophy until recently, for instance, that the Anglo-Saxon (or largely empirical) and the continental (or rationalistic) traditions were so distinct as to enable their respective practitioners to continue their speculations in isolation, oblivious to what was engaging the energies of colleagues across the water. So radically separate were they, indeed, that one side practically considered that the other was not doing philosophy at all. Within the last few years there has, however, been a change: British philosophers, under the inspired leadership of Stuart Hampshire, Alan Montefiore and Mary Warnock, have begun to look upon such continental developments as existentialism and phenomenology as offering something other than mere windy metaphysics; and a number of the younger French thinkers not only read English with sufficient understanding to tackle people like Ryle, Wisdom and Austin in the original, but have been induced by developments in the linguistic sciences to accept that some of our native forms of (largely linguistic) philosophy may offer possibilities for tackling traditionally vexing problems of epistemology and psychology in a non-trivial manner. We can expect the two traditions in philosophy to grow closer together as time goes on, but little hope exists at the moment that literary criticism will see a similar rapprochement; and this is serious, since there were, in a sense, two philosophies, but there can only be one literature. If the French read Balzac, Joyce or Kafka in ways which seem arcane and mandarin to English-speaking critics, and if our studies of Dickens, Proust or Mann strike continental colleagues as hopelessly unsystematic or insufficiently rigorous, the situation is grave indeed. Far from growing together, indeed, the two critical movements are, if anything, moving further apart, and we are finding ourselves progressively nearer to the true Babel, in which the other person appears to be speaking gibberish while seemingly intending sense.

Similarly, on the creative-writing side, reception of the French *nouveau roman* in English-speaking countries has on the whole been characterized by a marked feeling of bafflement. The theoretical writings of Alain Robbe-Grillet (*Towards a New Novel*, 1965) and of Nathalie Sarraute (*The Age of Suspicion*, 1963) have invited examination of a more searching kind, generally speaking, than their novels, which have tended to be somewhat cavalierly dismissed. In the December 1967 issue of *Encounter*, Gore Vidal castigated the 'rhetoric' of their theoretical pronouncements, pointed tellingly to inconsistencies and non-sequiturs, and concluded that they were in any case wasting their time since 'our lively vulgar and most human art [the novel] is at an end, if not the end'. Bernard Bergonzi, in *The Listener* dated 23 March 1967, argued that they were wasting their time not so much because the novel is finished as an art form, but because no amount of experimentation on the writer's part is going to alter the fact that 'the end product of his art will still be a small, hard, rectangular object, whose pages are bound along one edge into fixed covers, and numbered consecutively'.

A few Anglo-Saxon writers have taken a less negative view, notably Susan Sontag and Christine Brooke-Rose, but on the whole there seems to have been a failure in communication between French and English intellectuals on this question as on some others. I think the reason for this is that generally speaking English writers are not much concerned with formal questions; after all, the English novel has never troubled itself much up till now about the rationale of its aesthetic. Technical innovations have happened as it were incidentally, and by accident. In France, at least since Flaubert's time, the situation has been quite different. Novelists have been very concerned about the ideal form for the novel, and have sought it in their writing: Proust, Malraux, Camus, Sartre, Beckett have all developed individual structures to enable them to say something new in fictional terms. This is what Robbe-Grillet means when he says that Flaubert wrote the new novel of 1860 and Proust the new novel of 1910. So Robbe-Grillet, Nathalie Sarraute and the others are nothing new in French literature, however surprising they may seem over here. The French novel has always been experimental in nature—and not just in Zola's *roman expérimental*. The wider question, of course, remains unanswered. Has the novel, be it merely the novel as seen in the limited context of a French 'great tradition', any future at all? It would seem as if even Robbe-Grillet is not very sure of this: among his latest works have been 'cine-novels', hybrids that exist both on paper and on celluloid, *Last Year at Marienbad* and *The Immortal One*. Perhaps Gore Vidal has a point, that the novel really is finished. If so, Robbe-Grillet at least has insured his future by staking a claim in a rival and perhaps more vital medium.

This 'clerk's quarrel' throws up, of course, interesting reflections on intellectual relations between France and the English-speaking countries. In the latter, French culture is usually seen as impressive admittedly, but also as uncommonly arrogant and self-sufficient. French intellectuals have not helped matters by (for example) always talking of 'the novel' but meaning to all intents and purposes the French novel, with an occasional, and rather peculiar, side-glance at Poe, Dostoyevsky or Faulkner. The fact is that as often as not the French intellectual is monoglot, whereas the Anglo-Saxon blushes to call himself an intellectual if he only reads English. This perhaps explains certain historical quirks, such as the exaggerated praise given in France to Poe and Dos Passos, simply because they happened to be translated in a way that made them almost French, but not quite, at a time when French culture happened to feel the need for a little (but not too much) new blood.

This 'dialogue of the deaf' is not however the fault of the French alone. The *Times Literary Supplement* review of one of Francis Ponge's recent works, or D. J. Enright's *Listener* review of Michel Leiris's *Manhood* (1968), were marked by a tone of bewilderment and condescension that is, unhappily, echoed very frequently in Anglo-Saxon literary journals when French culture is discussed. In the particular case of Leiris, it is worth noting that Enright was answered by Richard Woll-heim, also in *The Listener* (issue dated 14 March 1968); but both writers failed to focus their discussion accurately. For his part Enright revealed ignorance of the tradition within which Leiris is working (out of Rousseau by Sade), while Wollheim overstressed Leiris's 'amorality'. Of course, Wollheim was far more sympathetic. Neither critic accepted however that Leiris is simply a moderately truthful, typical man: only his lucidity makes him rare, but far from unique. His book is partial, selective, sometimes silly (especially the introduction). But it is lucid and does try to be fair. Both articles, though Enright's more so, illustrate the incompre-hension which is often characteristic of British reactions to French intellectualism. Indeed, if the French on the whole appear blissfully unaware of other cultures, Anglo-Saxons tend to brush aside serious consideration of French work and prefer to go for the easy laugh at its expense.

Clearly there is something wrong here. Much needs to be done in Anglo-French intellectual relations; we need to start listening to each other, rather than shout volubly within our respective frontiers, unheard by the other side.

II

The best way to set about the difficult task of making dialogue possible is to try first to establish precisely what the differences are; and the most significant points of disagreement occur not so much in the consideration of past writing, but of the literature of our own time, and particularly of what is known universally by the French expression 'the avant-garde'. What then is the current state of thinking about the avant-garde?

The standard work on this subject, and the only objective commentary of which I am aware, is Renato Poggioli's *The Theory of the Avant-Garde* (1968). This offers an exhaustive account of the phenomenon from its origins to the present time; and Poggioli, as an Italian scholar resident in the United States, and a Slavist conversant with some ten languages, was ideally placed to analyse it. In an article which appeared shortly after his death ('The Artist in the Modern World', collected in *The Spirit of the Letter*, 1965), he stressed the schizophrenic position of the avant-garde, 'blessed in its freedom and cursed in its alienation', mainly because of the necessity it experiences to react simultaneously within a given society against both bourgeois and proletarian taste. 'The psychology of the avant-garde,' he commented, 'is dominated by an aristocratic or antiproletarian tendency and by an anarchical or antibourgeois tendency; on the sociological level as well as on the aesthetic level there is no conflict between the two tendencies,' since they converge in a single opposition to what Poggioli identifies as 'a common cult of the cliché'. But such opposition sets the avant-garde apart both from the bourgeois élites which it despises but who support it, and the proletarian masses, which it favours but to whom its aesthetic preoccupations are incomprehensible and even inimical. No wonder Poggioli concludes that all too often avant-gardism is 'condemned to a liberty which is slavery, and to serve the negative and destructive principle of art for art's sake'. Malcolm Bradbury (in *The Social Context of Modern English Literature*, 1971, pp. 17-18) agrees. The existence of the avant-garde derives largely, he says, 'from the fact that the arts have grown socially more marginal and the audience for them more dispersed'; there is a gain in independence, but the concomitant loss of 'a social overview' which tends to make the avant-garde culturally incestuous, in that its artistic products are consumed largely by fellow-artists. Nevertheless unlike Poggioli Bradbury can see a net benefit, since 'it is out of such environments that much of our most interesting art has come', but he qualifies this by noting that writers and artists have more commonly alternated between the avant-garde and 'other much more localized experiences, so that it represents a polarity of, rather than an absolute centre of, modern artistic activity'. This perhaps explains why modernism, according to Bradbury later in the same book, has been only one of several twentieth-century styles. Such a state of affairs can only exist when artistic chapels proliferate like biblical sects; when, in fact, there is no longer one dominant style (such as classicism or the baroque) but several, all competing for the attention of different sections of the public; and such a state pertains really only since the emergence of the concept of an artistic avant-garde, which occurred in the wake of the collapse of the values of the European Enlightenment, in the early decades of the nineteenth century.

So much, perhaps, for the more historical descriptions of the avant-garde. Equally 'objective' in this sense are two views from the United States, Edith Kern's and Bruce Kawin's. In *Telling It Again and Again*, his study of the role and function of repetition in literary and film aesthetics,[1] Kawin views the genuine avant-garde as being that which keeps us in the continuous present by devices of iteration. For, writes Kawin, 'in the continuous present there is no consciousness of repetition' (p. 151), and he bases his argument on such evidently modernist examples as Proust's timeless world of Combray, Robbe-Grillet's still and statuesque Marienbad, Genet's frozen symbol of the miraculous rose, Gertrude Stein's 'identical recurrences', and Beckett's *Waiting for Godot*, in which, it has been said, 'nothing happens, twice'. Edith Kern prefers instead to present the essence of the avant-garde as being contained in the *Künstlerroman*, or portrait-of-the-artist novel, making possible the fruitful fusion between fictional technique and existentialist thought which she sees as the achievement of the one pre-modernist and the two modernist writers she offers as exemplars: Kierkegaard, Sartre and Beckett.[2] 'To existentialist writers,' she claims 'the author-hero creating other author-heroes has proved a crucial device to lend perspective to an otherwise solipsistic world' (p. 241).

So rich has this vein turned out to be in the range of ironic techniques employed—from 'an array of "manuscripts discovered" by fictitious editors within editors to unreliable author or narrator heaped upon unreliable author or narrator' (p. 243)—that Mrs Kern is able to assert, like Bruce Kawin, that language in the avant-garde novel 'has come to be employed in rendering an eternal present, rather than a past or a future' (p. 242).

Mrs Kern's analysis is that of a scholar, not a socio-cultural commentator; nevertheless, I sense in my reading of her study that she believes those developments on the whole to be a 'good thing'. A similarly bland tone can be heard on the part of Leon S. Roudiez, who writes in *French Fiction Today: A New Direction* (1972) that the new literature 'aims to subvert, through its textual operations, the literary, political, social, and moral structures of Western culture' (p. 384). Someone who is not at all sure this should be welcomed is Gerald Graff, whose brilliant essay 'The Myth of the Postmodernist Break-through' appeared in the Winter 1973 issue of *TriQuarterly*. Graff, is, broadly speaking, on the side of Frank Kermode in seeing no radical divide between modernism and post- (or 'neo-') modernism; but he perceives sufficient danger in the fashionable radical mythos of 'nonrational energy opposing repressive rationalism and traditionalism' (p. 409) for us to need to be wary of 'perpetuating the nightmare we want to escape' (p. 417). This is because 'postmodernism signifies that the nightmare of history . . . has overtaken modernism itself' (p. 403). Graff is particularly disturbed by 'the narcissism and self-contempt which mark postmodernist aesthetics' (p. 399). This would not matter over-much, he says, if all forms of post-modernism were at one with the particular strain that includes Borges, Barth, Nabokov or Beckett and experiences a sense of the pathos of the demise of traditional Western rational humanism. But this is not the case: there is a more 'celebratory' brand of post-modernist enterprise which glorifies energy, energy 'conceived as pure immanence

and process' (pp. 393-4). This form clearly stands a long
distance away from Edith Kern's *Künstlerroman*; it is typified
rather by the work of Ken Kesey, who—it is hardly a coincidence—ends Tony Tanner's monumental study of contemporary American novelists, *City of Words*.[3] Tanner places
Kesey there, he says, because he pushes certain American
'possibilities and paradoxes' to their extremest conclusion.

Tony Tanner is, of course, a British observer of the American scene, but a deeply sympathetic one. He admits willingly
to a broad and eclectic tolerance, and rates highly the need
'constantly to renew one's sense of the various and wonderful
things which may be gathered together under the wide wings
of language' (p. 420). Not for him either the Kawin/Kern
scholarly detachment, nor Graff's rather Leavisite premoni-
tions of cultural calamity. Tanner is liberal in the best sense—
the one that cannot be ridiculed as flabby or permissive—and
it is this judicious openness which gives his book its particular
tone and makes it such a useful guide through the labyrinthine
paradoxes of its subject. Tanner, one feels, is unshockable,
and yet he is not to be hoodwinked. He deftly sorts out the
spurious, the modish and the meretricious from the genuinely
creative, however extreme its form, subject or tone; and this
is what makes him such a reliable pathfinder through rather
boggy terrain.

Ihab Hassan, the American theorist of the avant-garde, is
among those singled out by Gerald Graff as promulgating and
even encouraging the notion of a post-modernist breakthrough.
Hassan's most recent essay—one which represents for him the
beginning of a new framework of ideas—is entitled 'The New
Gnosticism' (*Boundary 2*, Spring 1973). Far from recoiling,
as Graff does, from the implications of the new temper,
Hassan asks rhetorically 'should we sever ourselves from the
sources of imagination and change in our time?' Or will we,
he wonders, 'continue to sustain ourselves on our own
traditions, with piety, scepticism, and complex hope?'
(p. 568). He openly admires Norman Mailer for 'his vaulting

ambition, imagination, irony [which] attempt to comprehend some final facts and fancies of our age', but even Hassan doubts whether Mailer will be enough to save literature, since in the natural inertia and conservatism of human affairs 'even the most extreme vision must hedge itself' (p. 568). Perhaps 'Imagination', Hassan hints darkly, will fail to find any longer its 'primary fulfilment in Literature' (p. 569); and his implication is that if it does so fail, he for one will not blame it. Graff and Hassan, it is clear, stand at opposite poles in their attitude to the avant-garde; the first cries wolf, the other urges us not to miss our connection.

To turn to the hearty common sense of John Weightman, especially after reading these American scrutators, is something of a tonic, even if the boost offered proves in the end to be a rather ephemeral pick-me-up. This is perhaps because the most useful aspects of his collection of reprinted essays, issued under the general title *The Concept of the Avant-Garde*,[4] are negative and even destructive. When he is not of the opinion that the avant-garde is little more than a lot of nonsense and well-organized ballyhoo, he clearly does not greatly enjoy it. His typical reaction is either to scoff or to yawn—in a most articulate manner. His bluff directness is seen at its most characteristic in a remark like this one, where the naïvety is so honestly expressed as to carry with it an aura of unquestioned authority:

> In spite of all the experimental films I have seen and experimental novels I have read, I am still of the opinion that if one begins telling a story, it should be told convincingly either on the imaginative or the realistic level. The author can be as oblique and allusive as he likes, provided that what he presents hangs together according to the mode he has chosen.
>
> (p. 162)

What gives utterances like these their force is that their eccentricity, which stands out sharply when they are quoted out of context, is effaced by the frequent rightness of the particular judgement they are supporting. In this instance Weightman is discussing Don Levy's film *Herostratus*, and he follows the statement I have just quoted by a straight-from-the-shoulder appraisal of Levy's movie which is pointedly just ('But this film doesn't make sense'), and by impressively neat demolitions of its improbabilities and pretensions. Weightman's wide culture, worn very lightly, enables him to undercut fatuity gracefully, as when he characterizes the behaviour of the glamour girl in the film (sent to seduce the hero) by this piece of devilish telegraphese: 'head thrown back, threads of saliva, cf. Jeanne Moreau in *Les Amants*'. If for nothing else, we need a critic like Weightman to remind us occasionally of the true score about the Emperor's vaunted new clothes. But the snag with his robust approach is that it can occasionally sound insensitive; nevertheless, it is an approach that offers its own particular insights. He is quite right, of course, that Warhol's *Flesh* is an oddly poetic and ingenuous film, while *Trash* is just that, vulgar and nasty. He is right, too, in asserting in his characteristic tone of voice, that Sade was 'obviously crazy', and he is typically shrewd in deducing that *Histoire d'O* is written not by a man as is often claimed, but by a woman who derives 'subjective pleasure from the spectacle of herself as victimized object, i.e. also satisfying a strong, narcissistic, masculine streak' (p. 278).

But what has Weightman to tell us that can be seen to make a positive contribution to our understanding of the avant-garde? For him 'avant-gardism, though international, is, in some important respects, a French invention' (p. 9), but this opinion cannot really excuse the omission from his discussion of virtually all avant-garde manifestations which are not French or Anglo-American. There is little generally on German (except for the *Marat-Sade*), Italian or Latin American writing; and little mention, in particular, of Günter Grass, Uwe Johnson, Borges or Cortázar. These omissions would not be too serious—after all, French critics like Ricardou

ignore virtually everything not written in their own language—
if Weightman offered in return a general analysis of the
aesthetics of the avant-garde which could be applied more
universally. His theoretical reflections are however largely
confined to the first essay, and this is too short and sketchy to
offer much beyond comments on the avant-garde's 'intellectual catastrophism' (i.e. its 'urge to throw the baby out with
the bath-water'), and on its uneasy containment of conflicting
impulses, progressive and reactionary (pp. 18, 24). But this
has been said before, and said better, by Poggioli and others.
In the essays on specific playwrights, film-makers and writers
Weightman stresses what he sees as the avant-garde's eroto-
mania, anarchy, 'self-indulgent doodling' (p. 323), and
confused thinking. He is, rightly, sharp on nonsense, and
particularly irrational nonsense, the sort he qualifies as
'emotional muddle' (p. 164) or 'neurotic self-revelation'
(p. 180 n.). He is justified, too, in castigating the avant-garde,
which survives by living off bourgeois clientèles, for being
facilely anti-society. The silliness of much that passes for
exciting experimentalism needs to be exposed. But this is the
job of the journalist, not the critic, who has other fish to fry.
It is for this reason that, for all its lively qualities, Weightman's
book will not really do as a serious study of the avant-garde,
chic or otherwise.

III

So much—or rather, perhaps, so little—by way of works that
set out to offer definitions (complete or partial) of the avant-
garde. To turn from the sturdy British pragmatism of John
Weightman to the austere theorizing of Ricardou and company
is not only to enter a different universe; it is to go a fair
distance towards understanding why dialogue is so difficult
between practitioners of the Anglo-Saxon and the French
brands of the criticism of literary modernism.

The German and even the Russian stance, if a couple of

random samples are anything to go by, are mild and a shade deferential in manner.[5] Most foreigners seem to take French assurance at its face value. And assurance, even arrogance, was the dominant chord struck at the 1971 conference at the chateau of Cerisy-la-Salle in Normandy, at which a number of French and foreign critics, together with some of the novelists themselves, set out to define the aesthetics of the new novel and to peer into the future to see what the 'new' new novel might look like. The theme of the symposium—'Nouveau roman: hier, aujourd'hui'—is also the title of the proceedings, published in their entirety by the Paris paperback firm '10-18' in two volumes a year after the colloquium took place. It is invaluable to have the total operation recorded cheaply and swiftly in this way. I do not think the adjective 'monumental' is misplaced in describing the work, which will certainly prove of considerable historical importance, if only because we get the deliberations 'warts and all'. Out of the dialectic of formal read papers and impromptu oral discussion, which magnetic tape recording can preserve in its fresh spontaneity, indeed out of the very excesses and extremes of clashing points of view, there emerges a quite sharp awareness of where the avant-garde of the novel is going in France. And while the critics and scholars present drew obvious benefit, so too probably did Alain Robbe-Grillet, the only leading novelist who stayed for the full ten days the conference lasted. He was present at nearly every session, and when there made frequent and pertinent interventions, all faithfully recorded in the '10-18' volumes (his comments would alone be enough, in fact, to make the book essential reading to all future students of the subject). And I suspect that those who attended will find the record more impressive than the actuality: partly because the often verbose interventions from the floor have been discreetly trimmed, and partly because embarrassing distractions, such as Robert Pinget's acute stage-fright during his replies to questions arising out of his paper, have not passed the print barrier. There has been no cosmetic surgery,

though; Ricardou pontificated in an almost totally humourless
fashion throughout the conference, and his ostensibly 'spon-
taneous' comments, delivered not to the speaker or the
audience but in reality to the microphone and therefore to
posterity, survive as equally pompous declarations in print.
Ricardou, I am sure, learned nothing and forgot nothing as a
result of the meetings. He even seemed to have a masochistic
awareness of his 'theoretical pretensions' (see the rather
heavy-humoured aside on p. 335 of Vol. II).

The real star of the show was not Ricardou, nor the
judicious and wise Françoise van Rossum-Guyon who occupied
the chair alternately with him, but Robbe-Grillet, elfish and
subtly leg-pulling, whose comments were distinguished by a
degree of intelligence rarely attained by other speakers.
Robbe-Grillet was clearly using the colloquium to formulate
his own poetics and to probe the views of others, colleagues
and critics alike. This perhaps betrayed a certain conflict
within the novelist himself; on the one hand he feels the need
to see his past work through the eyes of sympathetic but
perceptive readers in order to ascertain what processes of
composition are at work, and on the other he fears that such
activities, inevitably rather narcissistic on his part, will
sterilize his creative impulses. This conflict no doubt accounted
for the uncharacteristic note of acerbity which entered his
voice when he found himself face to face with the activities of
university-based critics (to whom, as he generously acknowledged, he owes his career). No wonder Gerald Graff can
write, in the article I referred to earlier, that 'much of the
literature of the last twenty years has been conditioned by the
wish to remain invulnerable to critical analysis', and can cite
the alleged 'opacity' of the new novel as a case in point (p. 386.)

A number of interesting details emerged over the period
the conference lasted. One was the close-knit (some might
say incestuous) quality of the new novel's enterprise, in
that its practitioners, or at least some of them, meet fairly
frequently and certainly read each other's work closely and

critically (I, p. 105). Another striking fact was that not once were non-French writers like Norman Mailer or Uwe Johnson even mentioned. Jean Alter, it is true, did upbraid Françoise van Rossum for failing to make any reference in her concluding remarks to the new novel in America, Germany or Italy, but he did not repair the omission himself (I, p. 419). As far as conference participants were concerned, indeed, literature today appeared to consist exclusively of French writing (and only a particular strain of French writing at that— Samuel Beckett and Marguerite Duras, usually considered part of the new novel, were barely discussed). A third point of significance was the way the speakers skirted round the uneasy question of the relationship between the new novelists and the *Tel Quel* group. Ricardou trod carefully over this heavily mined terrain; and no one was surprised, I am sure, when he finally broke with *Tel Quel* a few months after the conference ended. But at the time he was still associated with a review which had publicly denounced Robbe-Grillet, ostensibly for aesthetic reasons (his continued attachment to *le récit*, or story-telling), but in reality for political motives, since *Tel Quel* is now a more or less Maoist organ, devoted to the 'articulation of a politics connected logically with a non-representative dynamic of writing'.[6] At the time of the colloquium, people were talking as if the so-called 'new' new novel was being hatched by *Tel Quel*; I wonder what would be said about this now that the only figure at Cerisy who had a foot in both camps, Jean Ricardou, has been expelled from the Sollers circle.

But I do not want to give the impression that parochialism and sectarianism was all that emerged from the Cerisy colloquium. We learned a lot about the nature of the avant-garde, especially in the novel, and this is now enshrined within the pages of the proceedings. Jean Alter, for instance, wondered whether the *nouveau roman* was not the last novel, unconsciously echoing Gore Vidal's point which I mentioned earlier. He had particularly in mind Sollers's recent fiction, which he felt announced the death of the novel as we know it and the birth of the novel as play, or *jeu* (I, p. 54). And Françoise van Rossum, in her concluding remarks, offered a number of helpful criteria by which the new novel can roughly be defined: the disappearance of an organizing central character and the suppression of logically sequential actions as structural factors in fiction; the multiplication of partial or contradictory roles and angles in the novel; proliferation of anecdotes; the distortion of hallowed forms like 'story' or 'plot' and the development of fictions from generative themes and motifs instead; the elaboration of new logical patterns arising from the dual constriction of lexical and structural inhibitions; the systematic use of abstract (geometrical or anagrammatic) designs; exploitations of intertextuality (i.e. extensive quotation or pastiche of one text within another); and the multiplication of what Gerald Graff calls 'techniques of self-parody and structural involution' (article cited, p. 392). All these devices, Françoise van Rossum claims, draw the focus away from 'story' towards the 'global functioning of the text', and confirm Ricardou's comment that the novel today is not so much 'the writing of an adventure but the adventure of a writing' (I, pp. 402-3). After stressing the co-operation now expected in this enterprise on the part of the reader-critic, she concluded with this lapidary definition of the avant-garde novel: 'any text which poses within itself the problem of its own functioning' (p. 415). It would hardly be possible to put the matter better than that.

IV

After these French approaches to the new novel, most Anglo-Saxon attitudes to the same phenomenon must inevitably seem disappointingly flabby. One of the earliest, and the best, is Gore Vidal's *Encounter* essay mentioned above. Vidal has little time for Robbe-Grillet's theories (unlike Frank Kermode, who asserts in his 1968 essay 'Modernisms' that *Towards a New Novel* is 'one of the really important contributions to the theory of the novel'). Vidal sees the whole movement as so 'radical in its pronouncements yet traditional in its references' (p. 16) as to provoke amusement at its solemnities. It is also, he says, an interesting comment on our age that 'both Sarraute and Robbe-Grillet take for granted that the highest literature has always been made by self-conscious *avant-gardistes*', whereas great novelists of the past like Dostoyevsky, Conrad and Tolstoy 'were not much concerned with laboratory experiments' (p. 17). He deflates avant-garde pretensions by pointing out that enterprises like Robbe-Grillet's, which claim to reinvent man, are in fact in process of themselves being reinvented by the evolving world we inhabit. The avant-garde according to Vidal is thus much more a symptom than a cause. If traditional-style narrative is disappearing from the novel, this is not so much because the novelists are in the vanguard of civilization, but because 'people don't write letters any more: they use the telephone' (p. 16). (A telling confirmation of this is the Basildon Bond notepaper advertisement which shows a bundle of love-letters and comments: 'You can't tie a telephone call up in ribbon', but which very much gives a feeling of rowing against the tide.)

Other characteristically sceptical reactions to the French avant-garde can regularly be found in the columns of our literary reviews. Here are a few typical quips noted over the years: 'a *bête blanche* for me, this Carrollian soufflé' (of Pinget's *Mahu, or the Material*);[7] 'smells of the laboratory' (Anthony Burgess, no less, on Robbe-Grillet);[8] 'this investigator made an excuse and left' (Mary Sullivan on Klossowski's *Roberte ce soir*);[9] 'simply glance at it, you grovel' (Jim Hunter on Bataille's *My Mother*).[10] But in his book *The New Novel*,[11] Vivian Mercier not only presents sympathetically a whole panoply of writers, he also stresses the importance of two novelists virtually unread in English-speaking countries, Raymond Roussel, who has had an enormous influence on the *nouveau roman*, and Raymond Queneau, who has remained

largely distinct from the dominant French avant-garde (he is
virtually an avant-garde unto himself). Mercier accepts that
the new novel can be accused of being boring or trivial, but
claims that 'even if this is so, these writers have prepared the
soil for a new crop of French novelists—men and women who
can treat the genre with the greatest possible freedom because
the New Novelists have swept away restrictive conventions
and the crippling preconceptions of the average novel reader'
(p. 41). Mercier contemplates with equanimity, in other
words, the emergence of the *new* new novel which provoked
some unease among the Cerisy speakers and which Vidal and
others have declared to be an impossibility, or at the least an
arrant monstrosity. As for the achievement of the new novel
proper, Mercier, after naming half a dozen key works,
challenges the sceptic to 'produce six novels first published in
English anywhere in the world in 1957-62 that, on the one
hand, are as interesting in traditional novelistic ways as these
six and, on the other hand, illuminate the technical problems
and possibilities of the novel as searchingly' (p. 42). It is to be
noted that Stephen Heath makes a similar point in his own
study of the new novel when he states that 'in Britain realist
writing has hardly been challenged since Joyce', with the
clear implication that it ought to have been (p. 35).

As I have already suggested, Heath's view of the new novel
in France, and more particularly its Sollersian variant, is
wholeheartedly enthusiastic. One of Heath's points about the
nouveau roman, that it has 'nothing of the habitual rigid
distinction between novel and theoretical writing' (p. 12), is
precisely, I suspect, the sort of confusion between reflection
and creation which most worries other Anglo-Saxon critics of
the contemporary novel. Malcolm Bradbury, for instance,
quotes approvingly Robbe-Grillet's remark that 'a novel must
be something before it can *mean* anything' (*Possibilities*, p. 289),
but is distinctly tepid about the novels written according to
the theory of the logical anteriority of form over content. For
Bradbury these betray 'a highly reduced and formal realism';

and in order to accept them as reality 'there is much', he says, 'that you have to dismiss: the reality of the self as an active moral agent, the reality of the culture as a place of meanings commonly accrued out of individual living and speaking' (*Possibilities*, pp. 23-4).

He is quite right, of course: the sort of bathwater we observed Françoise van Rossum cheerfully throwing out contained at least one baby, the accommodation of the 'human' (which, for reasons that would repay investigation, is something of a dirty word in French intellectual circles). Bradbury counters the argument that British realist fiction is devoid of 'technical speculation' by pointing to the example of John Fowles, who seeks by 'an aesthetic marriage of phrases of style' to 'give us back reality by passing beyond the inert banality we have come to associate with [reality] in the deadening pages of the *nouveau roman*' (pp. 261-3). I would agree with this, and apply to other English-language novelists— like V. S. Naipaul whom I discussed earlier—the praise Bradbury justly accords to Fowles, who, he argues, 'not only registers the fictiveness of fiction, the spuriousness of structure, but also its inevitable claim and its psychic urgency,' in an attempt to 'create fresh and inquisitive new alignments of experience' (p. 271).

Critics of the avant-garde like Bradbury and Tanner are right to stress the vitality of non-*nouveau roman* modes of fiction. Tanner, for instance, perceptively demonstrates how profoundly sceptical American fiction is of 'verbal constructs which men call descriptions of reality' (*City of Words*, p. 27); so much so, indeed, that society itself comes to be seen as fiction. The American tension between a felt need for structure and a deep-seated suspicion of constraint is a profoundly fruitful one; and the way the American writer lays claim to his citizenship of the 'city of words', to an inherited language with all its multifarious energies, is an example to writers in older civilizations who are, perhaps, a little complacent about theirs. Such matters were not

animadverted to at Cerisy, the quite astonishing provin-
cialism of which becomes apparent the further one gets away
from it in time and space. A whole 'new novel' (Updike and
company[12]) and even a 'new new novel' (Barth and Hawkes)
have burgeoned in America during precisely the same period
as the *nouveau roman* in France, i.e. since about 1950; but the
thunder provoked by the 'energy of its fiction-building in the
face of immanent apocalypse'[13] was not heard by Ricardou or
Robbe-Grillet in their Normandy chateau.

V

It would be facile to say that it is their loss. Any such cultural
divide must sadden those who care for art. The Cerisy
proceedings and *City of Words* are phenomena of major literary
importance, as I hope to have shown. It is curious, but
seemingly inevitable, that only contemporary French and
contemporary American fiction—rather than, say, British,
German or Italian novels, for all their impressive qualities—
appear to be making the true running. And yet it is precisely
these two liveliest branches of western literary activity which
are the most remote from each other. In the thirties the
French novel was able to learn from the American novel, but
the relationship then was between patrician and client. Will
the French novel, now in a much less august position, be able
to humble itself to benefit from the rich and thriving experiments being conducted in fiction across the Atlantic? It looks
as if dialogue between the French- and English-speaking avant-
gardes will not be easy for some time to come, but, let us hope,
it will not be quite impossible. Angus Wilson, who has done as
much as anyone to interpret continental writing to the
English-speaking world, put the situation like this in a 'Forward into Europe' feature in *The Times* (2 January 1973):
'whether a writer speaks to one, or to a few, or to many is
often no more than an accident, especially where the gulf of
language has to be crossed' (p. xi). But he concluded more

optimistically. 'Talent,' he said, 'is widespread.' So much so, he felt, that 'out of it genius may come, so long as we do not congratulate ourselves upon our insularity'. Let us trust that the moral of that humane and reasonable wish carries into all embattled Cities of Words.

VI

Tony Tanner argues—and few would disagree—that the novel should be able to contain in language the whole destiny of man. Humanism and tragedy are the twin poles, too, to a famous essay of Robbe-Grillet's, reprinted in *Towards a New Novel*. And in his study, Stephen Heath questions the artificial dichotomy Sartre once sought to establish between literature and the death of a child. 'Without literature', Heath ripostes, 'that death is nothing: language and literature, as supreme moment of linguistic activity, define that death, realize its tragedy that we grasp not in spite of but because of literature . . . because of our capacity to make and remake meanings' (*The Nouveau Roman*, p. 32).

I have not made much reference to Claude Simon so far in this chapter. But my implication has been that his example is supremely relevant in the consideration of the avant-garde's contribution to the expression of our tragic condition. For when all is said and done, the only justification for fictional experiment, for the restless dissatisfaction with pre-existing forms and modes of expression, must be the more precise and exact formulation of what Claude Simon calls, in the dedicatory note in *La Corde raide*, 'la tragica i dolorosa inquietud' (p. 7), in so far as it besets mankind at every moment. For Simon eschews two extremes, set out on the one hand by Alain Robbe-Grillet when he says that by repudiating communion with the world of things man can escape tragedy, and on the other by George Steiner who has drawn attention to the tempting blandishments of what he calls in an arresting phrase 'the suicidal rhetoric of silence'.[14] Simon has not succumbed to this rhetoric; nor has he fallen either for Robbe-Grillet's easy optimism. 'Life is tragic for Claude Simon', writes Laurent LeSage, 'because human existence counts for so little in the universal order of things', and he compares Simon's vision to that of Ecclesiastes. There is in both works, LeSage argues, a perception of the essential vanity of human activity coupled with a strangely satisfying emphasis on the cyclical perenniality of the natural world in which 'to every thing there is a season . . . a time to be born, and a time to die' (Eccl. iii. 1-2). And Jean-Luc Seylaz has drawn attention to a fertile paradox in Simon's fiction between an impulse towards complete reconstitution and a tendency to nihilistic destruction, and between a powerfully evocative vision and hesitations about the solidity of things.[15]

It is this dual perception which drives Claude Simon to write novels in a vain (though for us fortunate) attempt to reconcile the conflict between the sceptical pessimism of the intellectual and the confident optimism of the artisan, between the Diogenes and the Daedalus aspects of his nature. It is this which causes him willy-nilly to explore the major permanent themes of the western novel in the wake of his masters, Dostoyevsky and Conrad. In offering an answer to the question 'what meaning, if any, can be discerned in human existence?' Claude Simon has been remarkably consistent over the years. From *Le Tricheur* of 1945 to *Triptyque* of 1973, the message of his novels has been the same. Let us listen, for a moment, to the voice of the narrator in these novels. For once, *pace* the intentional fallacy, we can be reasonably certain that this voice speaks for Simon himself. My evidence for this is derived to some extent from reported interviews, but mainly from his essay in autobiography *La Corde raide*, where he makes this statement (my translation):

I believe that every man is alone, whether he is a worker, bourgeois or intellectual, and whatever friends, companions or lovers surround him. He is irremediably alone and laden with an inalienable past in his journey towards the death he must face on his own. I have seen people die in different ways, surrounded by their nearest and dearest, or alone on a field of battle, but as far as I am concerned it comes to the same thing and that however you live or die, you are on your own.

(pp. 20-21)

La Corde raide contains a lot of comments like this one. So when the narrators of the fictional works make general remarks about life, death and human destiny which are in line with those in *La Corde raide*, we can be reasonably sure that they speak for Claude Simon himself.

In *Le Tricheur*, then, the lack of concern of the planet Earth is stressed. On an indifferent globe man attempts to correct the play of chance by cheating (hence the novel's title), even through a Gidean kind of 'gratuitous action', but in vain. Chance, as we are told in *Le Sacre du printemps*, is an 'eternal enigma' (p. 234) which we are unable to unravel. So we continue somehow, 'bearing our death within us like a woman carries her child' (*Le Tricheur*, p. 94), a death as absurd as our life because of the perpetual recommencement of things played out against a background of fundamentally unchanging reality (pp. 111, 181, 243).

There is a Dostoyevskian crime—a useless but somehow necessary murder—at the end of *Le Tricheur*. The next novel, *Gulliver*, is even more violent. Its atmosphere is more Faulknerian: sombre with a brooding sense of the end of things, as on a cold, long-dead planet 'continuing its aimless journey through the immensities of the constellations, a mineral lump on which matter solidified by temperatures making any form of life impossible rang hard and resonant like metal' (p. 168). In such a world man is made of 'soft and perishable stuff' (p. 306), violence and misery and insanity are of banal, even daily occurrence (p. 338), and tragedy can be read in hard, closed faces of people just as it must be seen in empty vastness of the sky (pp. 379, 373). It is a harsh universe projected in this novel: men die uselessly, illusions are lost and hopes are destroyed, and a harmless, gentle person like the Jew Herzog is made to suffer atrociously through the loss of his wife and daughter during the German occupation of France.[16] Unlike Malraux and some other tragic novelists, Simon is not detached; his refusal to accept is similar to Faulkner's, and his anger and resistance shines through his prose, especially in these early novels. Like Faulkner, Claude Simon broods over justice, or rather the lack of it, in human affairs; it is significant that the title he gave provisionally to *Gulliver* during its preparation was 'Les Juges'. His resentment against man's fate is motivated by the respect he feels for mankind in spite of everything, in spite of cowardice, cruelty and rapaciousness. Talking of the human skull, he calls it 'a fragile sphere of bone, a crumbly shell in which divinities are born, live and die' (p. 114).

Le Sacre du printemps takes as its epigraph in part two a remark of Trotsky's about the tragic nature of history and the grasshopper-like vulnerability of men. The novel—set partly in 1952 and partly in 1936—develops the many ironies of this notion. A man who is young and idealistic in 1936 has become a disillusioned realist by 1952; but then he comes up against another idealistic young man, a kind of mirror-image of himself as he was sixteen years before. He watches, sadly but knowingly, the youth losing a few illusions in his turn. But without cynicism; the novel appears to be saying that although man is vulnerable, he is not contemptible, and if life is anarchic, even luxuriantly, triumphantly so, if all it seems to offer are 'fresh mirages and fresh rebuffs' (p. 210), it is nonetheless continually recreated anew. And even at its most desperate life often holds in reserve a slightly malicious joke at our expense, as when the young hero at the very end of the book discovers that the precious ring, which means so much to him and Edith his idol and which had seemed irrevocably lost, is found to have been stuck in the bottom of his pocket after all.

After this lighter treatment of the theme of human destiny, we are back, in *The Wind*, with 'the irremediable existence of suffering and evil' (p. F235) which religion and philosophy attempt to disguise as benefits, just as they try to present the final corruption of the body as a deliverance, or at least as an insignificant mishap. But in reality, Simon argues, we progress, at least after the 'ephemeral glories of adolescence', from defeat to defeat, inexorably and irremediably (pp. F153, 83). The next novel (*The Grass*) plays up the grotesque aspects of this progression. Sabine and Pierre, in Louise's eyes, are figures both tragic and grotesque: tragic in the inevitability of their decline and approaching demise, grotesque in their undignified refusal to assume their condition. Or in the case of Sabine at least it is a matter of indignity: she paints her face and dyes her hair in a hideous parody of lost youth. But with Pierre it is rather different; like his peasant father, he is pursued by 'that insatiable and credulous thirst for dominance and knowledge which is mankind's way of expressing his repudiation of his condition' (p. F231). This point is taken up again in *The Flanders Road*. Pierre reacts in a characteristically intellectual fashion to the news of the destruction of the 'most precious library in the world' by writing to his POW son Georges in Germany that 'all of this is infinitely sad'. To which Georges replies, shrewdly enough, 'that if the contents of the thousands of books in that irreplaceable library had been impotent to prevent things like the bombing which destroyed them from happening, [he] didn't really see what loss to humanity was represented by the disappearance of those thousands of books and papers obviously devoid of the slightest utility' (p. 166). We can be sure that this debate, between Pierre the professor and the son whose interests revert to those of his illiterate ancestors, is one which Claude Simon conducts with himself. On the one hand, as a man of extensive culture, he regrets the loss of the books in the Leipzig collection, as does Pierre; on the other hand, with Georges, he is conscious of the fact that words merely serve, 'like those vaguely sugared pellets disguising a bitter medicine for children' (p. 137), to conceal from our awareness 'the whole dim and blind and tragic and banal imbroglio' of life (p. 205).

Tragic, yet banal: this sums up a lot in Claude Simon's attitude to human existence. *The Palace*, being about a political catastrophe, the Spanish civil war, concentrates on the images of disaster such an event throws up, 'the eternal and unchanging scenes of all catastrophes and all migrations' (p. 51). One of the characters, the American, imagines that a dead child lies putrefying in the sewers of Barcelona wrapped in newspaper, a 'shroud of words' (p. 21), and later the Student contemplates in the republican headquarters 'the bureaucratic accumulation of paper which always manages to soak up all violence and every act of revolt' (p. 216). Unavoidable in its ordinariness, commonplace in its inevitability: this is the nature, for Claude Simon, of the story of this failed revolution, and the true meaning of the dictionary definition of the word, quoted in the epigraph to the whole novel, as the locus of a moving body which, describing a closed curve, successively passes through the same points. The revolution, in other words, is cyclical like the rest of life. This notion, profoundly held by Claude Simon, is encapsulated in the brilliant image which closes the novel, that of children's coffins, a grotesque juxtaposition of birth and death, beginning and ending, renewal and decay.

Histoire, as we have seen, deals not with a political disaster, but with the break-up of a family and its fortunes. One can hear in the novel the murmurings of the old women, for whom 'all events, happy, unhappy or neutral occasions, Maman's illness, the bad harvests, the engagements of granddaughters, the trips, the suspicions about the estate-manager, births, deaths, misalliances, the wild oats of their children, the bankruptcies, were indiscriminately reduced to those snatches of desolate sentences, those commentaries hanging in the motionless air like those vibrations which persist long after the bells have stopped ringing . . .' (p. 16). Such familiar (and familial) catastrophes exist to demonstrate that 'at any moment the ordered and reassuring world can suddenly capsize . . . disclose the hidden surface in order to show that its other side is no more than a simple heap of garbage' (p. 52).

The sense of the epigraph to *Histoire*, a quotation from Rilke to the effect that we are perpetually engaged in organizing a chaos which engulfs us continually until we fall apart ourselves, recurs in *The Battle of Pharsalus* in the passage which contemplates the abandoned McCormick reaper,

> rusting, gradually falling to pieces in a ditch, in the corner of a field, in the barnyard of a ruined farm, apocalyptic and anachronistic, with those sprocket wheels, those jaws, those frail limbs, those cables, those chains forged in the deafening uproar of the steel mills of a remote continent, as if in very ancient times some earthquake, some gigantic tidal wave, it too from a great distance (like the legions of bronze which once crossed seas, mountains and plains to slaughter each other, to strew their corpses on an indifferent soil), had submerged the entire earth like a flood, carrying with it mules, cars, traveling salesmen, installment records and reaper-threshers, and then, withdrawing, had left them here, the salesmen surviving a while, filing their commissions and the installment checks signed on the table of a village café, emptying with a grimace the last glass of local wine, leaving behind as an artistic souvenir some gaudy advertisement embellished with machines and pretty girls, and departing at last to their empyrean of pastel skyscrapers, factories and giant airports—the bones of mules and the dismantled machines now strewing hills and plains.

> The former whitish, familiar and humble. The latter slowly devoured by rust, gradually revealing its incom-

prehensible, delicate, feminine anatomy with delicate and complicated articulations as well. The once-oiled, gently flexing joints are now jammed, stiffened. They lift to the sky, in an oratorical and interminable protest, vaguely ridiculous, like ancient divas, ancient fallen courtesans, their fleshless limbs: some rods, a rotten shaft, a seat on which no driver will ever sit and which now serves only as a perch for some skinny chickens with featherless bright-pink necks. Sometimes, as in this case, the farm itself having been abandoned, there are not even any chickens. Occasionally the wind stirs the weeds that have sprouted between the wheels and whistles in the links of the chains, between the cables, and among the narrow interstices of their carcasses.

(p. 104)

But if the machine (and man who makes it) is destined to decay and corruption, the same is not true of the natural world, as *Triptyque* makes clear, in speaking of 'the imperious, incessant circulation of the sap, the secret mutations of matter, the manifold breathing of the earth at night' (p. 208). Once again we find dominant the characteristically Simonian notion of cycle, of decay and regeneration: of paradox, in fact, at the very heart of things.

VII

A tragic sense of history, of the self, of human tenderness—in *Les Corps conducteurs*, for instance, the woman says 'We knew it from the start; all through the night we've known it' (p. 196)—pervades, even saturates Simon's world. Life's complex ironies are laid bare: the name of the battlefield of Pharsalus, which changed the destiny of the world, can today hardly be deciphered on the signposts in Thessaly, for instance; or a lost ring, the source of so many tragic misunderstandings, is found buried in a pocket where it had lain all the time.

8

These examples, macrocosmic and microcosmic respectively in significance, are typical of the way Simon highlights the vanity of human wishes. This might be melodramatic, romantic in the bad sense, if it were not brushed with a hint of comedy. It is not a cruel form of humour but, rather, a compassionate one. Those children's coffins, which I referred to earlier as constituting the final image in *The Palace*, are described by the narrator as 'absurd' (*dérisoires*). It is not that Simon considers children's coffins to be ridiculous in themselves: such an opinion would be callous and in poor taste. It is simply that objects such as these, which throw into sharp focus the cruelty and sadness of our condition—in this case, that children, so close to birth, do also sometimes die—are often so pathetic as to be comic, like the oppressed populations of Spain who are described as 'serious, taciturn, proud, humiliated and grim' (*The Palace*, p. 135), or like the tragic detritus which lines the roads in the wake of a retreat such as that portrayed in *La Route des Flandres*.

It is this dual perception of tragic absurdity which makes Simon's vision not only unsentimental but fully relevant to contemporary concerns. He is part of the avant-garde as I have been describing it in this chapter, but he is also preoccupied with the major themes of the humanistic novel since its rise in the eighteenth century. He pursues technical perfection because he is a moralist who wishes to convey intuitions about the human condition in a form that can command respect and admiration in today's world. He does not cultivate art for art's sake, but art for life's sake. What makes him a great novelist, what causes him to tower above most other writers of his generation, is that he has not impoverished the novel inherited from his forbears, but, on the contrary, enriched it. What Conrad did for the novel of the early 1900s, Claude Simon has done for the novel of the mid-century; he has enlarged its aesthetic range and has developed new possibilities of realism, but he has not caused it to abandon its permanent vocation: to exalt, in spite of everything, the heroic stature of

man, and so help us to understand our life, and come to terms
with our death.

CONCLUSION—NOTES

1 *Telling It Again and Again: Repetition in Literature and Film*, by Bruce F.
Kawin (Ithaca and London: Cornell University Press, 1972). Kawin's
thesis may seem too slender to justify book-length treatment; in any
case, to use his own distinction (p. 4), his discussion is, I am afraid,
'repetitious' rather than 'repetitive'.

2 *Existentialist Thought and Fictional Technique: Kierkegaard, Sartre, Beckett*, by
Edith Kern (New Haven and London: Yale University Press, 1970).

3 *City of Words: American Fiction 1950–1970*, by Tony Tanner (London:
Jonathan Cape, 1971).

4 *The Concept of the Avant-Garde: Explorations in Modernism*, by John Weightman (London: Alcove Press, 1973).

5 Julius Wilhelm's *Nouveau roman und anti-theâtre: eine Einführung* (Stutt-
gart: Kohlhammer, 1972) is just that, a convenient and comprehensive
expository guide: but it does not take us far towards a poetic of the new
novel. Karlheinz Stierle's interventions at Cerisy were naturally more
random, but more penetrating, advanced with the rigour and clarity one
associates with the younger German professors. A (perhaps uncharacter-
istically sympathetic) Russian reaction, from L. Andreev, was reported
upon in *Le Monde*, 9 August 1967, p. III (supplement).

6 Stephen Heath, *The Nouveau Roman*, p. 220; the 'logical' connection may
be evident to Heath, but not to me. For anyone interested in such
chinoiseries, further details about the aesthetic differences between the
(broadly speaking) *récit*-based *nouveau roman*, and the *texte*-based *Tel
Quel*, can be found in: Heath, pp. 226–7; the Cerisy proceedings, vol. II,
pp. 348–9; and in Ricardou, *Pour une théorie du nouveau roman*, pp. 264-5.

7 Hilary Corke, *The Listener*, 2 March 1967, p. 301.

8 *The Listener*, 20 January 1966, p. 109.

9 *The Listener*, 13 May 1971, p. 624.

10 *The Listener*, 13 April 1972, p. 493.

11 *The New Novel from Queneau to Pinget*, by Vivian Mercier (New York:
Farrar, Straus and Giroux, 1971). It is interesting that Mercier sees
Robert Pinget as possibly in the long term the greatest of all the novelists

he discusses. Robbe-Grillet, for his part, considers Pinget the furthest advanced towards the 'new' new novel (see the Cerisy proceedings, II, p. 325).

12 John Updike, who thinks that French theory has the merit of asking the right questions, sees himself as an experimental novelist: see 'John Updike talks to Eric Rhode about the shapes and subjects of his fiction' in *The Listener*, 19 June 1969, pp. 862-4.

13 This arresting phrase is used by Franz Kuna in an outstanding essay on Saul Bellow published in a recent number of *English Studies*. The re-volutionary nature of the American fictional avant-garde, which French critics either ignore, like Ricardou, or play down, like Hélène Cixous, is well stated by Ihab Hassan in his book *Contemporary American Literature 1945-1972* (New York: Frederick Ungar, 1973), where he writes that contemporary novelists in the United States are 'determined to re-conceive fiction—the very nature of language and narrative—in terms more adequate to crucial changes in American culture and consciousness' (p. 174).

14 *Language and Silence* (Penguin Books reprint), p. 71.

15 These comments are my translation or paraphrase of sentences in LeSage's and Seylaz's essays in *Un Nouveau Roman?*, ed. J. H. Matthews (Paris: Minard, 1964), pp. 222-3 and 239.

16 As Leon S. Roudiez writes in *French Fiction Today*, 'Not sympathy but bitterness pervades [*Gulliver*], and its title refers to the tone of Swiftian satire, not, as I see it, to any particular detail of the fiction' (p. 154). I would agree with this way of accounting for the book's curious title.'

BIBLIOGRAPHICAL NOTE

No adequate bibliography of Claude Simon's writings or of criticism devoted to his work exists, though it is badly needed. The only reasonably comprehensive one in print at the present moment is to be found in the Claude Simon special issue of *Entretiens* (Rodez: Subervie, 1972), pp. 181-92, but it is not fully accurate and there are omissions: in particular no attempt has been made to record all Simon's minor texts and pre-publication fragments. This is not the place to set about establishing an exhaustive bibliography; a number of doctoral theses, notably by Gérard Roubichou and Anthony Cheal Pugh, are starting to appear, and these should fill the gap. The present note is confined to listing the editions of Simon's fiction which I have used in preparing this study, and from which my quotations are drawn. Full bibliographical details about critical books and articles I have consulted will be found in the notes to individual chapters. Place of publication is Paris for the French texts, and for the English translations London, unless otherwise stated.

Le Tricheur. Editions du Sagittaire, 1945.
La Corde raide. Editions du Sagittaire, 1947.
Gulliver. Calmann-Lévy, 1952.
Le Sacre du printemps. Calmann-Lévy, 1954.
'Babel'. In *Les Lettres Nouvelles*, III, 31 (October 1955), pp. 391-413.
Le Vent: Tentative de restitution d'un retable baroque. Editions de Minuit, 1957.
L'Herbe. Editions de Minuit, 1958.

La Route des Flandres. Editions de Minuit, 1960.

Le Palace. Editions de Minuit, 1962.

Femmes, de Joan Miró. Texte de Claude Simon. Editions Maeght, 1966 (achevé d'imprimer: 27 November 1965).

Histoire. Editions de Minuit, 1967.

La Bataille de Pharsale. Editions de Minuit, 1969.

Orion aveugle. Geneva: Editions d'Art Albert Skira, 1970.

Les Corps conducteurs. Editions de Minuit, 1971.

Triptyque. Editions de Minuit, 1973.

English Translations (all by Richard Howard)

The Wind. New York: George Braziller, 1959.

The Grass. Jonathan Cape, 1961.

The Flanders Road. Jonathan Cape, 1962.

The Palace. Jonathan Cape, 1964.

Histoire. Jonathan Cape, 1969.

The Battle of Pharsalus. Jonathan Cape, 1971.

Triptyque. In preparation. Calder and Boyars.

Les Corps conducteurs. In preparation. Calder and Boyars.

INDEX

Absence, An See Johnson, Uwe

Ada See Nabokov, Vladimir

Adamov, Arthur 29

Age of Suspicion, The See Sarraute, Nathalie

A la recherche du temps perdu See Proust, Marcel

Albee, Edward 22

Allen, Walter
  Tradition and Dream 154-5 n. 11

All Quiet on the Western Front See Remarque, Erich Maria

Alter, Jean 12, 212

Amants, Les See Malle, Louis

'Ambiviolences' See Heath, Stephen

Andréas-Salomé, Lou 180, 181

Andreev, L. 227 n. 5

Angus Wilson See Halio, Jay L.

'Angus Wilson's Traditionalism' See Shaw, Valerie A.

Antonioni, Michelangelo 42
  Zabriskie Point 42

Apollinaire, Guillaume 181

Apuleius 179, 183, 190
  The Golden Ass 183

Aragon, Louis 21, 27

Arrabal, Fernando 22, 25

'Artist in the Modern World, The' See Poggioli, Renato

As I Lay Dying See Faulkner, William

Astier, Pierre A. G.
  La Crise du roman français 154 n. 10

August 1914 See Solzhenitsyn, Alexander

Austin, J. L. 199

'Babel' See Simon, Claude

Bachelard, Gaston 188

Bacon, Francis (painter) 15, 92

Bald Prima Donna, The See Ionesco, Eugène

Balzac, Honoré de 17, 31, 60, 199
  La Comédie humaine 60

Barth, John 22, 205, 217

Barthes, Roland 198

Bartok, Bela 21

Bassani, Giorgio 175

Bataille, Georges 23, 175, 180, 181, 184, 188, 190, 191, 193, 194, 214
  L'Erotisme 196 n. 4
  My Mother 214

Battle of Pharsalus, The See Simon, Claude

Baudelaire, Charles 34, 36, 185

Beckett, Samuel 12, 18, 22, 24, 25, 27, 28, 29, 30, 41, 49, 63, 72, 83, 154 n. 11, 179, 195, 200, 205, 212
  Molloy 28, 41, 49, 72
  Murphy 21, 83-4
  Waiting for Godot 204

Bellini, Vincenzo 176

Bellow, Saul 228 n. 13

Benn, Gottfried 21

Benstock, Bernard 55 n. 1
  Joyce-Again's Wake 55 n. 1

Berger, Yves 68

Bergman, Ingmar 42, 108
  Persona 42
  Wild Strawberries 108

Bergonzi, Bernard 19, 42, 151, 152, 200
  Innovations 19, 20

Bergonzi, Bernard (*continued*)
  The Situation of the Novel 154 n. 11
Between See Brooke-Rose, Christine
Bishop, Tom 96 n. 29
Blanchot, Maurice 23
Bleak House See Dickens, Charles
Böll, Heinrich 99
Bonaparte, Napoleon 17, 61
Borges, Jorge Luis 25, 49, 99, 205, 208
Bouvard and Pécuchet See Flaubert, Gustave
Bradbury, Malcolm 34, 105, 115 n. 6, n. 9, 131, 136, 148, 151, 154 n. 6, 198, 203-4, 215-16
  Possibilities 154 n. 6, 198, 215-16
  The Social Context of Modern English Literature 203
Braque, Georges 87
Brasillach, Robert 27
Brecht, Bertolt 97
Brooke-Rose, Christine 197, 200
  Between 197
Bryden, Ronald 165, 171
Burgess, Anthony 214
Burroughs, William 20, 22, 154 n. 11
Butor, Michel 22, 30, 49
  Passage de Milan 30

Caesar, Julius 179
Cage, John 20, 22, 23
Caldwell, Erskine 35
Camus, Albert 27, 28, 30, 37, 40, 43, 53, 74, 200
  'For five hours they shot French people' 27
  The Outsider 37, 74
Cancer Ward See Solzhenitsyn, Alexander
Carné, Marcel
  Le Jour se lève 89

Céline, Louis-Ferdinand 21, 27, 51
  Journey to the End of the Night 27

Cézanne, Paul 21
Chaplin, Charles 111
Chapsal, Madeleine
  Interviews with Claude Simon 95 n. 17, n. 22, n. 23
Chekhov, Anton
  Three Sisters 42

City of Words See Tanner, Tony
Cixous, Hélène 228 n. 13
Coe, Richard N. 63
Coindreau, Maurice Edgar 35, 52
Colet, Louise 94
Combat 27
Comédie humaine, La See Balzac, Honoré de
Concept of the Avant-Garde, The See Weightman, John
Connolly, Cyril 20
  The Modern Movement 20
Conrad, Joseph 34, 43-6, 51, 69, 70, 137, 214, 219, 226
  Heart of Darkness 45
  Lord Jim 45
  The Nigger of the Narcissus 44
  Nostromo 46
  Under Western Eyes 45, 69
Contemporary American Literature See Hassan, Ihab
Corde raide, La See Simon, Claude
Corke, Hilary 227 n. 7
Corps conducteurs, Les See Simon, Claude
Cortázar, Julio 208
Coward, Noel 151
Crise du roman français, La See Astier, Pierre A. G.

Daniel Deronda See Eliot, George

Days of Hope See Malraux, André
Debussy, Claude 21
'Declaration of the 121, The' 17, 31
Deeping, Warwick 166, 169
Delgove, Henri 52
Dickens, Charles 31-3, 137, 138, 151, 153, 170, 171, 178, 199
  Bleak House 33, 157
  Hard Times 31-3

Dismemberment of Orpheus, The See Hassan, Ihab
Doctor Zhivago See Pasternak, Boris
Dos Passos, John 21, 35, 127, 201
Dostoyevsky, Fyodor 43, 118, 121, 122, 137, 201, 214, 219, 220
Dream Play, A See Strindberg, August
Drieu La Rochelle, Pierre 27-8
Duchamp, Marcel 22
Duras, Marguerite 31, 212
  Hiroshima mon amour 31

Durrell, Lawrence 181, 194

Ecclesiastes 219
Eisenstein, Sergei 176
Eliot, George 137, 140, 153, 178
  Daniel Deronda 140

Eliot, T. S. 21
Eluard, Paul 27
Enright, D. J. 201-2
Entre Fantoine et Agapa See Pinget, Robert
Erasers, The See Robbe-Grillet, Alain
Erotisme, L' See Bataille, Georges
Esslin, Martin 24, 25
  The Theatre of the Absurd 24

Europeans, The See James, Henry

Farewell to Arms, A See Hemingway, Ernest
Faulkner, William 34, 51-4, 60, 63, 99, 115 n. 5, 137, 153, 201, 220, 221
  As I Lay Dying 55 n. 2
  Requiem for a Nun 53
  Sanctuary 52-4
  Sartoris 53
  Sound and the Fury, The 53, 55 n. 2

Femmes See Simon, Claude
Fernandez, Dominique 180
'Fiction mot à mot, La' See Simon, Claude
Fielder, Leslie 20, 23
  'The New Mutants' 20

Finnegans Wake See Joyce, James
First Circle, The See Solzhenitsyn, Alexander
Fitch, Brian T. 75, 95 n. 19
Flanders Road, The See Simon, Claude
Flaubert, Gustave 30, 31-4, 38, 75, 85, 94, 171, 172, 176, 178, 187, 200, 201
  Bouvard and Pécuchet 172
  Madame Bovary 31-32, 172
  Sentimental Education 33
  'A Simple Soul' 34
  Three Tales 85

Flesh See Warhol, Andy
Fletcher, John
  New Directions in Literature 13
Ford, John (film director) 42
'For five hours they shot French people' See Camus, Albert
Forster, E. M. 137
Fowles, John 216
French Fiction Today See Roudiez, Leon S.
French New Novel, The See Sturrock, John
Freud, Sigmund 176, 180
Fyvel, T. R. 119

Gabin, Jean 89
Gaiser, Gerd 98
Garibaldi, Guiseppe 177
Garrard, J. G. 134 n. 1, n. 2, n. 8
Genet, Jean 22, 41, 63, 204
Gide, André 21, 220
Ginsberg, Allen 22, 23
Golden Ass, The See Apuleius
Golden Fruits, The See Sarraute, Nathalie
Golding, William 152
Goncharov, Ivan 122
Graff, Gerald 205, 206, 207, 211, 213
  'The Myth of the Postmodernist Breakthrough' 205

Grass, Günter 99, 208
Grass, The See Simon, Claude
Gulliver See Simon, Claude

Halio, Jay L. 148
  Angus Wilson 154 n. 2

Hampshire, Stuart 199
Hard Times See Dickens, Charles
Hartley, L. P. 137
Hassan, Ihab 20, 22, 23, 24, 50, 55 n. 1, 206-7, 228 n. 13
  Contemporary American Literature 228 n. 13
  The Dismemberment of Orpheus 22
  'The New Gnosticism' 206
  'Paracritical Bibliography' (in New Literary History) 20

Hawkes, John 217
Heart of Darkness See Conrad, Joseph
Heath, Stephen 50, 55 n. 1, 198, 215, 218, 227 n. 6
  'Ambiviolences' 55 n. 1
  The Nouveau Roman 55 n. 1, 198, 218, 227 n. 6

Heitner, Robert R. 98
Hemingway, Ernest 21, 22, 23, 34-5, 99, 115 n. 5
  A Farewell to Arms 34-6, 37

Herostratus See Levy, Don
Hiroshima mon amour See Duras, Marguerite
Histoire See Simon, Claude
Histoire d'O See Réage, Pauline
Hitchcock, Alfred 42
Homer
  The Iliad 113
House for Mr Biswas, A See Naipaul, V. S.
House of Assignation, The See Robbe-Grillet, Alain
Howard, Richard 80, 154 n. 8, 230
Hunter, Jim 214

'Idea of Order at Key West, The' See Stevens, Wallace
Iliad, The See Homer
Immortal One, The See Robbe-Grillet, Alain
Innovations See Bergonzi, Bernard
Inquisitoire, L' See Pinget, Robert
Ionesco, Eugène 25, 28, 29
  The Bald Prima Donna 28

James, Henry 34, 58, 137, 140, 170
  The Europeans 170
  The Portrait of a Lady 140

Janvier, Ludovic 62
  Interview with Claude Simon 94 n. 6, n. 13, 95 n. 20, 96 n. 28

Jealousy See Robbe-Grillet, Alain
Johnson, B. S. 151, 156
Johnson, Uwe 97-115 passim, 208, 212

An Absence 100-1, 102
Speculations about Jakob 100
The Third Book About Achim 97-116 passim
Two Views 101-2, 105

Josipovici, Gabriel 197
The World and the Book 197

Journey to the End of the Night See Céline, Louis-Ferdinand
Jour se lève, Le See Carné, Marcel
Jouve, Pierre Jean 27
Joyce-Again's Wake See Benstock, Bernard
Joyce, James 11, 21, 22, 27, 34, 49-51, 55 n. 1, 63, 99, 137, 170, 199, 215
Finnegans Wake 22, 27, 49-50, 55 n. 1, 179, 198
A Portrait of the Artist 170
Work in Progress 29
Ulysses 22, 49

Kafka, Franz 22, 34, 99, 115 n.5, 170, 199
Kawin, Bruce 204-5, 206
Telling It Again and Again 204, 227 n. 1

Kermode, Frank 19, 20, 24, 42, 152, 205, 213
'Modernisms' 19-20, 213

Kern, Edith 204-5, 206
Kesey, Ken 206
Kierkegaard, Søren 204
Klee, Paul 21
Klossowski, Pierre 214
Roberte ce soir 214

Koestler, Arthur 17
Kuna, Franz 228 n. 13

Lampedusa, Giuseppe Tomasi di 175-95 passim
The Leopard 175-95 passim

Lanceraux, Dominique
'Modalités de la narration dans *La Route des Flandres*' 95 n. 19

Lang, Fritz 42
Last Year at Marienbad See Robbe-Grillet, Alain
Late Call See Wilson, Angus
Lawrence, D. H. 193, 194
The Rainbow 193

Leavis, F. R. 206
Leiris, Michel 51, 201-2
Manhood 201

Lemarchand, Jacques 58
Leopard, The See Lampedusa, Giuseppe
LeSage, Laurent 219, 228 n. 15
Levy, Don 208
Herostratus 208

Lord Jim See Conrad, Joseph
Lukács, Georg 117, 118, 119, 121, 130, 133

Madame Bovary See Flaubert, Gustave
Mahu, or the Material See Pinget, Robert
Mailer, Norman 13, 206-7, 212

Malle, Louis
Les Amants 208

Malraux, André 17, 21, 27, 31, 45, 66, 77, 200, 221
Days of Hope 31, 45
Man's Estate 27, 66

Mandiargues, André Pieyre de 185
Manhood See Leiris, Michel
Mann, Thomas 11, 21, 97, 199

Man's Estate See Malraux, André

Marat-Sade, The See Weiss, Peter

Marx, Karl 176

Maupassant, Guy de 171

Mauriac, Claude 24

Mauriac, François 27

Mercier, Vivian 61, 144, 154 n. 5, n. 8, 174 n. 3, 214-15, 227 n. 11
  The New Novel 94 n. 4, 154 n. 5, n. 8, 174 n. 3, 214, 227 n. 11

Middle Age of Mrs Eliot, The See Wilson, Angus

Miró, Joan 58, 181, 230

Mitchell, Julian 197

'Modalités de la narration dans *La Route des Flandres*' See Lanceraux, Dominique

Modern German Novel, The See Waidson, H. M.

'Modernisms' See Kermode, Frank

Modern Movement, The See Connolly, Cyril

Molloy See Beckett, Samuel

Montefiore, Alan 199

Moravia, Alberto 21

Moreau, Jeanne 208

Morgan, Michèle 89

Mulberry Bush, The See Wilson, Angus

Murdoch, Iris 152, 153
  The Sandcastle 153

Murphy See Beckett, Samuel

My Mother See Bataille, Georges

'Myth of the Postmodernist Breakthrough, The' See Graff, Gerald

Nabokov, Vladimir 12, 25, 49, 50, 99, 118, 170, 205
  Ada 170
  Pale Fire 50

Naipaul, V. S. 13, 14, 99, 156-74 *passim*, 216
  A House for Mr Biswas 156-73 *passim*

Nausea See Sartre, Jean-Paul

New Directions in Literature See Fletcher, John

'New Gnosticism, The' See Hassan, Ihab

'New Mutants, The' See Fielder, Leslie

New Novel, The See Mercier, Vivian

Nigger of the Narcissus, The See Conrad, Joseph

No Laughing Matter See Wilson, Angus

Nostromo See Conrad, Joseph

Nouveau Roman, The See Heath, Stephen

Nouveau roman: heir, aujourd'hui 14 n. 1, 95 n. 14, n. 22, 96 n. 28, n. 29, 210-13, 227 n. 6, 228 n. 11

Nouvea roman und anti-théâtre See Wilhelm, Julius

Novalis, Friedrich 22

O'Neill, Eugene 21

Orion aveugle See Simon, Claude

Orwell, George 17, 21

Outsider, The See Camus, Albert

Palace, The See Simon, Claude

Pale Fire See Nabokov, Vladimir

'Paracritical Bibliography' See Hassan, Ihab

Pascal, Blaise 37

Passage de Milan See Butor, Michel

Pasternak, Boris 118-34 *passim*, 144, 154 n. 8
  Doctor Zhivago 119-34 *passim*, 154 n. 8

Persona See Bergman, Ingmar

Picasso, Pablo 21, 50, 180, 181, 189

Pinget, Robert 30, 210, 214, 227-8n., 11
  Entre Fantoine et Agapa 30
  L'Inquistoire 30
  Mahu, of the Material 214

Pinter, Harold 22, 42

Pirandello, Luigi 21

Plath, Sylvia 144

Poe, Edgar Allan 36, 201

Poggioli, Renato 202-3, 209
  'The Artist in the Modern World' 203
  The Theory of the Avant-Garde 202-3

Ponge, Francis 201

Portrait of a Lady, The See James, Henry

Portrait of the Artist, A See Joyce, James

Possibilities See Bradbury, Malcolm

Pour une théorie du nouvea roman See Ricardou, Jean

Poussin, Nicolas 86

Powell, Anthony 169

Princes under the Volcano See Trevelyan, Raleigh

Project for a Revolution in New York See Robbe-Grillet, Alain

Proust, Marcel 11, 21, 34, 46-8, 50, 54, 59, 60, 63, 67, 78, 81, 137, 163, 199, 200, 201, 204
  A la recherche du temps perdu 46-8

Pugh, Anthony Cheal 174 n. 2, 229

Pushkin, Alexander 117

Queneau, Raymond 81, 214

Raimbault, R. N. 52

Rainbow, The See Lawrence, D. H.

Rattigan, Terence 151

Rauschenberg, Robert 15, 20, 86, 87, 92

Réage, Pauline
  Histoire d'O 208

Rebatet, Lucien 28

Remarque, Erich Maria
  All Quiet on the Western Front 27

Requiem for a Nun See Faulkner, William

Ricardou, Jean 62, 87, 198, 208, 209, 211, 212, 213, 217, 228 n. 13
  Pour une théorie du nouveau roman 198, 227 n. 6

Richardson, Samuel 137

Rilke, R. M. 21, 164, 224

Rimbaud, Arthur 22, 181

Roads to Freedom See Sartre, Jean-Paul

Robbe-Grillet, Alain 13, 29, 37-42, 50, 54, 57, 82, 194, 200, 201, 204, 210, 211, 212, 213, 214, 215, 217, 218, 219, 228 n. 11
  The Erasers 29
  The House of Assignation 39
  The Immortal One 201
  Jealousy 39
  Last Year at Marienbad 201
  Project for a Revolution in New York 50
  Snapshots and Towards a New Novel 37, 41-2, 200, 213-14, 218
  The Voyeur 39, 54

Roberte ce soir See Klossowski, Pierre

Ronsard, Pierre de 193

Rossum-Guyon, Françoise van, 211, 212, 213, 216

Roubichou, Gérard 229

Roudiez, Leon S. 59, 69, 76, 134 n. 10, 205, 228 n. 16

Roudiez, Leon S. (*continued*)
  French Fiction Today 94 n. 2, n. 12,
    95 n. 18, 96 n. 25, 134 n. 10,
    205, 228 n. 16

Rousseau, Jean-Jacques 202
Roussel, Raymond 214
Ryle, Gilbert 199

Sacre du printemps, Le See Simon,
  Claude
Sade, Marquis de 22, 195, 202, 208
Sanctuary See Faulkner, William
Sandcastle, The See Murdoch, Iris
Sand, George 178
Sarraute, Nathalie 25, 30, 38-9, 57,
    119, 200, 201, 214
  The Age of Suspicion 38, 200
  The Golden Fruits 25

Sartoris See Faulkner, William
Sartre, Jean-Paul 16, 21, 27, 28, 38,
    39, 40, 41, 45, 53, 63, 200,
    204, 218
  Nausea 21, 39
  Roads to Freedom 45
  Situations I 63
  What Is Literature? 21, 23, 28, 38

Sentimental Education See Flaubert,
  Gustave
Séparation, La See Simon, Claude
Seylaz, Jean-Luc 146, 154 n. 9, 219,
    228 n. 15
Shaw, Valerie A.
  'Angus Wilson's Traditionalism'
    155 n. 11

Simon, Claude
  'Babel' 58, 229
  The Battle of Pharsalus 18, 47, 50,
    60-1, 62, 67, 70, 72, 81, 85, 86,
    93, 175-94 *passim*, 224-5, 230
  Bibliography (in *Entretiens*) 229

Biographical Note 15-18
La Corde raide 43, 58, 76, 154 n.
    4, 169, 174 n. 5, 182, 183, 191,
    218, 219-20, 229
Les Corps conducteurs 18, 54, 60,
    62, 63, 67, 70, 73, 81, 86, 88,
    92, 186, 225, 230
Femmes 58, 67, 181, 185, 230
'La Fiction mot à mot' 95 n. 14, n.
    24
The Flanders Road 18, 45, 46, 59,
    60, 61, 62, 64, 65, 67, 68, 70, 72,
    78, 79, 85, 87, 88, 90, 94, 95 n.
    24, n. 26, 117-34 *passim*, 173,
    179, 185, 186, 187-8, 190, 193,
    222, 226, 230
The Grass 18, 46, 58, 59, 60, 62,
    63, 72, 78, 84, 86, 87, 88, 89,
    127, 135-53 *passim*, 181, 183,
    184, 186, 187, 195, 222, 229,
    230
Gulliver 17, 43, 53, 59, 65, 69,
    70, 76, 77, 84, 88, 89, 182, 186,
    220, 221, 228 n. 15, 229
Histoire 16, 18, 47, 48-9, 59, 60,
    61, 62, 67, 68, 72, 73, 79-81, 86,
    87, 88, 90-1, 95 n. 22, 127,
    156-73 *passim*, 179, 181, 182,
    186, 187, 190, 192, 193, 223,
    224, 230
Interviews See Chapsal, Madeleine
  and Janvier, Ludovic
Notes in the review *Minuit* 61
Notes in *Premier Plan* 96 n. 27
Orion aveugle 57, 60, 73, 86, 180,
    230
The Palace 17, 18, 31, 45, 46, 59,
    64, 65, 67, 68, 71, 72, 78, 85,
    87, 88, 93, 94 n. 2, 97-116
    passim, 184, 186, 223, 226, 230
Le Sacre du printemps 16, 17, 18,
    59, 65, 66, 68, 70, 71, 77, 84,

85, 89, 91, 94 n. 2, 181, 182, 184, 220, 221, 229
La Séparation 58, 135
Le Tricheur 17, 43, 53, 59, 60, 61, 67, 68, 70, 74, 75, 84, 88, 89, 94 n. 10, 182, 195, 219, 220, 229
Triptyque 13, 18, 54, 59, 68, 70, 73, 81, 82, 85, 86, 87, 88, 89, 91, 92, 93, 196 n. 5, 219, 225, 230
The Wind 17, 18, 43, 45-6, 59, 62, 65, 66, 69, 70, 72, 78, 84, 85, 88, 89, 91, 93, 137, 182, 184, 222, 229, 230

'Simple Soul, A' See Flaubert, Gustave
Situation of the Novel, The See Bergonzi, Bernard
Situations I See Sartre, Jean-Paul
Snapshots and Towards a New Novel See Robbe-Grillet, Alain
Social Context of Modern English Literature, The See Bradbury, Malcolm
Sollers, Philippe 23, 212, 215
Solzhenitsyn, Alexander 14, 118-34 *passim*, 152
August 1914 117-34 *passim*
Cancer Ward 130
The First Circle 130

Sontag, Susan 200
Sound and the Fury, The See Faulkner, William
Spark, Muriel 23, 152
Speculations about Jakob See Johnson, Uwe
Spencer, Sharon 87
Stein, Gertrude 204
Steiner, George 218
Stendhal 176, 178
Sterne, Laurence

Tristram Shandy 49

Stevens, Wallace 15, 19, 43
'The Idea of Order at Key West' 19

Stierle, Karlheinz 227 n. 5
Stravinsky, Igor 21
Strindberg, August 21
A Dream Play 42

Sturrock, John 62, 63, 74-5, 79, 94 n. 2
The French New Novel 94 n. 2, n. 5, n. 8, 95 n. 15, n. 21
Style in the French Novel See Ullmann, Stephen
Sullivan, Mary 214

Tanner, Tony 13, 206, 216, 218
City of Words 13, 206, 216, 217, 227 n. 3

Telling It Again and Again See Kawin, Bruce
Tel Quel 23, 55 n. 1, 58, 198, 212, 227 n. 6
Theatre of the Absurd, The See Esslin, Martin
Theory of the Avant-Garde, The See Poggioli, Renato
Third Book about Achim, The See Johnson, Uwe
Three Sisters See Chekhov, Anton
Three Tales See Flaubert, Gustave
Tolstoy, Leo 118, 119, 120, 121, 122, 124, 126, 214
War and Peace 120, 121

Towards a New Novel See *Snapshots and Towards a New Novel*
Tradition and Dream See Allen, Walter
transition 26, 29

Trash See Warhol, Andy
Trevelyan, Raleigh 178
   Princes under the Volcano 178

Tricheur, Le See Simon, Claude
Triptyque See Simon, Claude
Tristram Shandy See Sterne, Laurence
Trollope, Anthony 137
Trotsky, Leon 221
Two Views See Johnson, Uwe

Ullmann, Stephen
   Style in the French Novel 95 n. 19
Ulysses See Joyce, James

Under Western Eyes See Conrad, Joseph
Updike, John 217, 228 n. 12

Valéry, Paul 17, 21, 137
Verdi, Giuseppe 176
Vidal, Gore 200, 201, 212, 213, 214, 215
Visconti, Luchino 175
Voyeur, The See Robbe-Grillet, Alain

Waidson, H. M.
   The Modern German Novel 115 n. 6, n. 8

Wain, John 121
Waiting for Godot See Beckett, Samuel
Walser, Martin 99
War and Peace See Tolstoy, Leo
Warhol, Andy 23, 88, 208
   Flesh 208
   Trash 208

Warnock, Mary 199

Weightman, John 198, 207-9
   The Concept of the Avant-Garde 207, 227 n. 4

Weiss, Peter 22
   The Marat-Sade 208
What Is Literature? See Sartre, Jean-Paul
Wild Garden, The See Wilson, Angus
Wild Strawberries See Bergman, Ingmar
Wilhelm, Julius
   Nouveau roman und anti-théâtre 227 n. 5

Williams, Raymond 121, 198
Wilson, Angus 135-55 passim, 217
   Late Call 152
   The Middle Age of Mrs Eliot 135-55 passim
   The Mulberry Bush 135
   No Laughing Matter 151, 152
   The Wild Garden 147-8, 152, 154 n. 1, n. 3

Wilson, Edmund 122, 123
Wind, The See Simon, Claude
Wisdom, John 199
Wittgenstein, Ludwig 99
Wollheim, Richard 202
Woolf, Virginia 34, 49, 137, 153
Work in Progress See Joyce, James
World and the Book, The See Josipovici, Gabriel

Yeats, W. B. 21

Zabriskie Point See Antonioni, Michelangelo
Zola, Emile 137, 201